ENGLISH
FOR EVERYONE

LIBRO DE EJERCICIOS
BUSINESS ENGLISH

AUDIO GRATUITO
web y app
www.dkefe.com

Autores

Thomas Booth ha trabajado durante 10 años como profesor de inglés en Polonia y en Rusia. Actualmente vive en Inglaterra, donde ejerce como editor y autor de materiales para el aprendizaje de la lengua inglesa, principalmente manuales y vocabularios.

Trish Burrow ha trabajado durante siete años como profesora de inglés y formadora de profesores en escuelas de verano en Polonia y el Reino Unido. Tras un año dedicada a la enseñanza del inglés como profesora universitaria, ejerció como editora de materiales de examen y de materiales didácticos del inglés. Reside en el Reino Unido, donde presta servicios como escritora y editora independiente.

Consultor del curso

Tim Bowen ha enseñado inglés y ha formado profesores en más de 30 países en todo el mundo. Es coautor de libros sobre la enseñanza de la pronunciación y sobre la metodología de la enseñanza de idiomas, y autor de numerosos libros para profesores de inglés. Actualmente se dedica a la escritura de materiales, la edición y la traducción.
Es miembro del Chartered Institute of Linguists.

Consultora lingüística

La profesora **Susan Barduhn** cuenta con una gran experiencia en la enseñanza del inglés y la formación de profesores. Como autora ha participado en numerosas publicaciones. Además de dirigir cursos de inglés en cuatro continentes, ha sido presidenta de la Asociación Internacional de Profesores de Inglés como Lengua Extranjera y asesora del British Council y del Departamento de Estado de Estados Unidos. Actualmente es profesora de la School for International Training en Vermont, Estados Unidos.

ENGLISH
FOR EVERYONE

LIBRO DE EJERCICIOS NIVEL 1

BUSINESS ENGLISH

DK | Penguin Random House

Edición Estados Unidos Jenny Siklos, Allison Singer
Edición del proyecto Lili Bryant, Laura Sandford
Edición de arte Chrissy Barnard, Paul Drislane, Michelle Staples
Edición Ben Ffrancon Davies
Asistencia editorial Sarah Edwards, Helen Leech
Ilustración Edwood Burn, Michael Parkin, Gus Scott
Dirección editorial Daniel Mills
Dirección de la edición de arte Anna Hall
Dirección de la grabación de audio Christine Stroyan
Diseño de cubierta Ira Sharma
Edición de cubierta Claire Gell
Dirección editorial de cubierta Saloni Singh
Dirección de desarrollo del diseño de cubierta Sophia MTT
Producción, preproducción Andy Hilliard
Producción Mary Slater
Dirección editorial Andrew Macintyre
Dirección de arte Karen Self
Dirección general editorial Jonathan Metcalf

DK India
Dirección de la edición de arte sénior Arunesh Talapatra
Edición de arte sénior Chhaya Sajwan
Edición de arte Meenal Goel, Roshni Kapur
Asistencia de edición de arte Rohit Dev Bhardwaj
Ilustración Manish Bhatt, Arun Pottirayil,
Sachin Tanwar, Mohd Zishan
Coordinación editorial Priyanka Sharma
Dirección de preproducción Balwant Singh
Diseño sénior DTP Harish Aggarwal, Vishal Bhatia
Diseño DTP Jaypal Chauhan

Primera edición americana, 2018
Publicado en Estados Unidos por DK Publishing
345 Hudson Street, Nueva York, Nueva York 10014
DK es una División de Penguin Random House LLC

Nivel ❶ Contenidos

Cómo funciona el curso

English for Everyone está pensado para todas aquellas personas que quieren aprender inglés por su cuenta. La edición de inglés de negocios contiene las expresiones y construcciones inglesas imprescindibles para las situaciones de negocios más habituales. A diferencia de otros cursos, todo ello se practica y aprende de una forma enormemente visual. Los ejercicios de este volumen están pensados para consolidar lo aprendido en el libro de estudio. Los dos niveles del curso se incluyen en este libro. Sigue las unidades por orden y utiliza al máximo los audios disponibles en la web y la app.

LIBRO DE ESTUDIO

LIBRO DE EJERCICIOS

Número de unidad Este libro está dividido en unidades. En cada una de ellas se practica lo aprendido en la misma unidad del libro de estudio.

Qué vas a practicar La unidad comienza con un resumen de lo que practicarás en ella.

Módulos Cada unidad se compone de distintos módulos que debes seguir por orden. Puedes tomarte un descanso tras completar cualquiera de ellos.

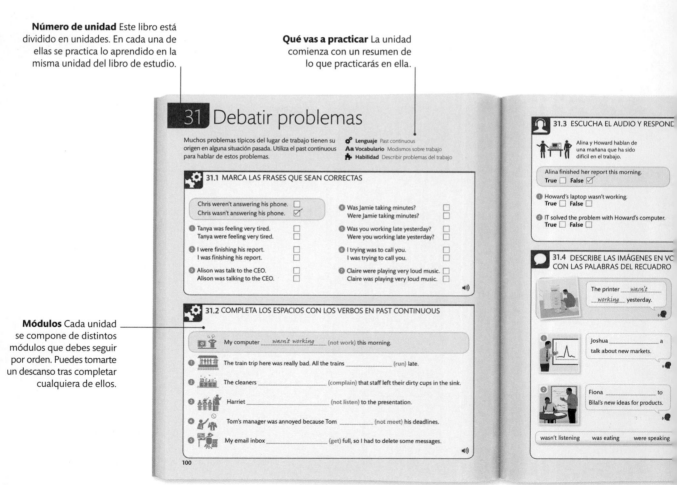

Vocabulario A lo largo del libro tienes páginas que recogen las palabras y las expresiones más útiles del inglés para los negocios, e incluyen pistas visuales que te ayudarán a recordarlas.

Guía visual Imágenes y gráficos te dan pistas visuales que te ayudan a fijar en la memoria las palabras más importantes.

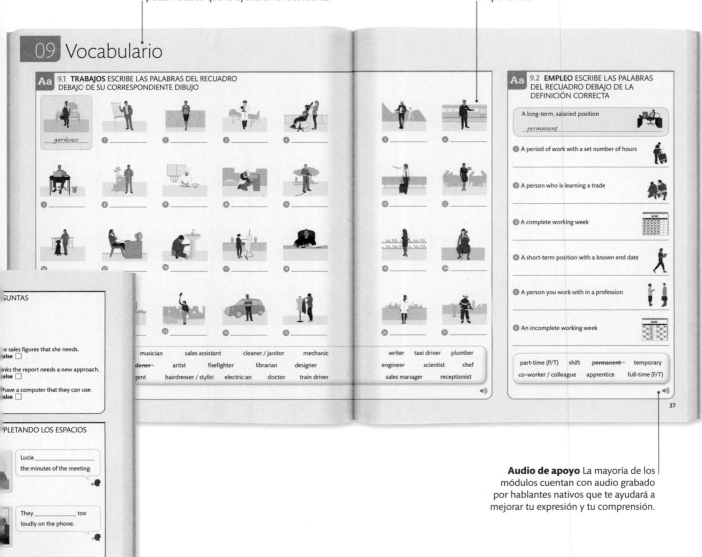

Audio de apoyo La mayoría de los módulos cuentan con audio grabado por hablantes nativos que te ayudará a mejorar tu expresión y tu comprensión.

AUDIO GRATUITO
web y app
www.dkefe.com

Módulos de ejercicios

Cada ejercicio está cuidadosamente graduado para que profundices y contrastes lo que has aprendido en la unidad. Si haces los ejercicios a medida que avanzas, asimilarás y recordarás mejor los conceptos, y tu inglés será más fluido. Cada ejercicio indica con un símbolo qué habilidad vas a practicar con él.

 GRAMÁTICA
Aplica las nuevas reglas en distintos contextos.

LECTURA
Analiza ejemplos del idioma en textos reales en inglés.

 ESCUCHA
Comprueba tu comprensión del inglés hablado.

 VOCABULARIO
Consolida tu comprensión del vocabulario clave.

ESCRITURA
Practica produciendo textos escritos en inglés.

 CONVERSACIÓN
Compara tu dicción con los audios de muestra.

Número de módulo Cada módulo tiene su propio número para que te sea fácil localizar las respuestas y el audio correspondiente.

Instrucciones En cada ejercicio tienes unas breves instrucciones que te dicen qué debes hacer.

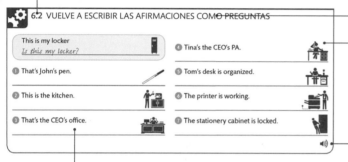

6.2 VUELVE A ESCRIBIR LAS AFIRMACIONES COMO PREGUNTAS

This is my locker
Is this my locker?

① That's John's pen.

② This is the kitchen.

③ That's the CEO's office.

④ Tina's the CEO's PA.

⑤ Tom's desk is organized.

⑥ The printer is working.

⑦ The stationery cabinet is locked.

Ayuda gráfica
Las ilustraciones te ayudan a entender los ejercicios.

Audio de apoyo Este símbolo indica que las respuestas a los ejercicios están disponibles en grabaciones de audio. Escúchalas tras completar el ejercicio.

Espacio para escribir Es útil que escribas las respuestas en el libro, pues te servirán para repasar lo aprendido.

Ejercicio de conversación Este símbolo indica que debes decir las respuestas en voz alta y compararlas a continuación con su audio correspondiente.

Respuesta de ejemplo
La primera respuesta ya está escrita, para que entiendas mejor el ejercicio.

Ejercicios de escucha Este símbolo te avisa de que debes escuchar el audio para poder responder a las preguntas.

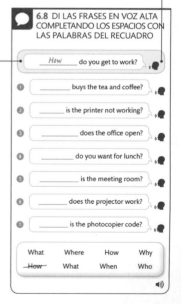

6.8 DI LAS FRASES EN VOZ ALTA COMPLETANDO LOS ESPACIOS CON LAS PALABRAS DEL RECUADRO

How do you get to work?

① _____ buys the tea and coffee?

② _____ is the printer not working?

③ _____ does the office open?

④ _____ do you want for lunch?

⑤ _____ is the meeting room?

⑥ _____ does the projector work?

⑦ _____ is the photocopier code?

| What | Where | How | Why |
| How | What | When | Who |

13.3 ESCUCHA EL AUDIO Y CONECTA LAS PERSONAS DE CADA IMAGEN CON EL ADJETIVO CORRECTO

organized

polite

calm

well dressed

creative

Audio

English for Everyone incorpora abundantes materiales en audio. Te recomendamos que los utilices al máximo, pues te ayudarán a mejorar tu comprensión del inglés hablado y a lograr una pronunciación y un acento más naturales. Escucha cada audio tantas veces como quieras. Páralo y vuelve atrás en los pasajes que te resulten difíciles, hasta que estés seguro de que has entendido bien lo que se dice.

EJERCICIOS DE ESCUCHA

Este símbolo indica que debes escuchar el audio para poder responder a las preguntas del ejercicio.

AUDIO DE APOYO

Este símbolo indica que dispones de audios adicionales que puedes escuchar tras completar el módulo.

 AUDIO GRATUITO
web y app
www.dkefe.com

Respuestas

Al final del libro tienes una sección con las respuestas correctas de todos los ejercicios. Consúltala al terminar cada módulo y compara tus respuestas con los ejemplos para comprobar si has entendido bien los contenidos que has estado practicando.

32

32.1 ◄))
1. I am so sorry I was late for the meeting with our clients today.
2. I would like to apologize for not finishing the report yesterday.
3. I'm really sorry. I forgot to charge the office cell phone and it has no power.
4. I'm really sorry this line is so bad. I hope we don't get cut off.
5. I'm afraid that's not good enough. I want a full refund on my ticket.

32.2 ◄))
1. No problem. I'll help you finish it now.
2. That's not good enough. Please heat it up.
3. Never mind. We're not very busy today.
4. No problem. I'll have tea instead.
5. Don't worry. I'll print off some more.

32.3
Ⓐ 4
Ⓑ 3
Ⓒ 1
Ⓓ 5
Ⓔ 2

32.4 ◄))
1. I'm really **sorry**. I forgot to send the agenda for the meeting.
2. I would like to **apologize** for the rudeness of the waitress.
3. I'm **afraid** that's not good enough. You missed an important meeting.
4. That's all **right**. I'll make you a copy right now.
5. Please **make** sure it doesn't happen again.

Respuestas Tienes las respuestas de todos los ejercicios al final del libro.

Número de ejercicio Para que las localices más fácilmente, las respuestas indican el número del ejercicio.

Audio Este símbolo indica que puedes escuchar el audio de las respuestas.

Puedes utilizar inglés formal o informal para presentarte o dar la bienvenida a nuevos colegas y compañeros de trabajo, según la situación y la persona de que se trate.

⚙ **Lenguaje** Abecedario y deletrear

Aa Vocabulario Presentaciones y saludos

🧩 **Habilidad** Presentarte a los colegas

⚙ 1.1 MARCA LAS FRASES CORRECTAS

It's pleasure to meet you. ☐
It's a pleasure to meet you. ☑

❶ My name Ali Patel. ☐
My name's Ali Patel. ☐

❷ Hi, I'm Jeff. ☐
Hi, I Jeff. ☐

❸ It good to meet you, Jane. ☐
It's good to meet you, Jane. ☐

❹ Pleased to meet you. ☐
Please to meet you. ☐

❺ I'm name is Deepak Kaur. ☐
My name is Deepak Kaur. ☐

❻ Great to meet you, Tanya. ☐
Pleasure to meet you, Tanya. ☐

❼ It's nice to meet you, too. ☐
It's nice meet you, too. ☐

❽ Good hello. My name is Ben Lewis. ☐
Good morning. My name is Ben Lewis. ☐

❾ It's a great to meet you, Gill. ☐
It's great to meet you, Gill. ☐

❿ Good evening. My name is Karen. ☐
Great evening. My name is Karen. ☐

🔊

⚙ 1.2 VUELVE A ESCRIBIR LAS FRASES PONIENDO LAS PALABRAS EN SU ORDEN CORRECTO

| name | afternoon. | is | Good | Tom. | My |

Good afternoon. My name is Tom.

❶ | my | Hill. | Fiona | name's | Hello, |

_____

❷ | too. | Nice | you, | meet | to |

_____

❸ | good | Jim. | you, | to | It's | meet |

_____

❹ | meet | Pleased | you. | to |

_____

❺ | a | to | meet | It's | you. | pleasure |

_____

❻ | name | Good | is | My | Roy. | evening. |

_____

🔊

1.3 ESCUCHA E_ AUDIO Y MARCA LOS NOMBRES QUE SE DELETREAN

1.4 DELETREA LOS NOMBRES EN VOZ ALTA

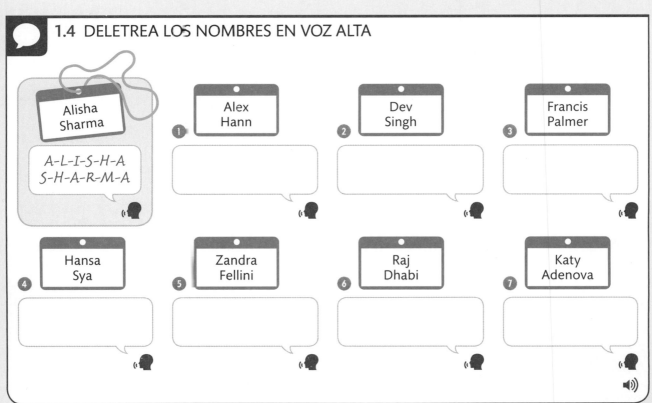

1.5 VUELVE A ESCRIBIR LAS FRASES CORRIGIENDO LOS ERRORES

> May you introduce Amy Daniels?
> _May I introduce Amy Daniels?_

1 This our new designer.

_____

2 Raj and I works together.

_____

3 I like you to meet our CEO.

_____

4 Hi, I'm name's Lola.

_____

5 It's great to meet to you, Emily.

_____

6 I may introduce Ewan Carlton?

_____

7 Farah, this my colleague, Leon.

_____

🔊

1.6 TACHA LA PALABRA INCORRECTA DE CADA FRASE

> Hi, Luke. This **is** / ~~meet~~ Emiko.

1 Good morning. **I'm** / **My** name's Saira Khan.

2 **Bye** / **I'm** Harry.

3 **I'm** / **I's** Andrew Shaw.

4 **It's** / **It** good to meet you.

5 Pleased **to** / **I** meet you.

6 It's a **pleased** / **pleasure** to meet you.

7 **May** / **This** I introduce our new HR assistant?

8 Keira, **meets** / **meet** John.

9 **Great** / **Greater** to meet you.

10 I **would** / **had** like you to meet Dan.

11 Colin and I **works** / **work** together.

🔊

1.7 ESCUCHA EL AUDIO Y NUMERA DESPUÉS LAS IMÁGENES EN EL ORDEN EN QUE LAS OIGAS

Julia acaba de empezar en un nuevo trabajo y conoce a algunos de sus nuevos compañeros en una fiesta de la empresa.

A Meet Jim. He's our CEO. ☐

B It's nice to meet you, Julia. ☐

C Hi, Jim. It's great to meet you, too. ☐

D And this is Gary, our Marketing Manager. ☐

E May I introduce Julia Parker? ☐ 1

F It's a pleasure to meet you, too, Claire. ☐

G Pleased to meet you, Julia. ☐

02 Actividades diarias en el trabajo

Utiliza el present simple para hablar de cosas que haces de manera habitual, como las tareas diarias o las rutinas del trabajo.

⚙ **Lenguaje** Present simple
Aa Vocabulario Actividades en el trabajo
Habilidad Hablar de rutinas del trabajo

⚙ 2.1 CONECTA LAS IMÁGENES CON LAS FRASES CORRECTAS

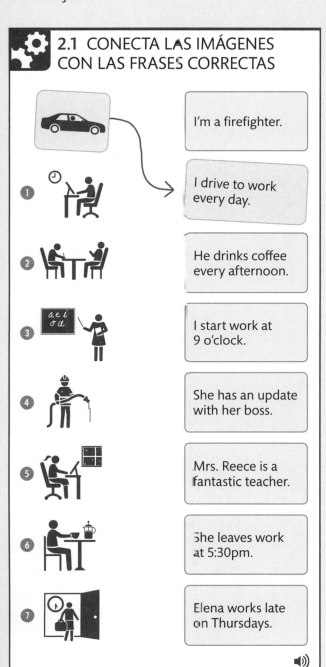

I'm a firefighter.

I drive to work every day.

He drinks coffee every afternoon.

I start work at 9 o'clock.

She has an update with her boss.

Mrs. Reece is a fantastic teacher.

She leaves work at 5:30pm.

Elena works late on Thursdays.

🔊

⚙ 2.2 VUELVE A ESCRIBIR LAS FRASES CORRIGIENDO LOS ERRORES

I **be** a teaching assistant at the local school.
I'm a teaching assistant at the local school.

❶ The IT Helpdesk **are** really good.
_____

❷ She **work** in a car factory.
_____

❸ I **eating** my lunch in the park.
_____

❹ We **takes** a break at 11am.
_____

❺ John **write** the minutes of our meetings.
_____

❻ Mrs. Rae **cleaning** the meeting rooms.
_____

❼ The CEO **bring** cake on his birthday.
_____

❽ I **prepares** presentations.
_____

❾ Jomir **stop** for tea at 3pm.
_____

🔊

2.3 MARCA LAS FRASES CORRECTAS

The office close at 7 o'clock. ☐
The office closes at 7 o'clock. ☑

1. The CEO arrive at work early. ☐
   The CEO arrives at work early. ☐

2. We have a hot-desking policy. ☐
   We has a hot-desking policy. ☐

3. My assistant opens my mail. ☐
   My assistant open my mail. ☐

4. Shazia be an engineer. ☐
   Shazia is an engineer. ☐

5. Hal working for his uncle. ☐
   Hal works for his uncle. ☐

6. I start work at 8:30am. ☐
   I starts work at 8:30am. ☐

7. They finish at 5pm. ☐
   They finishes at 5pm. ☐

8. They eating lunch in the cafeteria. ☐
   They eat lunch in the cafeteria. ☐

9. Kate only drinks coffee. ☐
   Kate only drink coffee. ☐

10. I calls the US office every Monday. ☐
    I call the US office every Monday. ☐

11. Andrew helps me with my PC. ☐
    Andrew help me with my PC. ☐

12. I replies to emails at 11am and 3pm. ☐
    I reply to emails at 11am and 3pm. ☐

🔊

2.4 ESCUCHA EL AUDIO Y RESPONDE A LAS PREGUNTAS

La jefa de Sarah le cuenta cómo es el día típico en su nuevo trabajo.

What happens at 9 o'clock?
The office opens ☐
The team starts work ☑
Sarah makes coffee ☐

1. Who makes the coffee at break time?
   Sales staff ☐
   Sales clients ☐
   The manager's PA ☐

2. When do staff call clients?
   At break time ☐
   Before the break ☐
   After the break ☐

3. How long can Sarah take for lunch?
   An hour ☐
   An hour and a half ☐
   Two hours ☐

4. What time can Sarah take her lunch break?
   11:30am ☐
   12:30pm ☐
   2:30pm ☐

5. What does the tech team do?
   They call sales ☐
   They analyze sales ☐
   They make sales ☐

6. How often do staff get training?
   Once a week ☐
   Twice a week ☐
   Three times a week ☐

2.5 TACHA LA PALABRA INCORRECTA DE CADA FRASE

Samia **takes** / ~~take~~ notes in our meetings.

1 The director **has** / **haves** an open door policy.

2 I **deal** / **deals** with all his emails.

3 Gavin **leaves** / **leave** work at 7pm.

4 They **works** / **work** evenings and weekends.

5 She **ride** / **rides** her bike to work.

6 Tim and Pat **bring** / **brings** their own lunch.

7 Deepak **turn** / **turns** off his phone after work.

8 Sobek and Kurt **plays** / **play** tennis after work.

9 My boss **plan** / **plans** my work for the week.

2.6 DI LAS FRASES EN VOZ ALTA COMPLETANDO LOS ESPACIOS CON LAS PALABRAS DEL RECUADRO

I ___write___ a list of my tasks every day.

1 Lulu always _____ to work early.

2 Our reps _____ clients at their office.

3 The CEO _____ to all new staff.

4 He's a nurse and he _____ weekends.

5 Imran _____ with all the contracts.

6 The printer _____ working late in the day.

7 The staff _____ to a nearby café for lunch.

8 Raj _____ a break at 11am.

9 Sophie _____ a travel agent.

deals	go	meet	stops	takes
talks	gets	~~write~~	works	is

17

03 Vocabulario

Aa 3.1 PAÍSES Y CONTINENTES ESCRIBE LAS PALABRAS DEL RECUADRO DEBAJO DE SU CORRESPONDIENTE DIBUJO

Poland

① _____

② _____

③ _____

④ _____

⑧ _____

⑨ _____

⑩ _____

⑪ _____

⑫ _____

⑯ _____

⑰ _____

⑱ _____

⑲ _____

⑳ _____

㉔ _____

㉕ _____

㉖ _____

㉗ _____

㉘ _____

18

5 _____

6 _____

7 _____

13 _____

14 _____

15 _____

21 _____

22 _____

23 _____

29 _____

30 _____

31 _____

Canada   Netherlands   Thailand

China   Japan   ~~Poland~~   Russia

India   Singapore   Mexico

Australia   New Zealand   Spain

France   Brazil   Asia   Africa

Europe   South Africa   Turkey

Argentina   Australasia

North America   Egypt

South Korea   South America

United States of America (US / USA)

Republic of Ireland (ROI)

United Kingdom (UK)

Pakistan   Mongolia

United Arab Emirates (UAE)

04 Empresas en todo el mundo

En inglés se utiliza "from" o adjetivos de nacionalidad para hablar del origen de los productos o las personas. "From" también sirve para hablar de tu empresa o departamento.

⚙ **Lenguaje** Expresiones negativas
Aa Vocabulario Países y nacionalidades
🧩 **Habilidad** Decir de dónde son las cosas

Aa **4.1** BUSCA EN LA PARRILLA LOS CINCO PAÍSES QUE CORRESPONDEN A LAS BANDERAS

```
A  D  R  T  R  K  L  I  J
K  U  U  I  N  D  I  A  A
Q  D  S  M  J  S  M  H  P
R  I  S  T  E  R  C  A  A
P  K  I  T  R  N  H  D  N
C  D  A  S  E  A  I  Z  T
B  Z  X  R  L  A  L  O  J
N  A  F  E  S  N  E  I  Z
T  G  R  E  E  C  E  G  A
```

❶ ❷ ❸ ❹ ❺

Aa **4.2** ESCRIBE LAS PALABRAS DEL RECUADRO EN LOS GRUPOS CORRECTOS

PAÍSES	
South Africa	_____
_____	_____
_____	_____

NACIONALIDADES	
Brazilian	_____
_____	_____
_____	_____

France   ~~South Africa~~   British   Greek   Italy   Canadian
Vietnam   Japanese   Switzerland   ~~Brazilian~~   Spanish   China

4.3 VUELVE A ESCRIBIR CADA FRASE EN SU OTRA FORMA

These new tablets are **from China**.	*These new tablets are Chinese.*
① _____	The new CEO is Australian.
② These new robots are **from Japan**.	_____
③ _____	We sell Portuguese leather bags.
④ _____	I'm Argentinian, but I work in the US.
⑤ The designer is **from Britain**.	_____
⑥ _____	Our sales director is South Korean.
⑦ Our best-selling rugs are **from India**.	_____
⑧ _____	These beautiful clothes are African.

🔊

4.4 MARCA LAS FRASES CORRECTAS

Our restaurant serves Japan food.	☐
Our restaurant serves Japanese food.	☑

① Our CEO is America. ☐
Our CEO is from America. ☐

② I've got a flight to Italy next Monday. ☐
I've got a flight to Italian next Monday. ☐

③ These sports cars are from French. ☐
These sports cars are from France. ☐

④ Most of our fabrics are from Africa. ☐
Most of our fabrics are from African. ☐

⑤ My PA is from Spanish. ☐
My PA is from Spain. ☐

🔊

4.5 TACHA LA PALABRA INCORRECTA DE CADA FRASE

Our best products are from **Russia** / ~~Russian~~.

① We sell smartphones from **Japan** / Japanese.

② The HR manager is from **America** / American.

③ My team follows the **China** / Chinese markets.

④ Travel to the **Greece** / Greek islands with us.

⑤ Our products are from **Vietnam** / Vietnamese.

⑥ Our CEO is **Canada** / Canadian.

⑦ Most of the sales team is from **Spain** / Spanish.

⑧ I'm British, but I work in **Italy** / Italian.

⑨ I have a lot of **Mexico** / Mexican co-workers.

⑩ My new assistant is from **France** / French.

🔊

4.6 VUELVE A ESCRIBIR LAS FRASES CORRIGIENDO LOS ERRORES Y UTILIZANDO CONTRACCIONES

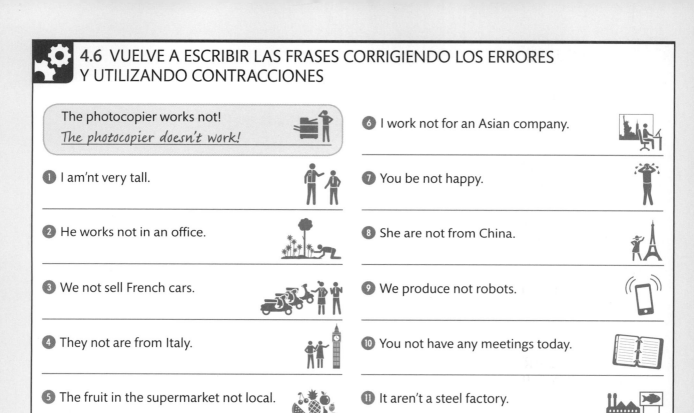

The photocopier works not!
The photocopier doesn't work!

1 I am'nt very tall.

2 He works not in an office.

3 We not sell French cars.

4 They not are from Italy.

5 The fruit in the supermarket not local.

6 I work not for an Asian company.

7 You be not happy.

8 She are not from China.

9 We produce not robots.

10 You not have any meetings today.

11 It aren't a steel factory.

4.7 DI LAS FRASES EN VOZ ALTA UTILIZANDO CONTRACCIONES

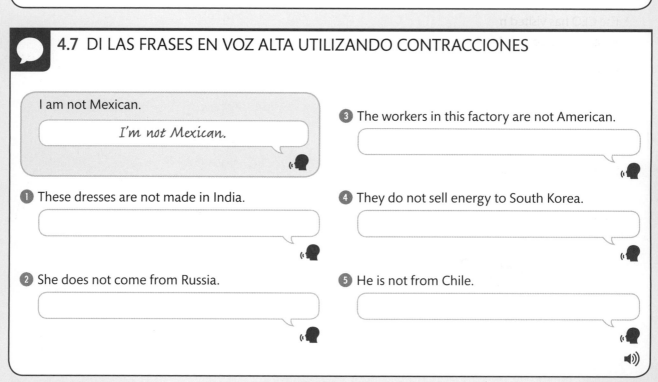

I am not Mexican.

I'm not Mexican.

1 These dresses are not made in India.

2 She does not come from Russia.

3 The workers in this factory are not American.

4 They do not sell energy to South Korea.

5 He is not from Chile.

4.8 ESCUCHA EL AUDIO Y RESPONDE A LAS PREGUNTAS

Nadia, Tim y Carlos asisten a una conferencia.

What department does Nadia work in?
Finance ☐ **Sales** ☑ **IT** ☐

❶ What department does Carlos work in?
Finance ☐ **Sales** ☐ **IT** ☐

❷ Who hasn't Nadia met before?
Carlos ☐ **Tim** ☐ **Neither of them** ☐

❸ What department does Tim work in?
Finance ☐ **Marketing** ☐ **IT** ☐

❹ Who has to report back to their team?
Tim ☐ **Nadia** ☐ **Carlos** ☐

❺ Where will Tim's company launch a brand?
China ☐ **Chile** ☐ **Japan** ☐

4.9 LEE EL ARTÍCULO Y RESPONDE A LAS PREGUNTAS

The company sells food from one country.
True ☐ **False** ☑ **Not given** ☐

❶ The CEO has visited many different countries.
True ☐ **False** ☐ **Not given** ☐

❷ He stayed with local people in each country.
True ☐ **False** ☐ **Not given** ☐

❸ All Fairtrade coffee comes from Chile.
True ☐ **False** ☐ **Not given** ☐

❹ Some Fairtrade products come from Kenya.
True ☐ **False** ☐ **Not given** ☐

❺ Food always tastes better if it's Fairtrade.
True ☐ **False** ☐ **Not given** ☐

❻ "Tasters" choose the food that the company sells.
True ☐ **False** ☐ **Not given** ☐

❼ "Selectors" find new foods to sell.
True ☐ **False** ☐ **Not given** ☐

COMPANY PROFILES

Foods from around the World

Founded in 2005, Foods from around the World brings you food from every corner of the globe. Their CEO, Johnathon Medway, had the idea for the company after he spent a year traveling around the world, eating exotic foods in each country that he visited.

Johnathon says, "We buy directly from our producers and all the food you buy from us has the Fairtrade guarantee. That means the food is from small-scale farmers in countries like India, Chile, and Egypt. Workers are treated fairly and paid a living wage. So Costa Rican coffee growers and Kenyan tea growers all earn enough to live on if you buy our products."

So, how does the company find new products to sell? They have a team of "tasters" who travel around a different region of the world, trying food in markets, cafés, and from shops and factories. The "tasters" then make a shortlist of their favorite products for the "selectors" to choose from at the head office. Finally, the "selectors" talk to the producer and agree a trade deal. So, next time you want to eat something interesting, go to Foods from around the World.

05 Vocabulario

Aa 5.1 **EN LA OFICINA** ESCRIBE LAS PALABRAS DEL RECUADRO DEBAJO DE SU CORRESPONDIENTE DIBUJO

photocopier

 1 _____

 2 _____

 3 _____

 4 _____

 8 _____

 9 _____

 10 _____

 11 _____

 12 _____

 16 _____

 17 _____

 18 _____

 19 _____

 20 _____

 24 _____

 25 _____

 26 _____

 27 _____

 28 _____

 5 _____

 6 _____

 7 _____

 13 _____

 14 _____

 15 _____

 21 _____

 22 _____

 23 _____

 29 _____

 30 _____

 31 _____

letter   adhesive tape

planner (US) / diary (UK)   notepad

computer   pencil   ruler

files / folders   stapler

lamp   hole punch

pencil sharpener   highlighter

laptop   pen   chair

eraser (US) / rubber (UK)

calendar   paper clips   headset

rubber bands   shredder

~~photocopier~~   clipboard

hard drive   scanner

telephone / phone   projector

envelope   printer   tablet

cell phone (US) / mobile phone (UK)

Preguntar cosas en el trabajo

Es importante utilizar el orden adecuado de las palabras y los pronombres interrogativos en las preguntas en inglés, especialmente si son preguntas abiertas.

⚙ **Lenguaje** Formular preguntas
Aa Vocabulario Material de oficina
🧩 **Habilidad** Preguntar a los colegas

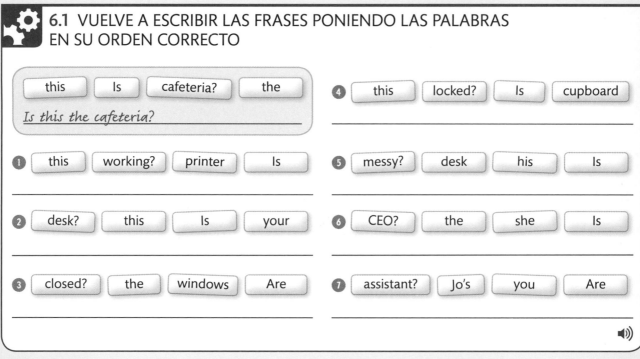

6.1 VUELVE A ESCRIBIR LAS FRASES PONIENDO LAS PALABRAS EN SU ORDEN CORRECTO

| this | Is | cafeteria? | the |

Is this the cafeteria?

① | this | working? | printer | Is |

② | desk? | this | Is | your |

③ | closed? | the | windows | Are |

④ | this | locked? | Is | cupboard |

⑤ | messy? | desk | his | Is |

⑥ | CEO? | the | she | Is |

⑦ | assistant? | Jo's | you | Are |

🔊

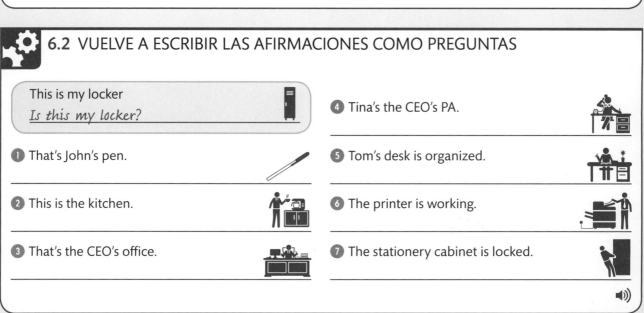

6.2 VUELVE A ESCRIBIR LAS AFIRMACIONES COMO PREGUNTAS

This is my locker
Is this my locker?

① That's John's pen.

② This is the kitchen.

③ That's the CEO's office.

④ Tina's the CEO's PA.

⑤ Tom's desk is organized.

⑥ The printer is working.

⑦ The stationery cabinet is locked.

🔊

6.3 COMPLETA LOS ESPACIOS CON "DO" O "DOES"

_____*Does*_____ she come in at 9am?

1. _____ you have an appointment?
2. _____ she work with Justin?
3. _____ your office have a scanner?
4. _____ you go to the finance meetings?
5. _____ Kish write the minutes?
6. _____ you have a stapler I can borrow?
7. _____ Saul work in your team?
8. _____ they know what to do?
9. _____ he know the CEO?
10. _____ we have a meeting now?

🔊

6.4 ESCUCHA EL AUDIO Y RESPONDE A LAS PREGUNTAS

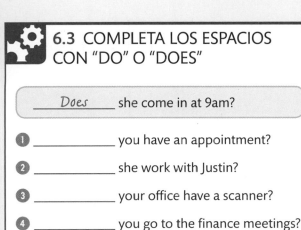

Rosa y Jordan se preparan para la presentación que deben hacer mañana.

All the meeting rooms are busy.
True ☐ **False** ☑

1. Room 203 is too small for the presentation.
True ☐ **False** ☐

2. There is a projector in the room.
True ☐ **False** ☐

3. Rosa and Jordan will use Rosa's laptop.
True ☐ **False** ☐

4. The video clips don't work.
True ☐ **False** ☐

6.5 CONECTA LAS SITUACIONES CON LAS PREGUNTAS CORRECTAS

I need to print this report.	Do you want tea or coffee?
1. We've run out of pens.	Do you know her phone number?
2. I'm going to make some hot drinks.	Is the printer working today?
3. I need to call Paola.	Do you have a laptop I can take home?
4. We should talk to our clients soon.	Is the stationery cabinet open?
5. I want to work from home tomorrow.	Are there any envelopes I can use?
6. You want to see a doctor.	Are they free for a meeting tomorrow?
7. I want to send a letter.	Does he usually arrive late?
8. Henry should be here by now.	Do you have an appointment?

🔊

6.6 TACHA LA PALABRA INCORRECTA DE CADA PREGUNTA

Where / ~~Which~~ are you going on vacation?

❶ How / Who does the scanner work?

❷ What / When is on the agenda for the meeting?

❸ Who / Why is the stationery cabinet locked?

❹ Who / When do we have a break for lunch?

❺ Where / What is the CEO's office?

❻ When / What is the door code?

❼ What / Who do I ask for ink for the printer?

🔊

6.7 MARCA LAS PREGUNTAS CORRECTAS

Does you know the door code? ☐
Do you know the door code? ☑

❶ Why does the cafeteria closed? ☐
Why is the cafeteria closed? ☐

❷ How do I scan this document? ☐
Who do I scan this document? ☐

❸ When are the fire alarm tested? ☐
When is the fire alarm tested? ☐

❹ Do you know where Faisal is? ☐
Does you know where Faisal is? ☐

❺ Are Sandra late again? ☐
Is Sandra late again? ☐

❻ Where is for lunch today? ☐
What is for lunch today? ☐

❼ Does the office stay open on weekends? ☐
Do the office stay open on weekends? ☐

❽ Who do you report to? ☐
Who you do report to? ☐

🔊

6.8 DI LAS FRASES EN VOZ ALTA COMPLETANDO LOS ESPACIOS CON LAS PALABRAS DEL RECUADRO

How do you get to work?

❶ _____ buys the tea and coffee?

❷ _____ is the printer not working?

❸ _____ does the office open?

❹ _____ do you want for lunch?

❺ _____ is the meeting room?

❻ _____ does the projector work?

❼ _____ is the photocopier code?

What	Where	How	Why
~~How~~	What	When	Who

🔊

28

07 Datos de contacto

Existen diversas expresiones para obtener y ofrecer información cuando se hacen nuevos contactos profesionales.

⚙ **Lenguaje** Respuestas cortas
Aa Vocabulario Información de contacto
🧩 **Habilidad** Intercambiar datos de contacto

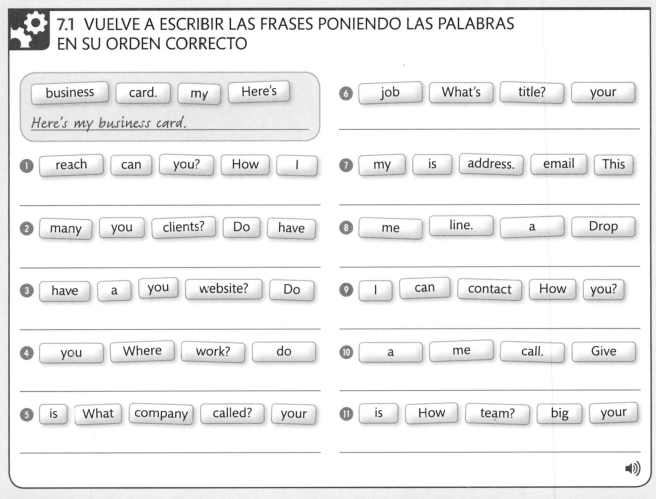

7.1 VUELVE A ESCRIBIR LAS FRASES PONIENDO LAS PALABRAS EN SU ORDEN CORRECTO

| business | card. | my | Here's |

Here's my business card.

1 | reach | can | you? | How | I |

_____

2 | many | you | clients? | Do | have |

_____

3 | have | a | you | website? | Do |

_____

4 | you | Where | work? | do |

_____

5 | is | What | company | called? | your |

_____

6 | job | What's | title? | your |

_____

7 | my | is | address. | email | This |

_____

8 | me | line. | a | Drop |

_____

9 | I | can | contact | How | you? |

_____

10 | a | me | call. | Give |

_____

11 | is | How | team? | big | your |

_____

7.2 ESCUCHA EL AUDIO Y NUMERA DESPUÉS LAS DIRECCIONES DE CORREO ELECTRÓNICO EN EL ORDEN EN QUE LAS OIGAS

Ⓐ paul_andrews@worldmail.co.jp ☐

Ⓑ pete_anderson@energo-mail.com

Ⓒ j.c.jones@digitalnetwork.co.uk

Ⓓ information@digimail.com ☐

Ⓔ maria.renzi@digi-tech.com [1]

Ⓕ claire.james@electrosolution.co.fr ☐

7.3 TACHA LA PALABRA INCORRECTA DE CADA FRASE

Do you have a ~~email~~ / business card?

1. How can I reach / touch you for more information?
2. Drop me a call / line when you're visiting next.
3. Does your company keep / have a website?
4. Please stay in reach / touch.

5. Is this your correct / precise phone number?
6. Line / Call me if you want further details.
7. Is this your present / current email address?
8. My job title / name is on the business card.
9. Do you have / got a portfolio with you?

7.4 MIRA LAS TARJETAS Y RESPONDE A LAS PREGUNTAS

Stronger Web Solutions is a café.
True ☐ False ☑ Not given ☐

1. Janice Strong is a web designer.
   True ☐ False ☐ Not given ☐

2. Stronger Web Solutions has a website.
   True ☐ False ☐ Not given ☐

3. Greybridge History Museum is 100 years old.
   True ☐ False ☐ Not given ☐

4. Dan has a website.
   True ☐ False ☐ Not given ☐

5. Dan works as an archaeologist.
   True ☐ False ☐ Not given ☐

6. Dan has an email address.
   True ☐ False ☐ Not given ☐

7. Paul is a web designer.
   True ☐ False ☐ Not given ☐

8. Consoul is based in Los Angeles.
   True ☐ False ☐ Not given ☐

Janice Strong
Web Designer
www.strongerweb.com

STRONGER WEB SOLUTIONS
Tel: 1 (545) 345-2342
info@strongerweb.com

GREYBRIDGE HISTORY MUSEUM
Seal Street, Daltry, Hertfordshire, H23 9NB
Dan Stone - Historian
Email: dstone@greybridge.co.uk
Tel: 0743 235 436

CONSOUL
Managing consultant, ConSoul

CONSOUL

PAUL@CONSOUL.COM
07853453452
23 Garden Walk
Cambridge
C43 7FD

7.5 CONECTA LAS FRASES CON LAS RESPUESTAS CORTAS CORRECTAS

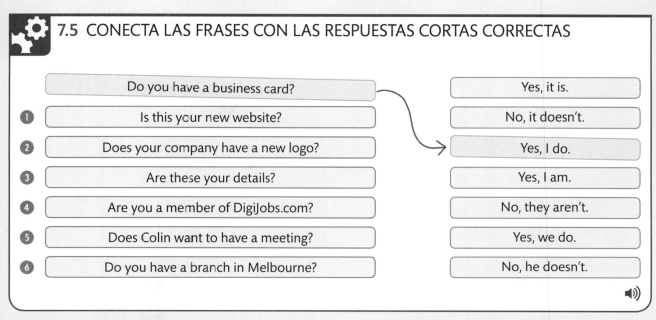

Do you have a business card? → Yes, I do.

① Is this your new website?
② Does your company have a new logo?
③ Are these your details?
④ Are you a member of DigiJobs.com?
⑤ Does Colin want to have a meeting?
⑥ Do you have a branch in Melbourne?

Yes, it is.
No, it doesn't.
Yes, I do.
Yes, I am.
No, they aren't.
Yes, we do.
No, he doesn't.

7.6 RESPONDE AL AUDIO EN VOZ ALTA UTILIZANDO LAS PALABRAS DEL RECUADRO

Do you have your portfolio?
No, _I don't_ .

① Is this your correct telephone number?
No, _____ .

② Does your company have a blog?
No, _____ .

③ Is this your email address?
Yes, _____ .

④ Does your company have a website?
Yes, _____ .

⑤ Do your employees work hard?
No, _____ .

⑥ Are you a member of a trade union?
No, _____ .

⑦ Do they have a branch in Mumbai?
Yes, _____ .

⑧ Does Mrs. Parry have an office?
Yes, _____ .

⑨ Do you want to go for lunch now?
Yes, _____ .

08 Capacidades y experiencia

En inglés se utiliza el verbo "have" para hablar de las capacidades, la experiencia y los atributos profesionales. También se usa "have got" en inglés británico informal.

Lenguaje "Have", "have got", artículos
Aa Vocabulario Trabajos y capacidades
Habilidad Redactar un perfil profesional

8.1 TACHA LAS PALABRAS INCORRECTAS DE CADA FRASE

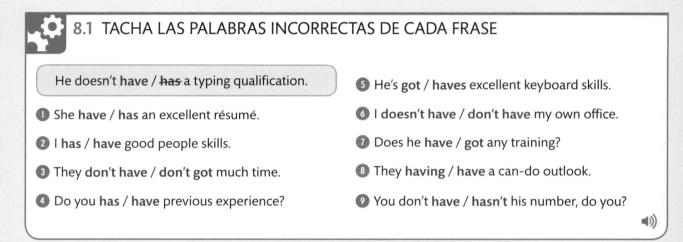

He doesn't **have** / ~~has~~ a typing qualification.

1. She **have** / **has** an excellent résumé.

2. I **has** / **have** good people skills.

3. They **don't have** / **don't got** much time.

4. Do you **has** / **have** previous experience?

5. He's **got** / **haves** excellent keyboard skills.

6. I **doesn't have** / **don't have** my own office.

7. Does he **have** / **got** any training?

8. They **having** / **have** a can-do outlook.

9. You don't **have** / **hasn't** his number, do you?

8.2 VUELVE A ESCRIBIR LAS FRASES PONIENDO LAS PALABRAS EN SU ORDEN CORRECTO

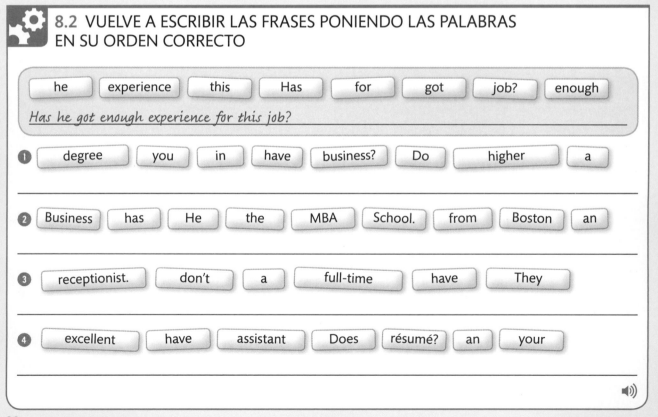

| he | experience | this | Has | for | got | job? | enough |

Has he got enough experience for this job?

1. | degree | you | in | have | business? | Do | higher | a |

2. | Business | has | He | the | MBA | School. | from | Boston | an |

3. | receptionist. | don't | a | full-time | have | They |

4. | excellent | have | assistant | Does | résumé? | an | your |

Hamid Syal

SALES AND MARKETING PROFESSIONAL

Experience

 I am a creative and proactive marketing professional who has varied experience in the travel industry. I love helping people realize their dreams of visiting new places and devising new ways to market vacations. I started work in the hotel industry as a receptionist before working my way up to deputy manager. I have worked in countries such as Japan, India, and South Africa and for well-known, prestigious hotels such as The Ritz. I have a passion for travel and often visit new countries. My next vacation is to Tanzania, where I hope to go on safari.

Achievements

- Advising Explore the World travel agency on how to grow new markets and existing ones.
- Investigating and taking forward new business ideas, providing strategic recommendations to the SMT (Senior Management Team).
- Acting as the public-facing representative of Safari Travels, giving presentations at industry events.

Skills

I have excellent people skills, learned from my time in the hotel sector.
I enjoy working in teams to market vacations on behalf of a wide range of clients.

Qualifications

- BS Business and Hospitality Management, London South Bank University, 2010
- Diploma in Marketing, CIM (Chartered Institute of Marketing), 2015

What job does Hamid have? **He's a sales rep** ☐ **He's the CEO** ☐ **He works in marketing** ☑

❶ What industry does Hamid work in? **Hotels** ☐ **Travel** ☐ **Airlines** ☐

❷ Where has Hamid worked before? **A department store** ☐ **A restaurant** ☐ **A hotel** ☐

❸ Who has Hamid advised on strategy? **Strategists** ☐ **Management** ☐ **The Chief Executive** ☐

❹ How does Hamid describe his people skills? **Average** ☐ **Good** ☐ **Excellent** ☐

❺ In what situation does Hamid say he enjoys working? **Alone** ☐ **In teams** ☐ **With clients** ☐

❻ What is the subject of Hamid's diploma? **Business** ☐ **Marketing** ☐ **Hospitality Management** ☐

8.4 MARCA LAS FRASES QUE SEAN CORRECTAS

I have excellent interpersonal skills. ✓
I have excellent the interpersonal skills. ☐

1. The new chef is very talented. ☐
   A new chef is very talented. ☐

2. Toby is a accountant. ☐
   Toby is an accountant. ☐

3. Search engines are invaluable. ☐
   The search engines are invaluable. ☐

4. She works for a leading company. ☐
   She works for leading company. ☐

5. Have you seen an ad I told you about? ☐
   Have you seen the ad I told you about? ☐

6. They are out of office. ☐
   They are out of the office. ☐

7. Did you see the new designs? ☐
   Did you see a new designs? ☐

8. They hired best candidate. ☐
   They hired the best candidate. ☐

9. What skills does the job require? ☐
   What a skills does the job require? ☐

10. Is there an office in India? ☐
    Is there a office in India? ☐

11. I have the certificate in sales. ☐
    I have a certificate in sales. ☐

12. He works for a biggest store. ☐
    He works for the biggest store. ☐

13. Interns are only paid expenses. ☐
    Interns are only paid the expenses. ☐

🔊

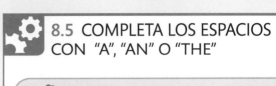 **8.5 COMPLETA LOS ESPACIOS CON "A", "AN" O "THE"**

He works in ____a____ phone store.

1. I worked as _____ intern at Beales.

2. I know _____ café you mean.

3. There's ____ printer on the second floor.

4. Jon hasn't got _____ diploma.

5. The CEO is in _____ NY office this week.

6. He's _____ amazing architect.

7. I just started _____ new job.

8. I'd like to put _____ ad in the paper.

9. Have you read _____ job description?

10. I work at _____ theater next door.

11. _____ new café does great coffee.

12. Where is _____ presentation?

13. The Tate is _____ art gallery.

14. I like _____ new CEO.

🔊

8.6 ESCUCHA EL AUDIO Y NUMERA DESPUÉS LAS IMÁGENES EN EL ORDEN EN QUE LAS OIGAS

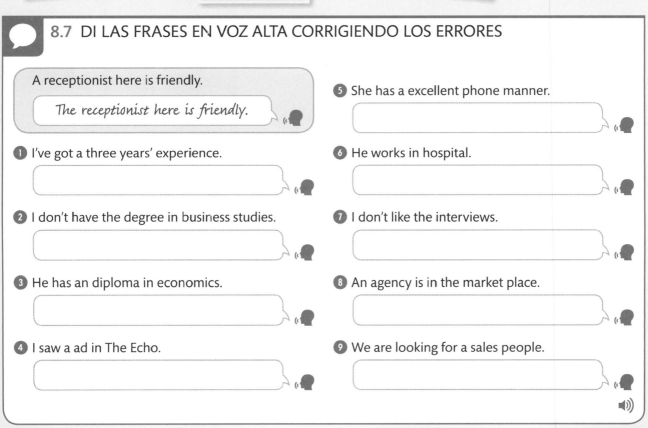

8.7 DI LAS FRASES EN VOZ ALTA CORRIGIENDO LOS ERRORES

A receptionist here is friendly.

The receptionist here is friendly.

1. I've got a three years' experience.

2. I don't have the degree in business studies.

3. He has an diploma in economics.

4. I saw a ad in The Echo.

5. She has a excellent phone manner.

6. He works in hospital.

7. I don't like the interviews.

8. An agency is in the market place.

9. We are looking for a sales people.

Aa 9.1 **TRABAJOS** ESCRIBE LAS PALABRAS DEL RECUADRO DEBAJO DE SU CORRESPONDIENTE DIBUJO

gardener

1 _____

2 _____

3 _____

4 _____

7 _____

8 _____

9 _____

10 _____

11 _____

14 _____

15 _____

16 _____

17 _____

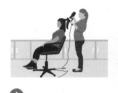
18 _____

21 _____

22 _____

23 _____

24 _____

25 _____

tour guide	judge	musician	sales assistant	cleaner / janitor	mechanic
vet	surgeon	~~gardener~~	artist	firefighter	librarian	designer
waitress	pilot	travel agent	hairdresser / stylist	electrician	doctor	train driver

5 _____   6 _____

12 _____   13 _____

19 _____   20 _____

26 _____   27 _____

writer   taxi driver   plumber

engineer   scientist   chef

sales manager   receptionist

A long-term, salaried position

permanent

❶ A period of work with a set number of hours

_____

❷ A person who is learning a trade

_____

❸ A complete working week

_____

❹ A short-term position with a known end date

_____

❺ A person you work with in a profession

_____

❻ An incomplete working week

_____

part-time (P/T)   shift   ~~permanent~~   temporary

co-worker / colleague   apprentice   full-time (F/T)

10 Elegir un trabajo

Los verbos "like", "enjoy" y "hate" expresan sentimientos sobre las cosas. Se utilizan a menudo para hablar sobre qué actividades se quieren desempeñar en el trabajo.

⚙ **Lenguaje** "Like", "enjoy" y "hate"
Aa Vocabulario Actividades del lugar de trabajo
🧩 **Habilidad** Encontrar el trabajo adecuado

⚙ 10.1 CONECTA LAS FRASES QUE VAN JUNTAS

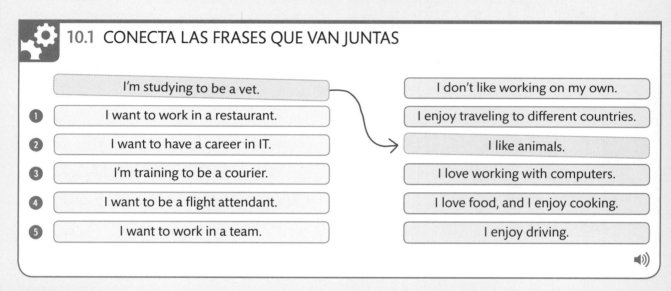

I'm studying to be a vet. ——→ I like animals.

① I want to work in a restaurant.

② I want to have a career in IT.

③ I'm training to be a courier.

④ I want to be a flight attendant.

⑤ I want to work in a team.

I don't like working on my own.

I enjoy traveling to different countries.

I like animals.

I love working with computers.

I love food, and I enjoy cooking.

I enjoy driving.

🔊

⚙ 10.2 VUELVE A ESCRIBIR LAS FRASES CORRIGIENDO LOS ERRORES

I like **work** outdoors.
I like working outdoors.

① She loves **meet** new clients.

② He **don't** enjoy giving presentations.

③ I hate **trained** big groups.

④ They like **work** in a team.

⑤ Jan **enjoy** working with children.

⑥ Ali doesn't **likes** long meetings.

⑦ We don't **liked** working weekends.

⑧ I love **solve** problems.

⑨ Jim doesn't **enjoying** business trips.

🔊

10.3 ESCUCHA EL AUDIO Y MARCA SI A QUIEN HABLA LE GUSTA O NO LA ACTIVIDAD DE CADA IMAGEN

Le gusta ☑ No le gusta ☐

① Le gusta ☐ No le gusta ☐

② Le gusta ☐ No le gusta ☐

③ Le gusta ☐ No le gusta ☐

④ Le gusta ☐ No le gusta ☐

⑤ Le gusta ☐ No le gusta ☐

⑥ Le gusta ☐ No le gusta ☐

⑦ Le gusta ☐ No le gusta ☐

10.4 TACHA LA PALABRA INCORRECTA DE CADA FRASE Y LUEGO DILAS TODAS EN VOZ ALTA

Does he like working / ~~work~~ weekends?

① I don't / doesn't enjoy work social trips.

② They like meet / meeting new people.

③ He doesn't like / likes working late.

④ She hates sitting / siting at a desk all day.

⑤ Do you enjoy work / working in a team?

⑥ We enjoy give / giving presentations.

⑦ Angus doesn't like use / using computers.

39

11 Describir el lugar de trabajo

Para explicar cosas de la empresa puedes utilizar "there is" y "there are". Utiliza "Is there...?" o "Are there...?" para formular preguntas sobre un lugar de trabajo.

⚙ **Lenguaje** "There is" y "there are"
Aa Vocabulario Material de oficina
🧩 **Habilidad** Describir un lugar de trabajo

11.1 MARCA LAS FRASES QUE SEAN CORRECTAS

There is a washroom on this floor? ☐
Is there a washroom on this floor? ☑

1 There are three printers in your department. ☐
There're three printers in your department. ☐

2 Are there ladies' toilets on the second floor? ☐
Is there ladies' toilets on the second floor? ☐

3 There isnt a cafeteria in the building. ☐
There isn't a cafeteria in the building. ☐

4 Is there a set time for lunch breaks? ☐
Is there any set time for lunch breaks? ☐

5 There are'nt any elevators in the office. ☐
There aren't any elevators in the office. ☐

6 Is there a dress code at this company? ☐
Are there a dress code at this company? ☐

7 There's photocopier on the first floor. ☐
There's a photocopier on the first floor. ☐

8 There aren't a trash cans in the office. ☐
There aren't any trash cans in the office. ☐

9 There are any interns on your team? ☐
Are there any interns on your team? ☐

10 There is a calendar on the notice board. ☐
There are a calendar on the notice board. ☐

🔊

11.2 CONECTA LAS IMÁGENES CON LAS FRASES CORRECTAS

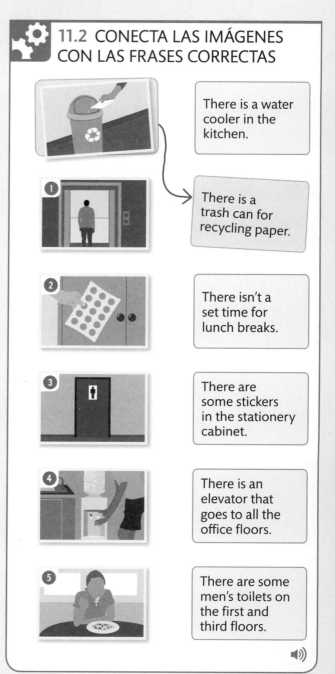

There is a water cooler in the kitchen.

There is a trash can for recycling paper.

There isn't a set time for lunch breaks.

There are some stickers in the stationery cabinet.

There is an elevator that goes to all the office floors.

There are some men's toilets on the first and third floors.

🔊

40

11.3 ESCUCHA EL AUDIO Y RESPONDE A LAS PREGUNTAS

Debbie le cuenta a Boris cómo fue el primer día en su nuevo trabajo.

There are five people on Debbie's team.
True ☑ False ☐ Not given ☐

❶ There is an elevator in Debbie's office.
True ☐ False ☐ Not given ☐

❷ There isn't a separate office for Debbie's team.
True ☐ False ☐ Not given ☐

❸ Debbie's office is on the third floor.
True ☐ False ☐ Not given ☐

❹ There is a printer in Debbie's office.
True ☐ False ☐ Not given ☐

❺ There is a casual dress code.
True ☐ False ☐ Not given ☐

❻ There's a deli near the office.
True ☐ False ☐ Not given ☐

11.4 TACHA LA PALABRA INCORRECTA DE CADA FRASE, Y DI LUEGO TODAS LAS FRASES EN VOZ ALTA

There is / are lots of great restaurants close to my office.

❶ There is / are two positions available at our company.

❷ There isn't a / any toaster in the kitchen, but there is a microwave.

❸ Is / Are there a spare computer I can use?

❹ Are there a / any pencils in the stationery cabinet?

❺ There is / are a big meeting room in our new office.

41

12 Vocabulario

Aa **12.1 DINERO** ESCRIBE LAS PALABRAS DEL RECUADRO DEBAJO DE SU CORRESPONDIENTE DIBUJO

debit card

 ❶ _____

 ❷ _____

 ❸ _____

 ❹ _____

 ❺ _____

 ❻ _____

 ❼ _____

 ❽ _____

 ❾ _____

 ❿ _____

 ⓫ _____

 ⓬ _____

 ⓭ _____

 ⓮ _____

 ⓯ _____

currency   credit card   receipt   cash register (US) / till (UK)   ~~debit card~~   bank

bills (US) / notes (UK)   invoice   cash machine / ATM   wallet   withdraw money

check (US) / cheque (UK)   online banking   safe   mobile banking   transfer money

Aa 12.2 SALARIO Y CONDICIONES ESCRIBE LAS PALABRAS DEL RECUADRO DEBAJO DE SU DEFINICIÓN

The amount of money paid per week or month

wage

① Additional pay for extra hours worked

② A fixed, regular payment every month, often expressed as an annual sum

③ Extras given to employees in addition to their usual pay

④ An increase in pay

⑤ To receive money in return for labor or services

⑥ Money added to a person's wages as a reward for good performance

⑦ Paid time off work granted by employers

⑧ The amount of money paid per hour

⑨ A reduction in pay

| a bonus | salary | annual vacation (US) / annual leave (UK) | | a pay cut | ~~wage~~ |
| to earn | hourly rate | overtime | a raise (US) / a pay rise (UK) | | benefits |

13 Cualidades personales

En el trabajo coincidirás con personas con personalidades y habilidades diferentes. Es muy útil poder describir a tus colegas y hablar de sus fortalezas y debilidades.

⚙ **Lenguaje** Adjetivos posesivos
Aa Vocabulario Rasgos de personalidad
🧩 **Habilidad** Describir a los colegas

 13.1 VUELVE A ESCRIBIR LAS FRASES CORRIGIENDO LOS ERRORES

I run a team great, but Kezia be really lazy.
I run a great team, but Kezia is really lazy.

❶ The new intern seems really bright and she is organized very.

_____

❷ My manager doesn't ask employees nervous to give presentations.

_____

❸ My director very bossy is and she is also hardworking.

_____

❹ Sue and Robin are sometimes rudes to our clients.

_____

❺ It's important to stay under pressure calm, even if you're very busy.

_____

❻ Mushira is very intelligente, and she will bring a great deal to the team.

_____

❼ It's impossible to feel relaxed when you work with people impatient.

_____

❽ The people on my team are all very motivateds, and it's great to work with them.

_____

❾ We are looking for a designer creative to join our busy production team.

_____

🔊

13.2 VUELVE A ESCRIBIR LAS FRASES PONIENDO LAS PALABRAS EN SU ORDEN CORRECTO

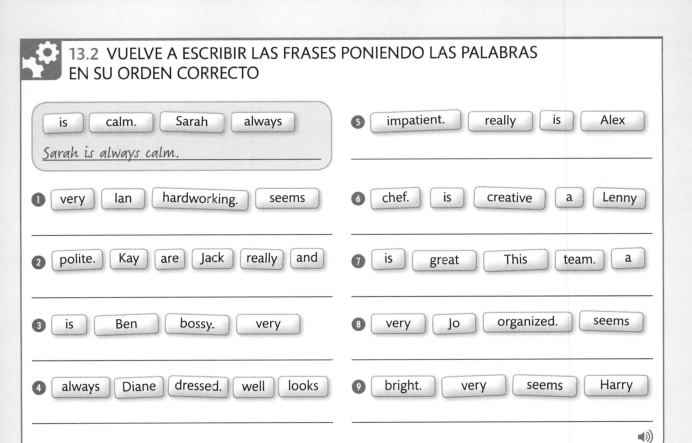

is · calm. · Sarah · always

Sarah is always calm.

1. very · Ian · hardworking. · seems

_____

2. polite. · Kay · are · Jack · really · and

_____

3. is · Ben · bossy. · very

_____

4. always · Diane · dressed. · well · looks

_____

5. impatient. · really · is · Alex

_____

6. chef. · is · creative · a · Lenny

_____

7. is · great · This · team. · a

_____

8. very · Jo · organized. · seems

_____

9. bright. · very · seems · Harry

_____

13.3 ESCUCHA EL AUDIO Y CONECTA LAS PERSONAS DE CADA IMAGEN CON EL ADJETIVO CORRECTO

organized · calm · creative

polite · well dressed

13.4 COMPLETA LOS ESPACIOS CON EL ADJETIVO POSESIVO QUE CORRESPONDE AL PRONOMBRE SUJETO QUE SE INDICA

James is very hardworking. _____His_____ (He) list of things to do is very long.

1 _____ (We) team meetings are always interesting.

2 Is this _____ (you) desk? It's very messy!

3 _____ (I) team is very motivated.

4 Is that _____ (they) design? It's great.

5 Kevin is talking to _____ (he) manager.

6 That's Tanya. _____ (She) phone manner is excellent.

7 The company is very proud of _____ (it) reputation.

 ## 13.5 TACHA LA PALABRA INCORRECTA DE CADA FRASE

This laptop is ~~my~~ / mine.

1 Is this **he** / his desk?

2 We don't like **theirs** / their product.

3 **My** / Mine manager is very smart.

4 This report is **your** / yours.

5 Jane does **her** / hers job well.

6 They are proud of **their** / theirs reputation.

7 Is this tablet **her** / hers?

8 **Their** / Theirs manager is never late.

9 Is this **your** / yours pen?

46

13.6 MARCA LAS FRASES QUE SEAN CORRECTAS

Toms secretary will take the minutes. ☐
Tom's secretary will take the minutes. ☑

❶ The interns have just finished college. ☐
The intern's have just finished college. ☐

❷ Jorges reputation is well deserved. ☐
Jorge's reputation is well deserved. ☐

❸ Nuala's assistant is very helpful. ☐
Nualas assistant is very helpful. ☐

❹ Helens manager often works late. ☐
Helen's manager often works late. ☐

❺ Maria's co-workers are really friendly. ☐
Marias co-workers are really friendly. ☐

❻ The team members' are hardworking. ☐
The team members are hardworking. ☐

❼ Look at this ad. I like it's design. ☐
Look at this ad. I like its design. ☐

❽ Leroy's work is very impressive. ☐
Leroys' work is very impressive. ☐

❾ Are there any file's in the cabinet? ☐
Are there any files in the cabinet? ☐

❿ Johns confidence has grown this year. ☐
John's confidence has grown this year. ☐

⓫ Sams' presentation went really well. ☐
Sam's presentation went really well. ☐

⓬ The CEO's new assistant is very bright. ☐
The CEOs' new assistant is very bright. ☐

⓭ Their products are very popular. ☐
Their product's are very popular. ☐

⓮ That's my bosses parking space. ☐
That's my boss's parking space. ☐

⓯ Pablo's report is almost finished. ☐
Pablos report is almost finished. ☐

⓰ The company is pleased with it's new logo. ☐
The company is pleased with its new logo. ☐

⓱ Ethans' team is working on a new project. ☐
Ethan's team is working on a new project. ☐

🔊

13.7 UTILIZA EL DIAGRAMA PARA CREAR 14 FRASES CORRECTAS Y DILAS EN VOZ ALTA

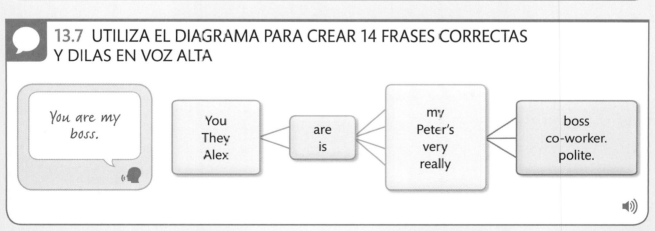

🔊

47

14 Describir tu trabajo

Una manera de explicar cosas de tu trabajo es utilizar adjetivos para describirlo. Los adjetivos te permiten comparar con otros cargos que hayas tenido.

⚙ **Lenguaje** Adjetivos y comparativos
Aa Vocabulario Dinero y salario
Habilidad Describirle tu trabajo a alguien

 14.1 TACHA LA PALABRA INCORRECTA DE CADA FRASE

Sean has a very ~~interested~~ / interesting proposal.

1 Vihaan is very **satisfied / satisfying** with his office.

2 The new login system is rather **annoyed / annoying**.

3 The quarterly results are **shocked / shocking**.

4 The economic situation is quite **worried / worrying**.

5 We're **excited / exciting** about the new office.

6 Simone was **tired / tiring** after the course.

7 The profits were **disappointed / disappointing**.

8 John is **confused / confusing** about the schedule.

9 We were **surprised / surprising** by the results.

10 We thought the meeting was **bored / boring**.

11 I'm often **exhausted / exhausting** by Friday.

🔊

Aa 14.2 CONECTA CADA DEFINICIÓN CON EL ADJETIVO QUE LE CORRESPONDE

very tired	boring
1 something that is not interesting	surprising
2 unable to understand or think clearly	exhausted
3 something that gives you enthusiasm	worried
4 something that is irritating	interesting
5 something that is not expected	exciting
6 something you want to know more about	annoying
7 sad that something is not as good as expected	confused
8 concerned or anxious about something	disappointed

🔊

14.3 COMPLETA LOS ESPACIOS CON LOS ADJETIVOS DEL RECUADRO Y SUS FORMAS COMPARATIVAS

Jan is _____excited_____ about the news, but is _____more excited_____ about her promotion.

❶ I am very _____ with the new project, but I'll be even _____ next week.

❷ Our new office building is _____ , but the office in Beijing is _____ .

❸ My job is very _____ , but being unemployed is _____ .

❹ The meeting was _____ , but last week's was even _____ .

❺ John's flight ticket was _____ , but mine was _____ .

❻ Our new photocopier is _____ , but the HR department's is _____ .

❼ Claire's news was _____ , but Peter resigning was _____ .

❽ My current job is _____ , but my old one was _____ .

❾ The new furniture is _____ , but the furniture at G-Tech is _____ .

❿ This test is _____ , but the next one will be _____ .

⓫ My commute is _____ ; it's only 10 minutes. Pete's is even _____ .

| comfortable | stressful | interesting | expensive | difficult | large |
| long | fast | ~~excited~~ | surprising | short | busy |

14.4 VUELVE A ESCRIBIR LAS FRASES CON LA FORMA COMPARATIVA DEL ADJETIVO QUE ESTÁ ENTRE PARÉNTESIS

This contract is (good) than the old one.
This contract is better than the old one.

❶ Your printer is (quick) than ours.

_____

❷ Today's meeting was (interesting) than usual.

_____

❸ Growth was (bad) than we had expected.

_____

❹ Sandra has been (successful) than last year.

_____

❺ I'm feeling (good) after a week off work.

_____

❻ There is (little) juice left than I thought.

_____

❼ My new apartment is (close) to the center.

_____

❽ The results are (good) than in the first quarter.

_____

❾ We will need to arrive (early) than usual.

_____

❿ I start work one hour (late) than my wife.

_____

⓫ This restaurant is (bad) than the others.

_____

⓬ The flight was (expensive) than I expected.

_____

14.5 CONECTA EL INICIO Y EL FINAL DE CADA FRASE

The new computer system

① The new intern is much

② Our hours are longer

③ The new computers are

④ I arrive at work earlier

⑤ Our new office design

⑥ The tickets

⑦ My raise was

⑧ My training this year was

⑨ The office is busier

more helpful than the old one.

faster than the old ones.

is more efficient than the last one.

now that the new train line has opened.

than those in the German branch.

are more expensive than they used to be.

is more modern than the previous one.

more interesting than last year.

since we merged with our competitors.

smaller than last year's.

14.6 ESCUCHA EL AUDIO Y RESPONDE A LAS PREGUNTAS

Anne y Patrick hablan de las nuevas oficinas a las que se han trasladado.

Patrick says the new office is more modern.
True ☑ **False** ☐ **Not given** ☐

① He thinks the old office was more comfortable.
True ☐ **False** ☐ **Not given** ☐

② He says the new computers are faster.
True ☐ **False** ☐ **Not given** ☐

③ He says the software is more complicated.
True ☐ **False** ☐ **Not given** ☐

④ Patrick likes the new café in the building.
True ☐ **False** ☐ **Not given** ☐

⑤ He says the building is closer to his apartment.
True ☐ **False** ☐ **Not given** ☐

⑥ He travels to work on the train.
True ☐ **False** ☐ **Not given** ☐

⑦ Patrick is going to a Chinese restaurant for lunch.
True ☐ **False** ☐ **Not given** ☐

⑧ Anne has been to the restaurant before.
True ☐ **False** ☐ **Not given** ☐

15 Rutinas del lugar de trabajo

Los empleados tienen agendas y los lugares de trabajo, rutinas y horarios propios. Es útil poder hablar con los colegas sobre cuándo suelen pasar las cosas.

Lenguaje Preposiciones de tiempo
Aa Vocabulario Desplazamientos y transporte
Habilidad Describir rutinas

15.1 VUELVE A ESCRIBIR LAS FRASES PONIENDO LAS PALABRAS EN SU ORDEN CORRECTO

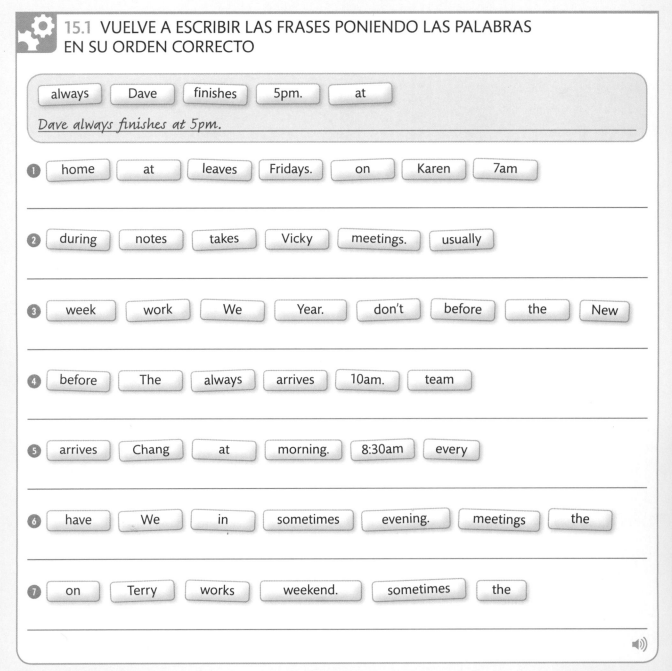

always · Dave · finishes · 5pm. · at

Dave always finishes at 5pm.

1. home · at · leaves · Fridays. · on · Karen · 7am

2. during · notes · takes · Vicky · meetings. · usually

3. week · work · We · Year. · don't · before · the · New

4. before · The · always · arrives · 10am. · team

5. arrives · Chang · at · morning. · 8:30am · every

6. have · We · in · sometimes · evening. · meetings · the

7. on · Terry · works · weekend. · sometimes · the

15.2 TACHA LA PALABRA INCORRECTA DE CADA FRASE Y DI LAS FRASES EN VOZ ALTA

The office is closed in / ~~on~~ the evening.

4 The café is open from / in 6am.

1 Everyone arrives until / by 9:30am.

5 I finish work at 4pm on / in Fridays.

2 Peter often works between / until 11pm.

6 The cafeteria is open in / from 1pm.

3 The office is closed about / during August.

7 Ann sends an agenda before / in each meeting.

15.3 LEE EL CORREO ELECTRÓNICO Y RESPONDE A LAS PREGUNTAS

John lives...
in the city. ☐   in the suburbs. ☑   in a village. ☐

1 John leaves the house at...
7am. ☐   8am. ☐   9am. ☐

2 The commute takes...
10 minutes. ☐   1 hour. ☐   30 minutes. ☐

3 John starts work at...
9am. ☐   8:30am. ☐   9am. ☐

4 On Fridays, John finishes at...
12am. ☐   2pm. ☐   4pm. ☐

5 John drives to work...
sometimes. ☐   every week. ☐   never. ☐

6 There are fewer traffic jams in the...
morning. ☐   afternoon. ☐   evening. ☐

✉
To: Andrew

Subject: Hello...

Hi Andrew,
It's great to hear from you! I have got quite a lot of news, too. Karen and I have just moved to a new house in the suburbs, so I have to commute to the center of town every day now. I leave the house at 7am, and take the bus at 7:20am. The commute takes about an hour, so it's quite a lot of traveling each day, but I don't mind. I start work at 8:30am and finish at 5pm, but on Friday I finish earlier, at 2pm. Sometimes I drive to work on Fridays because there aren't as many traffic jams in the afternoon.
You should come over and see us soon!
John

15.4 TACHA LA PALABRA INCORRECTA DE CADA FRASE

> Sarah **catches** / ~~jumps~~ the bus near the park.

1 I drive because it's so **comfortable** / **convenient**.

2 Jim **takes** / **drives** the bus every morning.

3 Jack travels **on** / **by** bike when he can.

4 The **rush** / **busy** hour starts at 7am in my city.

5 Sam **takes** / **makes** the metro home each evening.

6 Raymond **catches** / **drives** his car to work.

7 I get **on** / **in** the bus near the museum.

8 I missed my **connection** / **link**.

9 Janet prefers to travel **on** / **by** train to work.

10 Karl **takes** / **drives** the bus home at night.

11 There are a lot of traffic **blocks** / **jams** in the city.

12 You should get **off** / **from** the tram at the library.

13 It's much cheaper to **cycle** / **bike** than drive.

14 I like to **walk** / **walking** to work in the summer.

15 I prefer to **cycle** / **train** to my office.

🔊

 15.5 MARCA LAS FRASES QUE SEAN CORRECTAS

> I leave my house before 6am. ☑
> I leave my house in front of 6am. ☐

1 I car to work. ☐
I drive to work. ☐

2 We take the bus. ☐
We make the bus. ☐

3 Doug catches his bike to work. ☐
Doug rides his bike to work. ☐

4 I sometimes take a taxi home. ☐
I sometimes drive a taxi home. ☐

5 The buses run from 5am to 11pm. ☐
The buses run of 5am to 11pm. ☐

6 I go in train. ☐
I go by train. ☐

7 The train arrives on 5pm. ☐
The train arrives at 5pm. ☐

8 Sharon gets off the bus by the station. ☐
Sharon gets from the bus by the station. ☐

9 I like to go home from work on foot. ☐
I like to go home from work by foot. ☐

10 My train to work arrives on 7:45am. ☐
My train to work arrives at 7:45am. ☐

11 Traveling by train is comfortable. ☐
Traveling on train is comfortable. ☐

12 The train leaves at about 8pm. ☐
The train leaves at near 8pm. ☐

13 I travel on train every day. ☐
I travel by train every day. ☐

🔊

15.6 ESCUCHA EL AUDIO Y NUMERA DESPUÉS LAS IMÁGENES EN EL ORDEN EN QUE SE DESCRIBEN

A 1

B

C

D

E

F

G

H

15.7 CONECTA EL INICIO Y EL FINAL DE CADA FRASE

All the staff arrives	on the weekend.
❶ There aren't many buses	by 9:30am.
❷ Hank takes the bus because	until 10 in the evening.
❸ The office stays open	during the summer.
❹ I leave for work	it's cheaper than the train.
❺ Sally often walks to work	during meetings.
❻ I take the train to work because	between 7 and 8am.
❼ Ted takes notes	before 11pm.
❽ I always go to bed	it's faster than the bus.

16 Vocabulario

Aa 16.1 DÍAS DE LA SEMANA ESCRIBE LAS PALABRAS DEL RECUADRO DEBAJO DE SU CORRESPONDIENTE DIBUJO

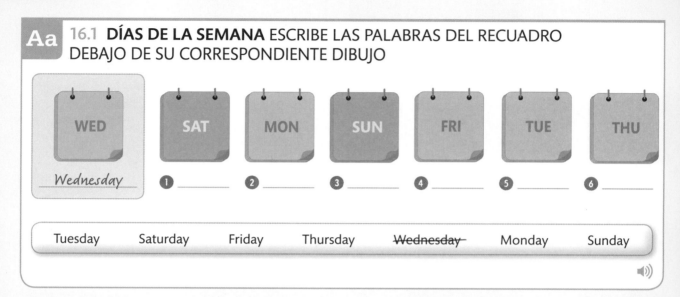

WED — *Wednesday*

SAT — **1** _____

MON — **2** _____

SUN — **3** _____

FRI — **4** _____

TUE — **5** _____

THU — **6** _____

Tuesday   Saturday   Friday   Thursday   ~~Wednesday~~   Monday   Sunday

Aa 16.2 EXPRESIONES DE FRECUENCIA ESCRIBE LAS PALABRAS DEL RECUADRO DEBAJO DE SU CORRESPONDIENTE DIBUJO

 *quarterly*

 **1** _____

 **2** _____

 **3** _____

 4 _____

 **5** _____

 **6** _____

 **7** _____

 **8** _____

 **9** _____

hourly   ~~quarterly~~   monthly   in the morning   before work

in the afternoon   in the evening   daily   three times a week   after work

go running

 ❶ _____

 ❷ _____

 ❸ _____

 ❹ _____

 ❺ _____

 ❻ _____

 ❼ _____

 ❽ _____

 ❾ _____

 ❿ _____

 ⓫ _____

 ⓬ _____

 ⓭ _____

 ⓮ _____

 ⓯ _____

 ⓰ _____

 ⓱ _____

 ⓲ _____

 ⓳ _____

---

visit a museum / art gallery   read   cook   meet friends   write   draw   watch a movie

go camping   take photos   see a play   go out for a meal   go cycling   play board games   do yoga

walk / hike   ~~go running~~   go shopping   stay (at) home   play sports   play an instrument

17 Aficiones y costumbres

Cuando hables con un colega de aficiones y costumbres, utiliza adverbios de frecuencia para indicar la periodicidad con la que realizas dichas actividades.

⚙ Lenguaje Adverbios de frecuencia
Aa Vocabulario Aficiones y costumbres
🧩 Habilidad Hablar sobre el tiempo libre

17.1 VUELVE A ESCRIBIR LAS FRASES PONIENDO LAS PALABRAS EN SU ORDEN CORRECTO

| visit | I | a | on | museum | Saturdays. | occasionally |

I occasionally visit a museum on Saturdays.

1. often | We | weekend. | camping | the | go | on

2. he | after | meets | work. | Doug | friends | finishes | sometimes

3. running | I | the | in | always | morning. | go

4. My | television. | watches | father | never

5. local | We | a | see | at | theater. | occasionally | our | play

6. he | Frank | rarely | lazy, | very | does | and | is | exercise. | any

7. sometimes | after | My | video | play | kids | school. | games

🔊

58

17.2 ESCUCHA EL AUDIO Y CONECTA CADA IMAGEN CON EL ADVERBIO DE FRECUENCIA QUE LE CORRESPONDE

rarely

often

usually

sometimes

never

17.3 CONECTA EL INICIO Y EL FINAL DE CADA FRASE

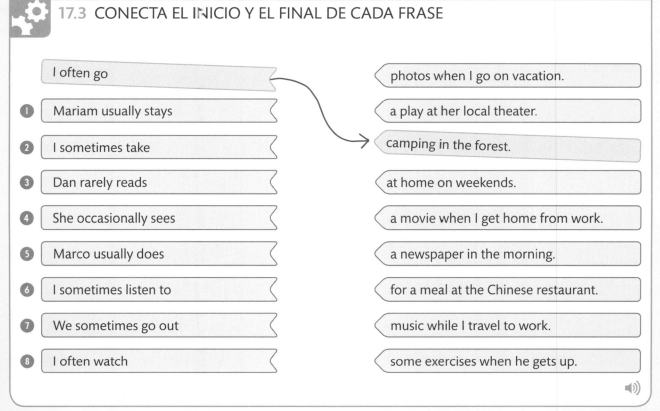

I often go — camping in the forest.

1 Mariam usually stays

2 I sometimes take

3 Dan rarely reads

4 She occasionally sees

5 Marco usually does

6 I sometimes listen to

7 We sometimes go out

8 I often watch

photos when I go on vacation.

a play at her local theater.

at home on weekends.

a movie when I get home from work.

a newspaper in the morning.

for a meal at the Chinese restaurant.

music while I travel to work.

some exercises when he gets up.

17.4 MARCA LAS FRASES QUE SEAN CORRECTAS

This is the best way to get home. ☑
This is the most good way to get home. ☐

1 The earliest flight is at 9am. ☐
The most early flight is at 9am. ☐

2 Sydney is the most largest city in Australia. ☐
Sydney is the largest city in Australia. ☐

3 Dubai is the hottest place I've visited. ☐
Dubai is the most hottest place I've visited. ☐

4 This is the most expensive software we sell. ☐
This is the expensivest software we sell. ☐

5 The most far I've flown is to New Zealand. ☐
The farthest I've flown is to New Zealand. ☐

6 Spanish is the most easiest language to learn. ☐
Spanish is the easiest language to learn. ☐

7 Kraków is the most beautiful city in Poland. ☐
Kraków is the more beautiful city in Poland. ☐

8 The train is the most affordable way to travel. ☐
The train is the affordablest way to travel. ☐

9 This is the most interesting gallery in town. ☐
This is the most interestingest gallery in town. ☐

10 Hiroshi is most intelligent person I know. ☐
Hiroshi is the most intelligent person I know. ☐

11 That was the scariest film I've seen. ☐
That was the most scary film I've seen. ☐

🔊

17.5 DI LAS FRASES EN VOZ ALTA CON LOS ADJETIVOS EN SU FORMA SUPERLATIVA

We had our ___worst___ (bad) results in 10 years.

1 The _____ (long) river in Brazil is the Amazon.

2 We'll have lunch at the _____ (close) café to the office.

3 I just watched the _____ (bad) presentation I've ever seen.

4 I think that snowboarding is the _____ (exciting) sport.

5 Sean lives the _____ (far) from the office.

6 Antonio is our _____ (loyal) employee.

7 This is the _____ (expensive) printer we have.

🔊

17.6 LEE EL ARTÍCULO Y RESPONDE A LAS PREGUNTAS

LEISURE WEEKLY

How do you spend your free time?

We speak to three different people about what
they do in their time away from work.

Chloe Smith, 21

I get up early most days and usually do some exercises. I'm not very sporty, to be honest, but I go jogging twice a week. On the weekend I like to relax; I work in a bank, which is stressful. I go to the theater quite often and I sometimes do yoga on Saturday afternoons. I never watch sports. It's the most boring thing possible!

Pete McManus, 30

I like martial arts. I'm a member of a karate club, and I try to go there as regularly as possible. I think karate is the most exciting sport. It involves a lot of self-discipline. What else? Well, I occasionally go jogging. Oh, and I play tennis with my wife from time to time. You could say that I'm a sporty person!

Dan Stevens, 47

I'm not the most active person. I like to play video games with my friends in the evening. I sometimes watch soccer with my friends on weekends. There's a gym at my workplace, but I go there pretty rarely. My wife thinks I should get more exercise, but I hate working out. I'd much rather relax at home.

Who goes jogging twice a week?   Chloe ☑ Pete ☐ Dan ☐

❶ Who rarely goes to the gym?   Chloe ☐ Pete ☐ Dan ☐

❷ Who plays tennis with his wife?   Chloe ☐ Pete ☐ Dan ☐

❸ Who is the most sporty?   Chloe ☐ Pete ☐ Dan ☐

❹ Who thinks karate is the most exciting sport?   Chloe ☐ Pete ☐ Dan ☐

❺ Who sometimes watches soccer?   Chloe ☐ Pete ☐ Dan ☐

❻ Who does exercise early in the morning?   Chloe ☐ Pete ☐ Dan ☐

❼ Who is a member of a sports club?   Chloe ☐ Pete ☐ Dan ☐

❽ Who doesn't go jogging?   Chloe ☐ Pete ☐ Dan ☐

❾ Who sometimes does yoga?   Chloe ☐ Pete ☐ Dan ☐

❿ Who likes to play video games?   Chloe ☐ Pete ☐ Dan ☐

18 Cosas del pasado

A menudo se utiliza el past simple al hablar sobre cosas que empezaron y acabaron en un momento concreto del pasado reciente o distante.

⚙️ **Lenguaje** El past simple
Aa Vocabulario Actividades fuera del trabajo
🧩 **Habilidad** Hablar sobre cosas del pasado

18.1 MARCA LAS FRASES QUE SEAN CORRECTAS

Chris played soccer after work. ✓
Chris playd soccer after work. ☐

① I didn't learn Spanish at school. ☐
I didn't learned Spanish at school. ☐

② We walking to the conference center. ☐
We walked to the conference center. ☐

③ John did lived in New York for 10 years. ☐
John lived in New York for 10 years. ☐

④ Did the team discussed the merger? ☐
Did the team discuss the merger? ☐

⑤ He went to the conference by car. ☐
He did went to the conference by car. ☐

⑥ My manager not visited the factory. ☐
My manager didn't visit the factory. ☐

⑦ Selma didn't walk to work today. ☐
Selma didn't walked to work today. ☐

⑧ Jimish posted the report a week ago. ☐
Jimish post the report a week ago. ☐

⑨ Did Tom finish the report? ☐
Finished Tom the report? ☐

🔊

18.2 COMPLETA LOS ESPACIOS PONIENDO LOS VERBOS EN PAST SIMPLE

Jenny ____studied____ (studied) hard, but she ___did not pass___ (not pass) the accounting exam.

① Akiko _____ (finish) her presentation, then she _____ (watch) some TV.

② I _____ (not watch) the game because I _____ (need) to prepare for the conference.

③ Derek _____ (want) to work somewhere interesting, so he _____ (move) to New York.

④ We _____ (arrive) late, but we _____ (not miss) the meeting.

⑤ Sally _____ (pass) her exams, and _____ (decide) to go to college.

🔊

18.3 VUELVE A ESCRIBIR LAS FRASES PONIENDO LAS PALABRAS EN SU ORDEN CORRECTO

get · explain · Dic · Peter · to · how · to · office? · the

Did Peter explain how to get to the office?

1 the · Fred · me · conference · center. · showed · new

_____

2 watched · about · We · documentary · an · Beijing. · interesting

_____

3 company · started · years · at · about · this · ago. · Ramon · five

_____

4 you · Did · presentation · enjoy · the · the · Indian economy? · about

_____

5 play · It · yesterday, · rained · we · soccer. · so · didn't

_____

6 cooked · Arnold · ast · me · dinner · a · night. · delicious

_____

7 about · Did · finish · Sam · report · the · product · new · range? · the

_____

8 table · I · in · a · the · center. · in · restaurant · a · booked

_____

9 the · Did Mike · tennis · on · with · CEO · new · Saturday? · play

_____

🔊

18.4 VUELVE A ESCRIBIR LAS FRASES EN FORMA DE PREGUNTA EN PAST SIMPLE

Claire finished the presentation on Thursday.
Did Claire finish the presentation on Thursday?

❶ Paul started working for us more than five years ago.

_____

❷ Sally explained how to use the new photocopier.

_____

❸ It rained while they were in Indonesia.

_____

❹ Clive picked up the guests from the railway station.

_____

❺ Mark joined you for lunch at the Chinese restaurant.

_____

❻ The team attended the conference in Paris last year.

_____

❼ Philip played golf with the consultants last weekend.

_____

❽ Carl and Marie walked to work again today.

_____

❾ You watched the game yesterday.

_____

❿ Janet showed you the new photocopier.

_____

⓫ Mo studied economics at Stanford University.

_____

⓬ The company invested $10 million in R&D.

_____

◀))

18.5 ESCUCHA EL AUDIO Y RESPONDE A LAS PREGUNTAS

Dos compañeros de trabajo hablan sobre el fin de semana.

Ben visited York with his family.
True ✓ **False** ☐ **Not given** ☐

1 York is a very modern city.
True ☐ **False** ☐ **Not given** ☐

2 The family stayed in a hotel.
True ☐ **False** ☐ **Not given** ☐

3 The castle is over 1,000 years old.
True ☐ **False** ☐ **Not given** ☐

4 Helen visited a shopping mall.
True ☐ **False** ☐ **Not given** ☐

5 They visited the circus.
True ☐ **False** ☐ **Not given** ☐

6 In the evening they went to see a movie.
True ☐ **False** ☐ **Not given** ☐

7 Helen didn't enjoy the food in the restaurant.
True ☐ **False** ☐ **Not given** ☐

18.6 DESCRIBE EN VOZ ALTA LO QUE HIZO CADA PERSONA, UTILIZANDO EL PAST SIMPLE DE LAS EXPRESIONES DEL RECUADRO

He played tennis.

1

2

3

4

5

walk to work   study for an exam   listen to the radio   ~~play tennis~~   travel to India   visit a friend

65

19 Fechas y horas

Cuando se hacen planes o se habla de cosas del pasado o del futuro, es importante decir bien la hora. En inglés se puede hacer de diversas maneras.

⚙️ **Lenguaje** Cuándo pasan las cosas
Aa Vocabulario Decir la hora
🧩 **Habilidad** Pedir citas

19.1 ESCUCHA EL AUDIO Y MARCA LAS HORAS CORRECTAS

19.2 DI LAS HORAS EN VOZ ALTA

05:15 It's (a) quarter past five.

1 9:17

2

3

4 3:22

5

19.3 VUELVE A ESCRIBIR LAS FRASES PONIENDO LAS PALABRAS EN SU ORDEN CORRECTO

August | on | begins | conference | The | 4.

The conference begins on August 4.

① ends | June | tournament | 20. | soccer | The | on

_____

② Independence | on | American | is | 4th | Day | July. | the | of

_____

③ December | is | Christmas | on | 25. | Day

_____

④ September | on | birthday | My | is | 5. | wife's

_____

⑤ August | My | born | on | was | 3. | daughter

_____

19.4 ESCUCHA EL AUDIO Y RESPONDE A LAS PREGUNTAS

Rachel habla de su vida y de los acontecimientos principales.

When was Rachel born?
1996 ☐ 1986 ✓ 1983 ☐

① What year did she move to New York?
2012 ☐ 2014 ☐ 2016 ☐

② When did she start working for her company?
August 2015 ☐ April 2015 ☐ April 2016 ☐

③ When is her best friend's birthday?
January ☐ June ☐ July ☐

④ Where does her best friend come from?
Scotland ☐ Switzerland ☐ Sweden ☐

⑤ When is Rachel's wedding anniversary?
May 1 ☐ May 3 ☐ May 4 ☐

20 Historia laboral

Al conocer nuevos colegas o en una entrevista, puede que te pregunten por trabajos anteriores. Al hablar del pasado es importante que utilices la forma verbal correcta.

🔧 **Lenguaje** Verbos irregulares en past simple
Aa Vocabulario Empleos y lugares de trabajo
🧩 **Habilidad** Hablar sobre trabajos anteriores

20.1 CONECTA LOS VERBOS CON SU FORMA DE PAST SIMPLE

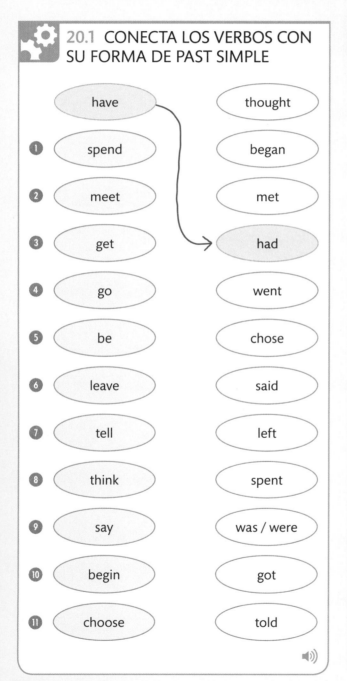

have — had
thought

1. spend — began
2. meet — met
3. get — had
4. go — went
5. be — chose
6. leave — said
7. tell — left
8. think — spent
9. say — was / were
10. begin — got
11. choose — told

20.2 VUELVE A ESCRIBIR CORRIGIENDO LOS ERRORES

I **haved** five colleagues on my team.
I had five colleagues on my team.

1. I **go** to Paris on a business trip last week.
_____

2. I **spended** all afternoon working on a report.
_____

3. I **beginned** working at Carter's last year.
_____

4. The CEO **telled** me that my work was excellent.
_____

5. I **thinked** this project was very difficult.
_____

6. Besim **were** off sick yesterday.
_____

7. I **meeted** the new Sales Director this morning.
_____

8. The staff **choosed** the name of the company.
_____

9. Kara **leaved** her last job because it was boring.
_____

20.3 COMPLETA LCS ESPACIOS CON LOS VERBOS INDICADOS EN PAST SIMPLE

My first job _____was_____ (be) in a supermarket.

1. I _____ (meet) the International Marketing Director last week.

2. I _____ (have) a demanding boss.

3. I _____ (leave) my last job because it was badly paid.

4. I _____ (get) to work very early today.

5. They _____ (go) to the New York office last month.

6. The staff _____ (choose) new chairs for the office.

7. Sally _____ (think) that Rohit's presentation went well.

🔊

 20.4 CONECTA LAS PREGUNTAS CON LAS RESPUESTAS CORRECTAS

How many people were on your team? → There were five of us.

I met many interesting people.

1. When did you start working at the café?

We had a black and white uniform.

2. Where did you work on your first job?

I took the children to school.

3. What did you do as a nanny?

I started work there after I left school.

4. Who did you meet as a journalist?

I worked in a bank at the start of my career.

5. How did you get your job as a director?

I worked hard and studied for an MBA.

6. What did you wear on your last job?

🔊

20.5 ESCUCHA EL AUDIO Y NUMERA DESPUÉS LAS IMÁGENES EN EL ORDEN EN QUE SE DESCRIBEN

 20.6 TACHA LA PALABRA INCORRECTA DE CADA FRASE Y DI TODAS LAS FRASES EN VOZ ALTA

We **had** / ~~haved~~ a very demanding boss in the marketing department.

1 I **feeled** / **felt** very well respected by my team leader.

2 The Head of Sales **taught** / **teached** me to give interesting presentations.

3 My brother **made** / **maked** a delicious cake, which I took to work for my birthday.

4 The staff **choosed** / **chose** the pictures for the meeting rooms, and they look great.

5 I **left** / **leaved** my last job because I didn't get along with the customers.

6 I **spended** / **spent** all of yesterday writing a sales report and now I'm very tired.

21 Historia de la empresa

Se puede utilizar el past simple para describir acciones individuales o recurrentes en la historia de una empresa. Estas acciones pueden ser de corta o larga duración.

⚙ **Lenguaje** Past simple con marcadores de tiempo
Aa Vocabulario Describir tendencias
🧩 **Habilidad** Describir la historia de una empresa

21.1 COMPLETA LOS ESPACIOS CON LAS PALABRAS DEL RECUADRO

I _____*founded*_____ Bee Designs in 2010.

started
ago
merged
launched
~~founded~~
first

1 We _____ a new range of apps last year.

2 At _____ , we only had four employees.

3 Two years _____ , we opened our tenth store.

4 The company _____ with a competitor a year ago.

5 A new Director of Marketing _____ working here last year.

◀))

21.2 VUELVE A ESCRIBIR LAS FRASES CORRIGIENDO LOS ERRORES

Maria Hill opened the first Hill Shoe Store past 2015.
Maria Hill opened the first Hill Shoe Store in 2015.

1 At the first, we only had one store.

_____

2 We open a new flagship store last month.

_____

3 We launch an exciting new app last year.

_____

4 A new Director of HR started working here six months before.

_____

◀))

21.3 LEE LA PÁGINA WEB Y RESPONDE A LAS PREGUNTAS

BUSINESS WORLD

HOME | ENTRIES | ABOUT | CONTACT

POSTED WEDNESDAY SEPTEMBER 16

Market leaders

This week, we look at the history of Bee Designs.

Bee Designs is now a successful company and one of the best-known names in online shopping. Last year, the company made a profit of $500,000 and sold over 10,000 bags.

The company started as a hobby business when Angela Lee couldn't find a bag that she wanted and she made her own. Friends asked her where she had bought it. When they found out that she had made it herself, they asked her to make bags for them. She decided to turn her garage into a workroom and launched Bee Designs in 2010.

The company went from strength to strength and now employs 50 people. Two years ago, Angela moved the operation of her business to a unit in the business park in her town.

Most of the company's business comes from online orders, but Angela started going to craft fairs five years ago. She sold out of bags at the first fair, so she took on 5 extra sewing machinists. The company makes over a hundred bags a week and its turnover for 2015 was more than $1.2 million.

What does Bee Designs make? **Bags** ✓ **Shoes** ☐ **Hats** ☐

❶ How many bags did the company sell last year? **Over 1,000** ☐ **Over 10,000** ☐ **Over 100,000** ☐

❷ Where did Angela originally make the bags? **In a business unit** ☐ **In a factory** ☐ **In her garage** ☐

❸ How many employees does the company currently have? **5** ☐ **50** ☐ **150** ☐

❹ When did Angela move the operation of her business? **Two years ago** ☐ **Five years ago** ☐ **2012** ☐

❺ Where does Bee Designs sell bags directly? **At wedding fairs** ☐ **At craft fairs** ☐ **At vintage fairs** ☐

72

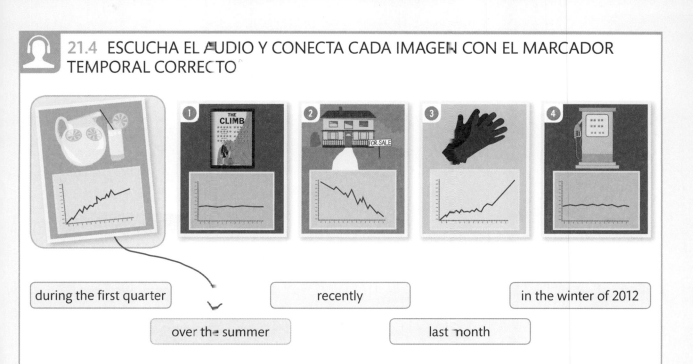

21.4 ESCUCHA EL AUDIO Y CONECTA CADA IMAGEN CON EL MARCADOR TEMPORAL CORRECTO

during the first quarter

recently

in the winter of 2012

over the summer

last month

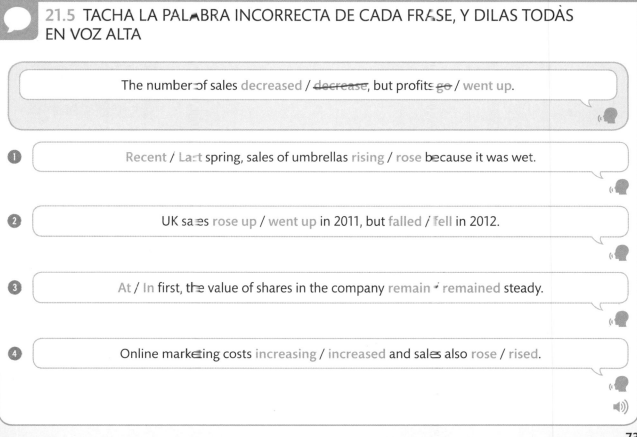

21.5 TACHA LA PALABRA INCORRECTA DE CADA FRASE, Y DILAS TODAS EN VOZ ALTA

The number of sales decreased / decrease, but profits go / went up.

1 Recent / Last spring, sales of umbrellas rising / rose because it was wet.

2 UK sales rose up / went up in 2011, but falled / fell in 2012.

3 At / In first, the value of shares in the company remain / remained steady.

4 Online marketing costs increasing / increased and sales also rose / rised.

22 Vocabulario

Aa 22.1 HACER PLANES ESCRIBE LAS PALABRAS DEL RECUADRO DEBAJO DE SU CORRESPONDIENTE DIBUJO

to book a
meeting room

1 _____

2 _____

3 _____

8 _____

9 _____

10 _____

11 _____

16 _____

17 _____

18 _____

19 _____

Aa 22.2 ACEPTAR Y DECLINAR ESCRIBE LAS EXPRESIONES DEL RECUADRO BAJO LAS DEFINICIONES CORRECTAS

To be convenient

to suit someone

1 To occur unexpectedly

_____

4 Cannot go to

_____

5 To be pleased about something that is going to happen

_____

4  _____

5  _____

6  _____

7  _____

12  _____

13  _____

14  _____

15  _____

to miss a meeting   refreshments   café   to invite someone   agenda   restaurant

to attend a meeting   evening   ~~to book a meeting room~~   morning   calendar

to decline an invitation   appointment   running late   reception   boardroom

conference room   to accept an invitation   afternoon   office

🔊

---

2 To decide that a planned event will not happen

_____

3 To have lots to do

6 To decide on a new time and date for a meeting

_____

to cancel   ~~to suit someone~~   to come up

to reschedule   to look forward to

to be busy   to be unable to attend

🔊

23 Hablar sobre los planes

Una manera de hacer planes con un compañero de trabajo o un cliente es utilizar el present continuous para hablar de lo que estás haciendo ahora o de los planes de futuro.

⚙️ **Lenguaje** El present continuous
Aa Vocabulario Hacer planes
🧩 **Habilidad** Hablar sobre los planes

23.1 COMPLETA LOS ESPACIOS CON LOS VERBOS EN PRESENT CONTINUOUS

Steve is _____*working*_____ (work) from home today. He is _____*writing*_____ (write) the report.

1. The company _____ (lose) money, so we _____ (plan) a restructure.

2. Stacy _____ (not work) in the office today. She _____ (visit) the factory.

3. Dan _____ (meet) a new client. They _____ (chat) in the meeting room.

4. Colin _____ (start) a new project. He _____ (work) with Angela.

5. The head office _____ (relocate) to Delhi. We _____ (move) this week.

6. Profits _____ (fall) this year, and the team _____ (feel) nervous.

7. Anika _____ (work) late tonight. She _____ (prepare) a presentation.

8. Sue and Clive _____ (have) lunch downtown. They _____ (eat) Chinese.

9. I _____ (go) on vacation next week. I _____ (miss) the training day.

10. Our company _____ (sell) a lot to India. We _____ (open) an office in Mumbai.

11. Our secretary _____ (retire). We _____ (recruit) a new one.

12. Sam and Sue are _____ (discuss) the report. They _____ (plan) a meeting about it.

13. Chrissie _____ (choose) a new team. She _____ (consider) Paul for a position.

14. Alex _____ (leave) the company. He _____ (move) to New York.

🔊

23.2 VUELVE A ESCRIBIR LAS FRASES PONIENDO LAS PALABRAS EN SU ORDEN CORRECTO

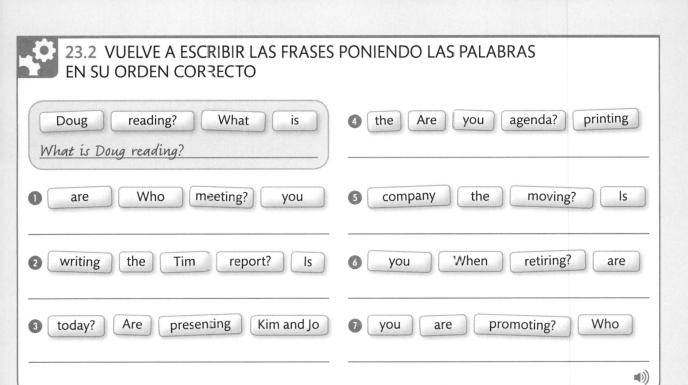

Doug | reading? | What | is

What is Doug reading?

1 are | Who | meeting? | you

_____

2 writing | the | Tim | report? | Is

_____

3 today? | Are | presenting | Kim and Jo

_____

4 the | Are | you | agenda? | printing

_____

5 company | the | moving? | Is

_____

6 you | When | retiring? | are

_____

7 you | are | promoting? | Who

_____

23.3 VUELVE A ESCRIBIR LAS AFIRMACIONES EN FORMA DE PREGUNTAS EN PRESENT CONTINUOUS

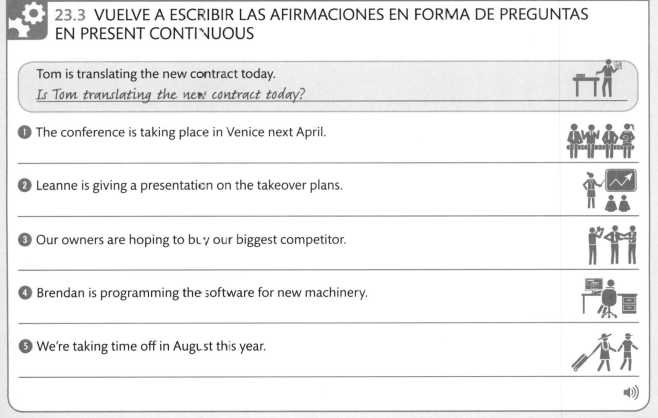

Tom is translating the new contract today.
Is Tom translating the new contract today?

1 The conference is taking place in Venice next April.

_____

2 Leanne is giving a presentation on the takeover plans.

_____

3 Our owners are hoping to buy our biggest competitor.

_____

4 Brendan is programming the software for new machinery.

_____

5 We're taking time off in August this year.

_____

23.4 MARCA LAS FRASES QUE SEAN CORRECTAS

Where are you working on Friday? ☑
Where does you work on Friday? ☐

1. Are you have lunch at 1pm today? ☐
   Are you having lunch at 1pm today? ☐

2. Tom will going to the conference today. ☐
   Tom is going to the conference today. ☐

3. Is John working until 7pm again? ☐
   Does John working until 7pm again? ☐

4. We are traveling to New York again. ☐
   We are travel to New York again. ☐

5. Is you coming to the meeting on Friday? ☐
   Are you coming to the meeting on Friday? ☐

6. Will you visiting the factory next month? ☐
   Are you visiting the factory next month? ☐

7. I'm not taking time off in August. ☐
   I amn't taking time off in August. ☐

8. The head office will moving in the spring. ☐
   The head office is moving in the spring. ☐

9. Fran aren't coming to the office tomorrow. ☐
   Fran isn't coming to the office tomorrow. ☐

10. What are you doing on Tuesday? ☐
    What you are doing on Tuesday? ☐

11. Sam be meeting the client this afternoon. ☐
    Sam is meeting the client this afternoon. ☐

12. Tim is leaving work at 5pm today. ☐
    Tim leaving work at 5pm today. ☐

🔊

23.5 ESCUCHA EL AUDIO Y RESPONDE A LAS PREGUNTAS

Clare llama a su colega, Frank, para concertar una reunión con él.

Clare needs to arrange a meeting about...
the new sales strategy. ☑
the new recruits. ☐
the health and safety presentation. ☐

1. On Monday morning, Frank is...
   attending a course. ☐
   going to the dentist. ☐
   visiting the factory. ☐

2. On Monday afternoon, Clare is...
   free. ☐
   attending a course. ☐
   giving a presentation. ☐

3. On Tuesday, Frank is...
   celebrating his birthday. ☐
   celebrating his wedding anniversary. ☐
   going on vacation. ☐

4. In the evening, he is...
   going to a film. ☐
   going to a restaurant. ☐
   going to the theater. ☐

5. On Thursday at 2pm, Clare is...
   meeting Pete. ☐
   having lunch. ☐
   visiting the factory. ☐

6. They are both available at...
   2:30pm on Thursday. ☐
   3:30pm on Thursday. ☐
   2:30pm on Friday. ☐

23.6 LEE LA AGENDA Y RESPONDE AL AUDIO EN VOZ ALTA

July

Monday	Tuesday	Wednesday	Thursday	Friday
10am Give presentation to the interns		12 noon Flight to Edinburgh departs	11:30am Return to London	
2pm Have lunch with the IT team				
	3pm Meet the new clients from Germany		3pm Give report to CEO	
				7pm Sandra's leaving party

What are you doing on Monday morning?

I'm giving a presentation to the interns at 10am.

③ Where are you going on Wednesday?

① Where are you going on Monday afternoon?

④ What time are you returning on Thursday?

② What time are you meeting the clients?

⑤ Where are you going on Friday evening?

79

24 Dar opiniones

En inglés a menudo se utilizan expresiones para indicar que se quiere interrumpir sin ser maleducado. Hay diversas maneras de dar tu opinión de manera educada.

⚙ **Lenguaje** Interrupciones y opiniones
Aa Vocabulario Cuestiones medioambientales
🧩 **Habilidad** Dar opiniones educadamente

⚙ 24.1 MARCA SI LA INTERRUPCIÓN ES EDUCADA O NO

I'm sorry, but I can't agree with you there.
Educada ☑ **No educada** ☐

1 Excuse me, but I agree with Stacey here.
Educada ☐ **No educada** ☐

2 What are you talking about? That's wrong.
Educada ☐ **No educada** ☐

3 I'm afraid I have to disagree with you about that.
Educada ☐ **No educada** ☐

4 Could I just say that there are other options.
Educada ☐ **No educada** ☐

5 Sorry to interrupt, but I have different figures.
Educada ☐ **No educada** ☐

6 That's absolute nonsense.
Educada ☐ **No educada** ☐

7 If I could just come in here, Robert.
Educada ☐ **No educada** ☐

🔊

🎧 24.2 ESCUCHA EL AUDIO Y RESPONDE A LAS PREGUNTAS

Dan y Susan hablan en una reunión.

The meeting is about a new policy.
True ☑ **False** ☐ **Not given** ☐

1 Susan wants the company to develop new vehicles.
True ☐ **False** ☐ **Not given** ☐

2 Dan agrees with Susan's suggestion.
True ☐ **False** ☐ **Not given** ☐

3 The company leaves a bad carbon footprint.
True ☐ **False** ☐ **Not given** ☐

4 Dan thinks the workers should use the metro.
True ☐ **False** ☐ **Not given** ☐

5 Agrocorp are developing a motorcycle.
True ☐ **False** ☐ **Not given** ☐

6 The company will develop electric vehicles soon.
True ☐ **False** ☐ **Not given** ☐

7 Agrocorp employees recycle at home.
True ☐ **False** ☐ **Not given** ☐

This will lead to a fall in profits.

Sorry to _____*disagree*_____ , but my figures are different.

① The company might lose millions of dollars.

I'm sorry. I'm not sure I _____ .

② These clothes won't appeal to people in China.

Sorry, but in my _____ they will sell well.

③ We need to increase our focus on the youth market.

I can see your _____ , but I still think senior citizens are more important.

④ We had exactly the same problem last year.

If I could just _____ in here and mention the good news from France.

⑤ The figures show a dramatic fall this year.

_____ me, but my figures tell a different story.

⑥ We need to employ two new team members.

_____ I just say...? The budget won't cover it.

⑦ India will be our biggest market in 2050.

I'm not _____ I agree. Sales to China are growing faster.

⑧ And if we sell our new software...

Sorry to _____ , but the software is not ready yet.

| come | interrupt | agree | excuse | point | ~~disagree~~ | could | sure | opinion |

24.4 TACHA LA PALABRA INCORRECTA DE CADA FRASE

Claire's ~~timed~~ / scheduled a meeting for later. She'll send the agenda to everyone soon.

1 I'm afraid Sean can't make it to the meeting and has given / sent his apologies.

2 Shall we take / make a vote on the new strategy to see what course of action to take?

3 Ramona will take / recall the minutes and email them to everyone after the meeting.

4 I agree with the motion. How about / for you? What do you think about it?

5 If I could just disturb / interrupt for a moment. I think we need to take a vote on this.

6 That sums up most of the issues we are facing. I just have a few finishing / closing remarks.

7 Claude is the chair, so he has the casting / choosing vote if there is a tie.

8 The chair / seat of our budget meetings likes to keep his closing remarks very short.

9 I read through / up the agenda before the meeting, so I know what we will be talking about.

🔊

Aa **24.5 CONECTA CADA DEFINICIÓN CON LA PALABRA CORRECTA**

make something usable again	footprint
1 the mark or effect something leaves behind	reuse
2 environmentally friendly	recycle
3 to use something again	green
4 natural products you can use	environment
5 things we do not need or want	reduce
6 the natural world around us	resources
7 make an amount smaller	waste

🔊

25 Acuerdos y desacuerdos

Cuando reaccionas a la opinión de alguien, es importante hacerlo de manera educada y respetuosa, especialmente si no estás de acuerdo con esa persona.

⚙ **Lenguaje** Reaccionar a las opiniones
Aa Vocabulario Acuerdos y desacuerdos
🧩 **Habilidad** Debatir opiniones

⚙ 25.1 MARCA LA MEJOR RESPUESTA PARA CADA INTERVENCIÓN

I don't like the new offices.
Me too. ☐
Me neither. ✓

① I didn't understand Juan's presentation.
Me too. ☐
Me neither. ☐

② I don't like the new product designs.
So do I. ☐
Neither do I. ☐

③ I thought this year's report was very positive.
So did I. ☐
Neither did I. ☐

④ I didn't enjoy Pavel's presentation.
So did I. ☐
Neither did I. ☐

⑤ I'm going to the cafeteria for lunch.
Me too. ☐
Me neither. ☐

⑥ I like Derek's new tie.
So do I. ☐
Neither do I. ☐

⑦ I don't like taking the metro.
Me too. ☐
Me neither. ☐

⑧ I think the software needs updating.
So do I. ☐
Neither do I. ☐

⑨ I like the new team members.
Me too. ☐
Me neither. ☐

🔊

Aa 25.2 CONECTA LAS INTERVENCIONES CON LAS RESPUESTAS

	I think the new interns are great.	So did I. He's so entertaining.
1	We should buy a new photocopier.	I'll ask the secretary to send it again.
2	I loved Pablo's presentation.	Me too. They are really helpful.
3	We need to invest more in training.	I suppose so. It will be expensive though.
4	I didn't receive the agenda.	Exactly. I didn't understand it at all.
5	I don't like the cafeteria much.	I agree. The team could improve their skills.
6	I like the new office furniture.	Absolutely. We should promote her.
7	The presentation was really confusing.	I agree. I learned some new skills.
8	The training was useful.	Me neither. The food's very bland.
9	The new HR assistant is really hard working.	So do I. It's very comfortable.

🔊

25.3 COMPLETA LOS ESPACIOS CON LAS PALABRAS DEL RECUADRO

I'm sorry, but we disagree ___*with*___ the price.

1 I'm _____ we'll have to cancel the meeting.

2 I'm sorry, but I _____ with you.

3 I _____ disagree with you about this.

4 I'm really not _____ about that design.

5 I'm _____ , Pete, but I don't agree with you.

6 I don't agree at _____ . It won't work.

7 I'm not _____ about this. Can we talk later?

8 I'm afraid I _____ agree with you at all.

9 I don't _____ at all with the merger.

10 You _____ be right, but I'm not sure.

11 Sorry, but I disagree _____ this plan.

with	totally	afraid	sorry	don't	sure
could	all	disagree	sure	agree	~~with~~

🔊

84

25.4 ESCUCHA EL AUDIO Y RESPONDE A LAS PREGUNTAS

Dos colegas, Jenny y Greg, valoran
los candidatos para un puesto.

How does Jenny feel about the candidates?
She likes all of them. ☑
She likes some of them. ☐
She dislikes all of them. ☐

③ Greg thinks they need someone with experience.
Jenny strongly agrees. ☐
Jenny disagrees. ☐
Jenny strongly disagrees. ☐

① Jenny thinks it's going to be an easy choice.
Greg strongly agrees with her. ☐
Greg agrees with her. ☐
Greg disagrees with her. ☐

④ Jenny thinks Paula could be a good candidate.
Greg agrees. ☐
Greg strongly agrees. ☐
Greg disagrees. ☐

② Jenny thinks John is a strong candidate.
Greg thinks he has lots of enthusiasm. ☐
Greg thinks he doesn't have enough experience. ☐
Greg thinks he has enough qualifications. ☐

⑤ Greg suggests they send Paula on a course.
Jenny agrees. ☐
Jenny strongly agrees. ☐
Jenny strongly disagrees. ☐

25.5 TACHA LA PALABRA INCORRECTA DE CADA FRASE Y DI LAS FRASES EN VOZ ALTA

I agree / ~~argue~~ with you about the new IT system.

① We totally / perfectly agree about the redesign.

② I can't agree with you in / at all about the downsizing.

③ We're frightened / afraid we totally disagree.

④ You could / would be right, but I need more evidence.

⑤ I'm not sure about / with the latest business plan.

26 Salud y seguridad

Muchas empresas tienen directrices para evitar accidentes y trabajar de manera segura. En inglés este tema se trata con vocabulario especializado y pronombres reflexivos.

⚙ **Lenguaje** Pronombres reflexivos
Aa Vocabulario Salud y seguridad en el trabajo
🧩 **Habilidad** Hablar sobre seguridad en el trabajo

26.1 MARCA LAS FRASES QUE SEAN CORRECTAS

Anita signed herself up for the course. ✓
Anita signed itself up for the course. ☐

1 Roger hurt him when he slipped. ☐
Roger hurt himself when he slipped. ☐

2 She burned herself on the coffee maker. ☐
She burned himself on the coffee maker. ☐

3 Ron blames itself for the accident. ☐
Ron blames himself for the accident. ☐

4 Jan cut herself on the machinery. ☐
She cut itself on the machinery. ☐

5 We enjoyed ourselves at the office party. ☐
We enjoyed ourself at the office party. ☐

6 Juan cut yourself in the kitchen. ☐
Juan cut himself in the kitchen. ☐

7 We need to protect himself from risks. ☐
We need to protect ourselves from risks. ☐

🔊

26.2 TACHA LAS PALABRAS INCORRECTAS DE CADA FRASE Y DI TODAS LAS FRASES EN VOZ ALTA

We locked ourselves / ~~themselves~~ in the factory last week. 🗣

1 I hurt yourself / myself when I moved the photocopier. 🗣

2 They should prepare themselves / themself for the course. 🗣

3 Claire's cut herself / itself on the equipment. 🗣

4 Have you all signed yourself / yourselves up for the course? 🗣

5 Sam is teaching himself / hisself Japanese. 🗣

🔊

26.3 LEE EL ARTÍCULO Y RESPONDE A LAS PREGUNTAS

Many employees are afraid of a fire in their building.
True ☑ False ☐ Not given ☐

1 You should leave the building as quickly as possible.
True ☐ False ☐ Not given ☐

2 You should turn off electrical appliances.
True ☐ False ☐ Not given ☐

3 If you smell a fire, activate the fire alarm.
True ☐ False ☐ Not given ☐

4 If you find a large fire, use an extinguisher to fight the fire.
True ☐ False ☐ Not given ☐

5 You should take care to close doors behind you.
True ☐ False ☐ Not given ☐

6 You should make sure you take your belongings with you.
True ☐ False ☐ Not given ☐

7 You should go to the assembly point and wait.
True ☐ False ☐ Not given ☐

8 You can go back to your office when the alarm stops.
True ☐ False ☐ Not given ☐

DAILY NEWS

A Burning Issue

What to do when you hear the fire alarm

A fire in the workplace is what 63% of employees fear the most. But there are some simple steps that you can follow to make sure you stay safe. First of all, don't panic: remember the instructions from your fire drill. If you smell smoke, activate the fire alarm. You should only use a fire extinguisher on a small fire. You should stay calm and leave the building using the stairs. Don't use the elevator, even if you are not fit. You should also leave all your belongings at your desk—don't waste time. Then, go to the nearest assembly point and stay there (even if the alarm has stopped) until the fire officer tells you it is safe to return.

Fire extinguisher

Aa 26.4 COMPLETA LOS ESPACIOS CON LAS PALABRAS DEL RECUADRO

If you discover a fire, set off the _fire alarm_ .

1 An _____ is used to stop small fires.

2 If you hear the fire alarm, go to the _____.

3 Medical equipment is kept in the _____.

4 Each fire _____ has a sign above the door.

5 You practice leaving the building during a _____.

| fire drill | extinguisher | escape | ~~fire alarm~~ | first aid kit | assembly area |

🔊

27 Sugerencias y consejos

Cuando aparecen problemas del día a día en el lugar de trabajo, es útil saber cómo realizar sugerencias y ofrecer consejos. En inglés se puede hacer de diversas maneras.

⚙ **Lenguaje** Prefijos y sufijos
Aa Vocabulario Problemas diarios en el trabajo
Habilidad Realizar sugerencias

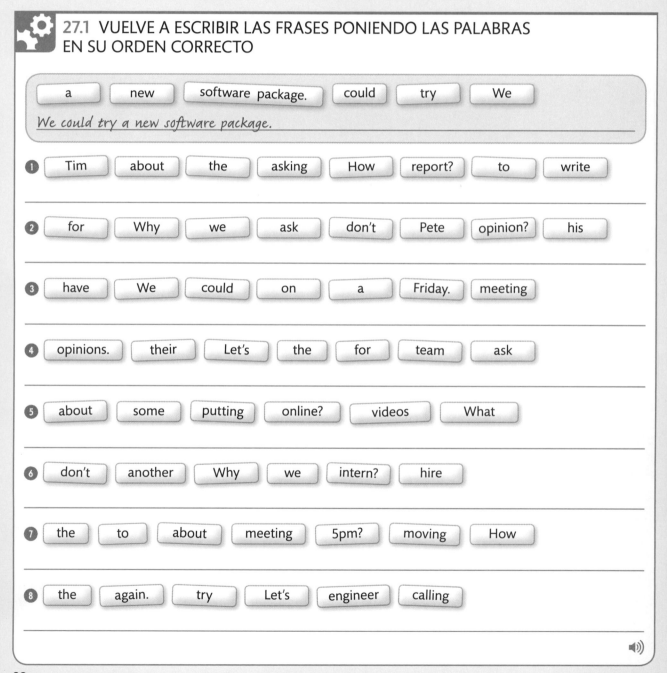

27.1 VUELVE A ESCRIBIR LAS FRASES PONIENDO LAS PALABRAS EN SU ORDEN CORRECTO

| a | new | software package. | could | try | We |

We could try a new software package.

❶ Tim | about | the | asking | How | report? | to | write

❷ for | Why | we | ask | don't | Pete | opinion? | his

❸ have | We | could | on | a | Friday. | meeting

❹ opinions. | their | Let's | the | for | team | ask

❺ about | some | putting | online? | videos | What

❻ don't | another | Why | we | intern? | hire

❼ the | to | about | meeting | 5pm? | moving | How

❽ the | again. | try | Let's | engineer | calling

27.2 CONECTA LOS PROBLEMAS DEL TRABAJO CON LAS SUGERENCIAS Y CONSEJOS

I've been at my desk all day.

1 Sally doesn't feel well.

2 I've lost my copy of the agenda.

3 I don't understand the new program.

4 There's no more coffee.

5 Karl's computer keeps crashing.

6 The photocopier's jammed.

7 My deadline is tomorrow.

8 The metro isn't running tomorrow.

She should go home and rest.

You should go on a training course.

You should go for a walk.

You should order some more.

You should ask the secretary for another.

You should call the engineer.

You should take the bus.

He should call IT.

You should ask for an extension.

27.3 COMPLETA LOS ESPACIOS CON LAS PALABRAS DEL RECUADRO

Susan _____*misspelled*_____ my name. It's Catherine with a "C."

1 Where have the reports gone? They've _____ .

2 Pete _____ me. He thought I said 3 o'clock.

3 Cathy isn't coming in today. She's feeling _____ .

4 You should be _____ crossing the road.

5 Doug is really _____ . He gets angry so easily.

6 I'm _____ to come to the training because I have a meeting.

7 Don't forget to _____ the machine after you've used it.

8 I'm _____ with that program. I don't know it.

9 Jean is so _____ . She's always making mistakes.

10 This morning is _____ for me. Can we meet later?

unable

impractical

careful

unfamiliar

~~misspelled~~

misunderstood

impatient

careless

disappeared

unwell

disconnect

27.4 TACHA LAS PALABRAS INCORRECTAS DE CADA FRASE Y DI TODAS LAS FRASES EN VOZ ALTA

What about arranging a meeting to discuss some practical / ~~impractical~~ solutions?

1. We should make sure no one understood / misunderstood the instructions.

2. How about organizing training for everyone who is unfamiliar / familiar with the program?

3. Let's make sure no one on the team spells / misspells the name wrongly again.

4. Why don't we ask Pete to help if Laura isn't well / unwell tomorrow?

5. I think we should disconnect / connect the machine since it's not working.

6. I don't think you should be so patient / impatient with the new recruits.

7. Let's send a memo to everyone who isn't able / unable to come to the meeting.

8. Let's explain to Tim that he should be more careful / careless with financial information.

9. Why don't we try to find a time that is convenient / inconvenient for everyone?

28 Hacer una presentación

Cuando prepares una presentación, asegúrate de que sea clara y fácil de seguir. Puedes utilizar diversas expresiones para que el público te siga durante la charla.

⚙ **Lenguaje** Lenguaje corporal
Aa Vocabulario Material para presentaciones
🧩 **Habilidad** Estructurar un discurso

28.1 ESCUCHA EL AUDIO Y RESPONDE A LAS PREGUNTAS

El director general de una empresa de confección se dirige a sus empleados.

The presentation is about...
marketing. ☑ **TV ads.** ☐ **websites.** ☐

❶ The speaker wants to focus on...
retired men. ☐ **young adults.** ☐ **children.** ☐

❷ Young adults between 18 and 23 are buying...
sports wear. ☐ **business wear.** ☐ **casual wear.** ☐

❸ Young adults between 24 and 30 buy more...
jackets. ☐ **suits.** ☐ **sneakers.** ☐

❹ What percentage of Europeans wear sports wear?
50% ☐ **60%** ☐ **65%** ☐

❺ What percentage of Americans wear sports wear?
70% ☐ **80%** ☐ **85%** ☐

❻ The speaker is disappointed with growth in...
England. ☐ **China.** ☐ **the US.** ☐

❼ The speaker hopes that growth will occur in...
South Africa. ☐ **India.** ☐ **New Zealand.** ☐

28.2 VUELVE A ESCRIBIR LAS FRASES PONIENDO LAS PALABRAS EN SU ORDEN CORRECTO

we'll | Next, | benefits. | explore | the
Next, we'll explore the benefits.

❶ about | Today | going | I'm | talk | profit. | to
_____

❷ anyone | questions? | Does | have | any
_____

❸ up, | facing | To | we | are | issues. | sum
_____

❹ happy | I'm | to | questions. | answer
_____

❺ the | Last, | look | let's | future. | at
_____

🔊

28.3 CONECTA EL INICIO Y EL FINAL DE CADA FRASE

Today, I want to talk   by showing you this graph.

① I'd like to begin   questions or comments?

② I'm happy to   about something really important.

③ Does anyone have any more   answer any questions.

④ Let's move   been an excellent quarter for the company.

⑤ After that, I would   on to the next topic.

⑥ To sum up, it's   like to talk about the merger.

🔊

Aa 28.4 COMPLETA LOS ESPACIOS CON LAS PALABRAS DEL RECUADRO

Can you please look at the graph on your _____*handout*_____ ?

① The _____ is black. We can't see the graph.

② If you use a _____ , you can introduce graphs and visuals.

③ I'll write down the company's name on the _____ .

④ There are programs to help you make professional-looking _____ .

⑤ If you use a _____ , the people at the back will hear you.

| projector | slides | ~~handout~~ | flipchart | microphone | screen |

🔊

28.5 TACHA LAS PALABRAS INCORRECTAS DE CADA FRASE Y DI TODAS LAS FRASES EN VOZ ALTA

Feel free to ask / ~~answer~~ any questions at the end.

1 I'd want / like to start with our factory in Vietnam.

2 To sum up / in, we need to invest more in infrastructure.

3 I'll explore / travel the benefits of investing in web technology later.

4 Let's begin in / by looking at the sales figures.

5 In short / small, we need to develop new products.

6 Let's take a look / view at the second graph.

7 So we've completed / covered all the topics I wanted to discuss.

8 Turning to / on the previous quarter's profits.

9 Then I'm going to talk / discuss about the situation in China.

10 For / To start, let's look at this year's performance.

11 Moving on / up, let's look at our main competitors.

12 First, I'm going to look at / in last year's results.

13 I'm happy to ask / answer any questions at the end.

14 I'd like to end in / by thanking you all for your attention today.

29 Normas y peticiones

Utiliza "can" y "have to" para hablar sobre normas en el trabajo, y verbos como "could" para pedir de manera educada a tus colegas que te ayuden con un problema.

🔧 **Lenguaje** Verbos modales
Aa Vocabulario Pedir cosas educadamente
🧩 **Habilidad** Hablar sobre normas y reglas

29.1 TACHA LAS PALABRAS INCORRECTAS DE CADA FRASE

 There's a formal dress code here. You **can't** / ~~have to~~ wear shorts to work.

1 You **can't** / **don't have to** stay late tonight. It's very quiet.

2 Is your phone broken? You **can** / **have to** use mine if you like.

3 We **can't** / **have to** wear a jacket and tie when we meet clients.

4 You **can't** / **don't have to** park there. It's a space for disabled drivers.

🔊

29.2 CONECTA LAS FRASES QUE VAN SEGUIDAS

You have to turn off the lights. ——→ There's tea and coffee in the kitchen.

1 You can't leave early tonight. —→ It saves energy.

2 You don't have to pay for lunch. That's the fire alarm.

3 You can make yourself a hot drink. There's a formal dress code.

4 We have to wear business clothes. Staff eat for free in the cafeteria.

5 We have to leave the building now. We have an important meeting at 5pm.

🔊

29.3 ESCUCHA EL AUDIO Y RESPONDE A LAS PREGUNTAS

Peter mantiene una conversación difícil con su jefe.

Peter can take long lunch breaks.
True ☐ **False** ☐ **Not given** ☑

❶ Staff can take their lunch break at 12:00.
True ☐ **False** ☐ **Not given** ☐

❷ Peter can wear jeans to work.
True ☐ **False** ☐ **Not given** ☐

❸ Women can't wear dresses to work.
True ☐ **False** ☐ **Not given** ☐

❹ Men don't always have to wear a tie.
True ☐ **False** ☐ **Not given** ☐

❺ Staff don't have to clean up the meeting rooms.
True ☐ **False** ☐ **Not given** ☐

29.4 VUELVE A ESCRIBIR LAS FRASES CORRIGIENDO LOS ERRORES

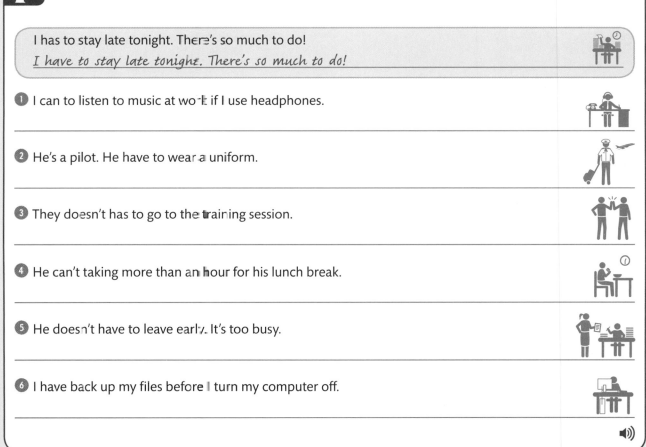

I has to stay late tonight. There's so much to do!
I have to stay late tonight. There's so much to do!

❶ I can to listen to music at work if I use headphones.
_____

❷ He's a pilot. He have to wear a uniform.
_____

❸ They doesn't has to go to the training session.
_____

❹ He can't taking more than an hour for his lunch break.
_____

❺ He doesn't have to leave early. It's too busy.
_____

❻ I have back up my files before I turn my computer off.
_____

29.5 CONECTA LAS IMÁGENES CON LAS FRASES CORRECTAS

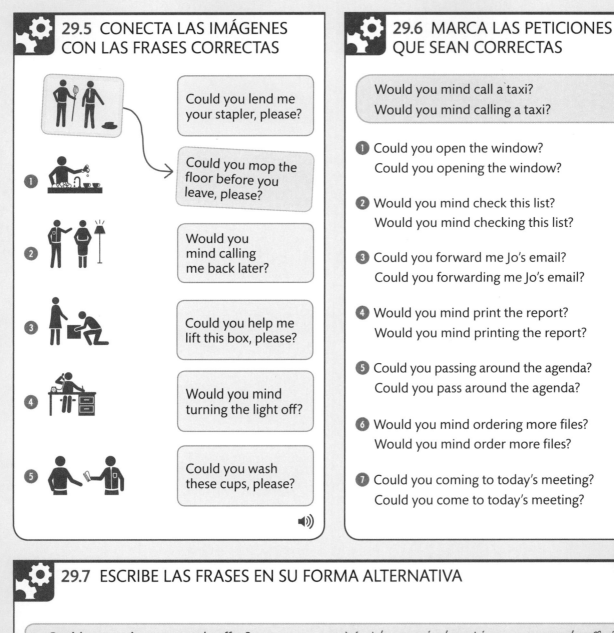

Could you lend me your stapler, please?

Could you mop the floor before you leave, please?

Would you mind calling me back later?

Could you help me lift this box, please?

Would you mind turning the light off?

Could you wash these cups, please?

29.6 MARCA LAS PETICIONES QUE SEAN CORRECTAS

Would you mind call a taxi? ☐
Would you mind calling a taxi? ☑

1 Could you open the window? ☐
Could you opening the window? ☐

2 Would you mind check this list? ☐
Would you mind checking this list? ☐

3 Could you forward me Jo's email? ☐
Could you forwarding me Jo's email? ☐

4 Would you mind print the report? ☐
Would you mind printing the report? ☐

5 Could you passing around the agenda? ☐
Could you pass around the agenda? ☐

6 Would you mind ordering more files? ☐
Would you mind order more files? ☐

7 Could you coming to today's meeting? ☐
Could you come to today's meeting? ☐

29.7 ESCRIBE LAS FRASES EN SU FORMA ALTERNATIVA

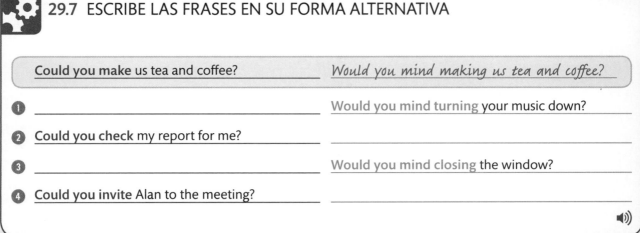

Could you make us tea and coffee?	Would you mind making us tea and coffee?
1 _____	Would you mind turning your music down?
2 Could you check my report for me?	_____
3 _____	Would you mind closing the window?
4 Could you invite Alan to the meeting?	_____

29.8 VUELVE A ESCRIBIR LAS PETICIONES PONIENDO LAS PALABRAS EN SU ORDEN CORRECTO

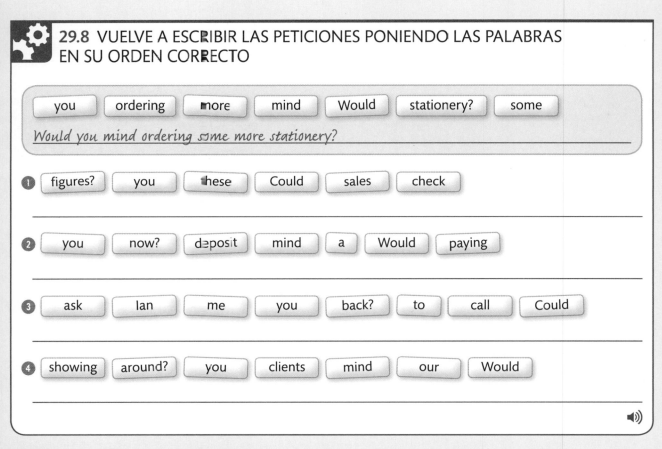

| you | ordering | more | mind | Would | stationery? | some |

Would you mind ordering some more stationery?

1 | figures? | you | these | Could | sales | check |

_____

2 | you | now? | deposit | mind | a | Would | paying |

_____

3 | ask | Ian | me | you | back? | to | call | Could |

_____

4 | showing | around? | you | clients | mind | our | Would |

_____

29.9 DI LAS PETICIONES EN VOZ ALTA COMPLETANDO LOS ESPACIOS CON LAS PALABRAS DEL RECUADRO

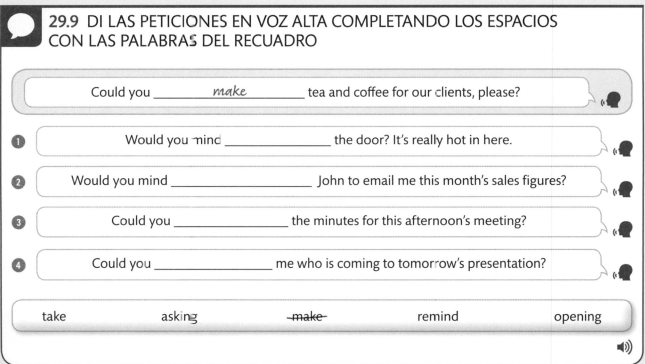

Could you _____ _make_ _____ tea and coffee for our clients, please?

1 Would you mind _____ the door? It's really hot in here.

2 Would you mind _____ John to email me this month's sales figures?

3 Could you _____ the minutes for this afternoon's meeting?

4 Could you _____ me who is coming to tomorrow's presentation?

| take | asking | ~~make~~ | remind | opening |

97

30 Vocabulario

Aa **30.1 MODISMOS EN EL TRAJAJO** ESCRIBE LAS EXPRESIONES DEL RECUADRO DEBAJO DE SU DEFINICIÓN

To start something

to get the ball rolling

❶ To think about a something in an original way

_____

❸ Administration, paperwork, or rules and regulations

_____

❹ To relax or calm down

_____

❻ To gradually relax

_____

❼ The normal daily routine at a company

_____

❾ A situation with no negative outcome

_____

❿ To owe money

_____

⓬ It is your turn to do or say something

_____

⓭ To delay or avoid something

_____

⓯ Wasting money

_____

⓰ To be really busy

_____

2 To start work on something that needs doing

_____

5 To be busy doing something else

_____

8 To not be working

_____

11 To work very long hours

_____

14 Not acting or behaving as it should

_____

17 To do a fair share of work

_____

to work around the clock   going haywire

to be out of order   ~~to get the ball rolling~~

to think outside the box   to take it easy

throwing money down the drain   red tape

to pull your weight   to be in the red

a win-win situation   to be swamped

to wind down   the ball is in your court

business as usual   to get down to business

to be tied up with   to put something off

31 Debatir problemas

Muchos problemas típicos del lugar de trabajo tienen su origen en alguna situación pasada. Utiliza el past continuous para hablar de estos problemas.

⚙ **Lenguaje** Past continuous
Aa Vocabulario Modismos sobre trabajo
🧩 **Habilidad** Describir problemas del trabajo

⚙ 31.1 MARCA LAS FRASES QUE SEAN CORRECTAS

Chris weren't answering his phone. ☐
Chris wasn't answering his phone. ☑

❶ Tanya was feeling very tired. ☐
Tanya were feeling very tired. ☐

❷ I were finishing his report. ☐
I was finishing his report. ☐

❸ Alison was talk to the CEO. ☐
Alison was talking to the CEO. ☐

❹ Was Jamie taking minutes? ☐
Were Jamie taking minutes? ☐

❺ Was you working late yesterday? ☐
Were you working late yesterday? ☐

❻ I trying was to call you. ☐
I was trying to call you. ☐

❼ Claire were playing very loud music. ☐
Claire was playing very loud music. ☐

🔊

⚙ 31.2 COMPLETA LOS ESPACIOS CON LOS VERBOS EN PAST CONTINUOUS

My computer ___wasn't working___ (not work) this morning.

❶ The train trip here was really bad. All the trains _____ (run) late.

❷ The cleaners _____ (complain) that staff left their dirty cups in the sink.

❸ Harriet _____ (not listen) to the presentation.

❹ Tom's manager was annoyed because Tom _____ (not meet) his deadlines.

❺ My email inbox _____ (get) full, so I had to delete some messages.

🔊

31.3 ESCUCHA EL AUDIO Y RESPONDE A LAS PREGUNTAS

 Alina y Howard hablan de una mañana que ha sido difícil en el trabajo.

Alina finished her report this morning.
True ☐ **False** ☑

① Howard's laptop wasn't working.
True ☐ **False** ☐

② IT solved the problem with Howard's computer.
True ☐ **False** ☐

③ Alina has the sales figures that she needs.
True ☐ **False** ☐

④ Howard thinks the report needs a new approach.
True ☐ **False** ☐

⑤ They don't have a computer that they can use.
True ☐ **False** ☐

31.4 DESCRIBE LAS IMÁGENES EN VOZ ALTA COMPLETANDO LOS ESPACIOS CON LAS PALABRAS DEL RECUADRO

The printer ___wasn't___ ___working___ yesterday.

③ Lucia _____ the minutes of the meeting.

① Joshua _____ a talk about new markets.

④ They _____ too loudly on the phone.

② Fiona _____ to Bilal's new ideas for products.

⑤ Helen _____ her lunch at her desk.

| wasn't listening | was eating | were speaking | was giving | ~~wasn't working~~ | was taking |

🔊

101

Louise's Blog

HOME | ENTRIES | ABOUT | CONTACT

Having a bad day at work is something that happens to all of us. Delayed trains, co-workers who annoy you, printers that don't work; it all adds up to stress for the best of us.

Take last week, for example. I missed an important meeting with a new supplier. My boss was sick, so I had to go instead, but my train was running late. I also had a cold because my co-workers were always leaving the windows next to the fire doors and the elevators open. To make matters worse, the people in my pod were talking really loudly and it was hard to concentrate. I knew it was Ben's last day and that they were having drinks and snacks to say goodbye, but I had lots of work to do.

Later that week, I had a long meeting with my boss. I tried to tell him that it didn't help that my assistant was copying me into lots of emails I didn't need to see. My boss said I needed to talk to my assistant and ask him to talk to me first if he was unsure of anything. I felt better after my update meeting, but when I got back to my desk, my USB cable and headphones were missing. Someone was borrowing them without asking. This was always happening. I was fed up.

So what should you do when you have a week like mine? When everything is going haywire, talking to a co-worker for ten minutes can help. It's good to share problems, but don't turn it into a complaining session. Complaining is negative and uses up our energy. Having a quick walk outside should clear your head. Our bodies like to be in the open air and sunlight for half an hour a day, so go for a walk after lunch instead of reading those reports. Then you can tackle a full inbox with a positive perspective.

Why did Louise miss her meeting? **She was sick** ☐ **It was canceled** ☐ **Her train was running late** ☑

❶ What were Louise's co-workers always opening? **The windows** ☐ **The doors** ☐ **The elevators** ☐

❷ How were Louise's co-workers making it difficult for her to focus? **Talking** ☐ **Eating** ☐ **Drinking** ☐

❸ Who was sending Louise too many emails? **Her boss** ☐ **Her assistant** ☐ **Her co-workers** ☐

❹ What was missing from Louise's desk? **Her laptop** ☐ **Her files** ☐ **Her USB cable** ☐

❺ What should you do if you're stressed? **Complain** ☐ **Talk to a co-worker** ☐ **Use up energy** ☐

❻ What does Louise say a walk outside can help us do? **Think clearly** ☐ **Get fit** ☐ **Enjoy nature** ☐

32 Disculpas y explicaciones

En inglés dispones de diversas expresiones educadas para disculparte por cualquier error. Utiliza el past continuous y el past simple juntos para dar explicaciones sobre un error.

⚙ **Lenguaje** Past continuous y past simple
Aa Vocabulario Errores en el lugar de trabajo
🧩 **Habilidad** Disculparse y dar explicaciones

⚙ 32.1 MARCA LAS FRASES QUE SEAN CORRECTAS

I like to apologize for keeping you waiting so long. ☐
I would like to apologize for keeping you waiting so long. ☑

1. I am so sorry I was late for the meeting with our clients today. ☐
   I so sorry I was late for the meeting with our clients today. ☐

2. I would like to apologize for not finish the report yesterday. ☐
   I would like to apologize for not finishing the report yesterday. ☐

3. I'm sorry really. I forgot to charge the office cell phone and it has no power. ☐
   I'm really sorry. I forgot to charge the office cell phone and it has no power. ☐

4. I'm really apologize this line is so bad. I hope we don't get cut off. ☐
   I'm really sorry this line is so bad. I hope we don't get cut off. ☐

5. I'm afraid that's not enough good. I want a full refund on my ticket. ☐
   I'm afraid that's not good enough. I want a full refund on my ticket. ☐

🔊

Aa 32.2 CONECTA LAS DISCULPAS CON LAS RESPUESTAS CORRECTAS

I'm very sorry if the waiter was rude. — That's all right. I could see he was very busy.

No problem. I'll help you finish it now.

1. I'm so sorry. My presentation isn't ready.

That's not good enough. Please heat it up.

2. I apologize if your food was cold.

3. I'm really sorry, but I have to leave early.

Don't worry. I'll print off some more.

4. I'm very sorry the coffee machine's broken.

Never mind. We're not very busy today.

5. I'm really sorry. I left the reports at home.

No problem. I'll have tea instead.

🔊

32.3 ESCUCHA EL AUDIO Y NUMERA DESPUÉS LAS IMÁGENES EN EL ORDEN EN QUE SE DESCRIBEN

A ☐ B ☐ C ☐ 1 D ☐ E ☐

32.4 DI LAS FRASES EN VOZ ALTA COMPLETANDO LOS ESPACIOS CON LAS PALABRAS DEL RECUADRO

I really ___*must*___ apologize for not calling you back earlier.

4 That's all _____ . I'll make you a copy right now.

1 I'm really _____ . I forgot to send the agenda for the meeting.

5 Please _____ sure it doesn't happen again.

2 I would like to _____ for the rudeness of the waitress.

6 Never _____ . It's only a cup.

3 I'm _____ that's not good enough. You missed an important meeting.

7 I would _____ to apologize for the delay to your train this evening.

| ~~must~~ | like | mind | apologize | sorry | afraid | make | right |

104

32.5 TACHA LAS PALABRAS INCORRECTAS DE CADA FRASE

I ~~wrote~~ / **was writing** a report when my computer **crashed** / ~~was crashing~~.

1. Harry **practiced** / **was practicing** his presentation when I **called** / **was calling** him.

2. Sam's cell phone **rang** / **was ringing** when Tom **described** / **was describing** the sales for this quarter.

3. The elevator **got** / **was getting** stuck while they **waited** / **were waiting** for it.

4. Tina **didn't listen** / **wasn't listening** when the CEO **said** / **was saying** all staff would get a raise.

5. The fire alarm **went** / **was going** off when we **had** / **were having** our update meeting.

6. I **worked** / **was working** late when I **heard** / **was hearing** a strange noise.

7. I **edited** / **was editing** the report when the fire alarm **went** / **was going** off.

🔊

32.6 COMPLETA LOS ESPACIOS PONIENDO LOS VERBOS EN PAST CONTINUOUS O PAST SIMPLE

I __was driving__ (🚗 drive) to a meeting when someone __crashed__ (🚗 crash) into me.

1. The photocopier _____ (break) while I _____ (copy) your sales report.

2. We _____ (listen) to Janet's presentation when the power _____ (go) off.

3. John _____ (sign) the contract when the lawyer _____ (call) him.

4. Anna _____ (be) furious when she found out George _____ (copy) her ideas.

5. Simon _____ (edit) the report when his computer _____ (crash).

6. We _____ (wait) for the bus when two buses _____ (arrive).

🔊

105

33 Tareas y objetivos

Utiliza el present perfect para que tus compañeros sepan cómo vas de trabajo cuando se acerquen las fechas de entrega y trabajes bajo presión.

 Lenguaje Present perfect y past simple

Aa Vocabulario Tareas del trabajo

Habilidad Debatir logros en el trabajo

33.1 COMPLETA LOS ESPACIOS PONIENDO LOS VERBOS EN PRESENT PERFECT

I ___*have written*___ (**write**) the report you wanted.

1. I _____ (**call**) eight customers this morning.

2. Gareth _____ (**make**) coffee for the visitors.

3. Piotr _____ (**cut**) the hair of many famous people.

4. I _____ (**not finish**) checking my emails.

5. Carl _____ (**not email**) me the sales data.

🔊

33.2 TACHA LA PALABRA INCORRECTA DE CADA FRASE

I've **just** / ~~yet~~ sent him the files.

1. She hasn't sent the invoice **just** / **yet**.

2. We have **yet** / **just** heard the CEO is leaving.

3. I haven't met the new director **yet** / **just**.

4. Has Tom finished fixing my laptop **just** / **yet**?

5. George has **just** / **yet** called me.

6. The painters haven't finished **yet** / **just**.

7. Have you had a meeting with Ann **yet** / **just**?

8. The trainer has **just** / **yet** arrived.

9. Have you **just** / **yet** finished the report?

🔊

33.3 VUELVE A ESCRIBIR LAS FRASES PONIENDO LAS PALABRAS EN SU ORDEN CORRECTO

| just | preparing | have | my | I | presentation. | finished |

I have just finished preparing my presentation.

1 | the | haven't | stationery | yet. | I | ordered |

_____

2 | the | They | packaging. | just | new | introduced | have |

_____

3 | answered | you | emails | yet? | those | Have |

_____

4 | our | minutes | has | written | from | Derinda | the | meeting. | just |

_____

33.4 LEE LA LISTA DE TAREAS PENDIENTES DE LAILA Y RESPONDE A LAS PREGUNTAS

Laila has emailed the CEO.
True ☐ **False** ☐ **Not given** ☑

1 Laila has organized the team meeting.
True ☐ **False** ☐ **Not given** ☐

2 Laila has photocopied the expenses claims.
True ☐ **False** ☐ **Not given** ☐

3 Laila hasn't updated the database.
True ☐ **False** ☐ **Not given** ☐

4 Accounts has found the missing invoice.
True ☐ **False** ☐ **Not given** ☐

To do list

- ~~Organize team meeting~~
- ~~Write FAQs for new staff~~
- Photocopy boss's expenses claims
- Update the database
- ~~Call Accounts about missing invoice~~
- Get bus timetables for visitors

33.5 VUELVE A ESCRIBIR LAS FRASES CORRIGIENDO LOS ERRORES

> Tim **has given** a great presentation yesterday afternoon.
> *Tim gave a great presentation yesterday afternoon.*

1 Daniel **has sent** your package last Friday.

_____

2 Jenny **has shown** me the new designs yesterday.

_____

3 Babu and Zack **hasn't finished** their research yet.

_____

4 Kate **has spoken** to the HR manager last week.

_____

33.6 ESCUCHA EL AUDIO Y MARCA QUÉ COSAS REALMENTE TUVIERON LUGAR

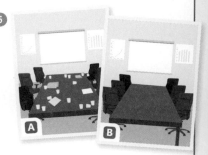

33.7 MARCA LAS FRASES QUE SEAN CORRECTAS

I've finished the reports last week. ☐
I finished the reports last week. ☑

① I has done all the invoices for June. ☐
I have done all the invoices for June. ☐

② He met the Chinese partners last month. ☐
He has met the Chinese partners last month. ☐

③ He hasn't sent the salaries to payroll yet. ☐
He hasn't sended the salaries to payroll yet. ☐

④ They not started the audit yet. ☐
They have not started the audit yet. ☐

⑤ He has left this morning. ☐
He left this morning. ☐

⑥ I have yet heard about your promotion. ☐
I have just heard about your promotion. ☐

⑦ She have sold the most products. ☐
She has sold the most products. ☐

⑧ Have you designed that box yet? ☐
You have designed that box yet? ☐

⑨ They have given him a verbal warning. ☐
They have gived him a verbal warning. ☐

⑩ Mark hasn't scanned it just. ☐
Mark hasn't scanned it yet. ☐

⑪ I have speaked to your team. ☐
I have spoken to your team. ☐

◀))

33.8 RESPONDE AL AUDIO EN VOZ ALTA UTILIZANDO LAS PALABRAS DEL RECUADRO

Have you finished the reports?

No, I haven't finished them _yet._

① Have you scanned the photos?

Yes, I've _____ scanned them.

② Has Philip audited the books?

No, he _____ done them yet.

③ Where are the contracts?

_____ filed them all in the cabinet.

④ Why are there no newspapers?

We've_____ the delivery.

I've   just   stopped
hasn't   ~~yet~~

◀))

109

34 Tratar las quejas

Si un cliente se queja de un problema, se le puede ofrecer una solución, igual que hacer predicciones o promesas, utilizando el future con "will".

⚙ **Lenguaje** El futuro con "will"
Aa Vocabulario Quejas y disculpas
🧩 **Habilidad** Tratar las quejas

34.1 MARCA LAS FRASES QUE SEAN CORRECTAS

The company wills offer you a discount. ☐
The company will offer you a discount. ☑

❶ We will replace your tablet free of charge. ☐
We will to replace your tablet free of charge. ☐

❷ The chef will cooks you another pizza. ☐
The chef will cook you another pizza. ☐

❸ I'll talk to the boss about it. ☐
I'll talking to the boss about it. ☐

❹ The manager be will with you soon. ☐
The manager will be with you soon. ☐

❺ I contact our courier immediately. ☐
I'll contact our courier immediately. ☐

❻ We will give you a full refund. ☐
We will to give you a full refund. ☐

❼ I promise that your order arrive today. ☐
I promise that your order will arrive today. ☐

❽ I'm afraid we won't finish the project on time. ☐
I'm afraid we willn't finish the project on time. ☐

❾ I'm sorry, but we don't will cancel your order. ☐
I'm sorry, but we won't cancel your order. ☐

🔊

34.2 CONECTA LAS QUEJAS CON LAS RESPUESTAS CORRECTAS

My bus was three hours late.

❶ My luggage didn't arrive.

❷ This food is cold.

❸ You have charged me twice.

❹ I've been waiting for a taxi for 40 minutes.

❺ There is no hot water in our bathroom.

We'll move you to another room.

I will call the driver immediately.

We'll refund you the price of your ticket.

We'll send it to your hotel when it gets here.

I'll ask the chef to cook it properly.

I'll refund the money to your credit card.

🔊

110

34.3 LEE LA CARTA Y RESPONDE A LAS PREGUNTAS

Dear Mr. Vance,

Thank you for your letter of March 3. I am sorry to hear you were not happy with the service provided by our hotel during your two-day business trip to Rome last month. First of all, I sincerely apologize that there was no receptionist when you arrived at midnight. We will ask our receptionists to work late when travelers are delayed so that there is always someone to welcome our guests in the future. I am also sorry to hear that the bathroom in your hotel suite had not been cleaned. I agree that this was unacceptable, and I will speak to the cleaning services manager. Regarding breakfast, I am sorry that there was no bread and that you had to ask for hot coffee. I will speak to the catering staff to ensure this does not happen again. With reference to the hotel's policy on guaranteeing residents a good night's sleep, I am so sorry to hear that you were kept awake by guests in the adjoining room. Given all the above, I would like to offer a full refund of what you paid for your two-night hotel stay.

I hope this is satisfactory.
Yours sincerely,
Mr. J Silvano

Why did Mr. Vance write to the hotel?

To complain about the food in Rome ☐

To thank them for a pleasant stay ☐

To complain about his stay there ☑

1 What was the problem when Mr. Vance checked in?

The security guard arrived after midnight ☐

The security guard was rude ☐

There was no receptionist ☐

2 What will the hotel do in the future?

They will ask receptionists to work late ☐

Receptionists will go to the airport ☐

Receptionists will not work late ☐

3 What was wrong with Mr. Vance's hotel suite?

It was noisy at night ☐

The light didn't work ☐

The bathroom was dirty ☐

4 How will this complaint be addressed?

Mr. Silvano will clean the bathrooms ☐

Mr. Silvano will apologize to the cleaner. ☐

He will speak to the cleaners' manager ☐

5 What was wrong with the breakfast?

There wasn't any hot coffee ☐

There wasn't any juice ☐

There wasn't any cereal ☐

6 What was the problem that evening?

Mr. Vance had to work late ☐

Mr. Vance went to a party ☐

Mr. Vance was kept awake ☐

7 What does Mr. Silvano offer Mr. Vance?

A discount off his next stay ☐

A full refund ☐

A refund for one night's stay in the hotel ☐

34.4 VUELVE A ESCRIBIR LAS FRASES PONIENDO LAS PALABRAS EN SU ORDEN CORRECTO

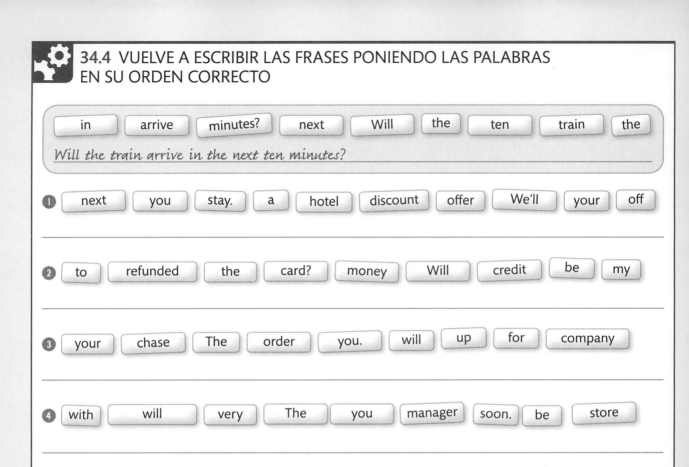

`in` `arrive` `minutes?` `next` `Will` `the` `ten` `train` `the`

Will the train arrive in the next ten minutes?

① `next` `you` `stay.` `a` `hotel` `discount` `offer` `We'll` `your` `off`

② `to` `refunded` `the` `card?` `money` `Will` `credit` `be` `my`

③ `your` `chase` `The` `order` `you.` `will` `up` `for` `company`

④ `with` `will` `very` `The` `you` `manager` `soon.` `be` `store`

⑤ `the` `washing` `Will` `machine?` `broken` `on` `part` `my` `replace` `you`

34.5 ESCUCHA EL AUDIO Y MARCA SI ESTAS SITUACIONES TENDRÁN LUGAR HOY O NO

Sí ☑
No ☐

① Sí ☐ No ☐

② Sí ☐ No ☐

③ Sí ☐ No ☐

④ Sí ☐ No ☐

34.6 RESPONDE AL AUDIO EN VOZ ALTA COMPLETANDO LOS ESPACIOS CON LAS EXPRESIONES DEL RECUADRO

My train was an hour late.

I do apologize. We _'ll refund_ the fare to your credit card.

① The concert was canceled when we got to the venue last night.

I'm very sorry about that. _____ you a refund.

② My pasta is cold.

I really must apologize. I _____ it back to the kitchen.

③ Where is the sales assistant? I want to try these shoes on.

She _____ with you in a minute.

④ The receptionist was rude.

I _____ to her about this.

⑤ Your assistant didn't finish that report I asked him to prepare.

It _____ again.

⑥ There aren't any vegetarian options on this menu.

I _____ the chef to make you something vegetarian.

won't happen   'll take   'll refund   'll ask   We'll offer   'll be   'll talk

Aa 35.1 TRANSPORTE ESCRIBE LAS PALABRAS DEL RECUADRO DEBAJO DE SU CORRESPONDIENTE DIBUJO

metro

1 _____

2 _____

3 _____

4 _____

5 _____

6 _____

7 _____

8 _____

9 _____

10 _____

11 _____

car	taxi	bus stop	train station	bus	helicopter
tram	taxi stand (US) / taxi rank (UK)	airport	~~metro~~	bicycle	plane

one-way ticket

 ① _____

 ② _____

 ③ _____

 ④ _____

 ⑤ _____

 ⑥ _____

 ⑦ _____

 ⑧ _____

 ⑨ _____

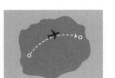 ⑩ _____

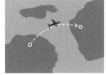 ⑪ _____

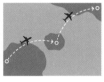 ⑫ _____

 ⑬ _____

 ⑭ _____

 ⑮ _____

 ⑯ _____

 ⑰ _____

 ⑱ _____

 ⑲ _____

---

passport   aisle seat   terminal   passport control   board a plane   check-in   ~~one-way ticket~~

international flight   round trip ticket (US) / return ticket (UK)   window seat   late   boarding pass

on time   domestic flight   delay   luggage   connecting flight   seat reservation   security   hotel

🔊

36 Planear un viaje

Cuando haces planes de viaje es útil poder hablar sobre los posibles resultados de nuestras acciones o elecciones.

Lenguaje Zero conditional y first conditional
Aa Vocabulario Viajes
Habilidad Hablar sobre acciones y resultados

36.1 COMPLETA LOS ESPACIOS PONIENDO LOS VERBOS EN EL TIEMPO CORRECTO PARA FORMAR FRASES EN EL FIRST CONDITIONAL

If you _____*book*_____ (book) in advance, you _____*will get*_____ (get) a discount.

1. If we _____ (not hurry), we _____ (miss) the flight.

2. If we _____ (meet) in Berlin, it _____ (save) us some time.

3. We _____ (take) on a new intern if we _____ (win) the contract.

4. If the train _____ (be) late, we _____ (miss) the meeting.

5. If the bank _____ (be) closed, we _____ (not have) any money.

6. We _____ (pay) for your flight if you _____ (fly) to Denver.

7. If you _____ (work) hard, you _____ (pass) the exam.

8. The firm _____ (pay) expenses if you _____ (be) delayed.

9. If I _____ (go) to Rome, I _____ (visit) the Colosseum.

10. If I _____ (lose) my job, I don't know what I _____ (do).

36.2 CONECTA EL INICIO Y EL FINAL DE CADA FRASE

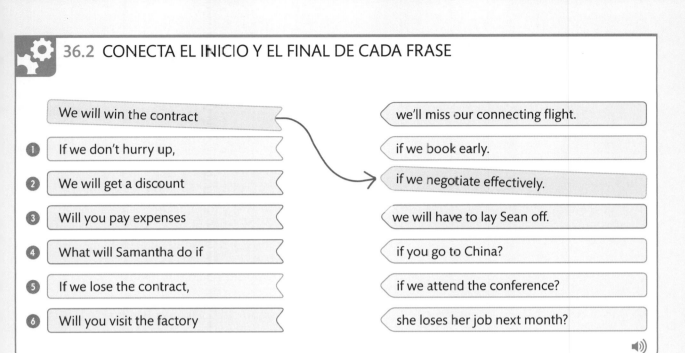

We will win the contract — if we negotiate effectively.

1. If we don't hurry up,
2. We will get a discount
3. Will you pay expenses
4. What will Samantha do if
5. If we lose the contract,
6. Will you visit the factory

we'll miss our connecting flight.

if we book early.

if we negotiate effectively.

we will have to lay Sean off.

if you go to China?

if we attend the conference?

she loses her job next month?

36.3 MARCA LAS FRASES QUE SEAN CORRECTAS

If the flight is delayed, we will definitely miss the meeting. ☑
If the flight will be delayed, we definitely miss the meeting. ☐

1. Will you have a celebration if you get the job? ☐
   Do you have a celebration if you get the job? ☐

2. If you'll buy the ticket online, it will be cheaper. ☐
   If you buy the ticket online, it will be cheaper. ☐

3. If we visit Paris, we probably go sightseeing. ☐
   If we visit Paris, we will probably go sightseeing. ☐

4. What will we do if we don't win the contract? ☐
   What do we do if we won't win the contract? ☐

5. If we'll take on a new intern, where do they sit? ☐
   If we take on a new intern, where will they sit? ☐

6. How will you travel to Berlin if the flight is canceled? ☐
   How do you travel to Berlin if the flight will be canceled? ☐

36.4 ESCUCHA EL AUDIO Y RESPONDE A LAS PREGUNTAS

Clara habla por teléfono con Jane para comentar los detalles de su próximo viaje.

Clara has already booked the flights.
True ☐ False ✓ Not given ☐

❶ If they book the flights online, they will be cheaper.
True ☐ False ☐ Not given ☐

❷ They both agree to take a taxi.
True ☐ False ☐ Not given ☐

❸ The Hotel Ritz is more expensive.
True ☐ False ☐ Not given ☐

❹ The Hotel Grande is closer to the convention hall.
True ☐ False ☐ Not given ☐

❺ The Hotel Ritz includes breakfast.
True ☐ False ☐ Not given ☐

❻ The company will pay for all meals.
True ☐ False ☐ Not given ☐

36.5 VUELVE A ESCRIBIR LAS FRASES PONIENDO LAS PALABRAS EN SU ORDEN CORRECTO

| pay | travel | to | class, | you | more. | If | you | first | have |

If you travel first class, you have to pay more.

❶ | If | to | nice | work. | walk | it's | a | day, | I |

_____

❷ | water, | If | heat | it | boils. | you |

_____

❸ | for | late | boss | isn't | work, | you're | If | unhappy? | your |

_____

❹ | that | press | If | machine | button, | the | you | stops. |

_____

🔊

36.6 TACHA LAS PALABRAS INCORRECTAS DE CADA FRASE Y DI TODAS LAS FRASES EN VOZ ALTA

If you press / ~~will press~~ the red button here, the machine stops immediately.

1. Will you visit Red Square if you go / will go to Moscow?

2. People use public transportation if it is / be cheap.

3. What will we do if we lose / will lose the contract?

4. The ticket will be / is more expensive if we buy it later.

5. If you pay / will pay staff more, they work harder.

6. Will / Do you pick me up from the station if I give you my details?

7. We'll miss the train if we won't / don't hurry.

8. If trains / will rain, the event is always moved indoors.

9. Sharon won't / doesn't go on vacation if she loses her job.

10. Does / Will Doug resign if the company loses the deal?

37 Preguntar direcciones

Cuando viajes a congresos y reuniones es posible que tengas que preguntar direcciones. En tal caso es esencial saber cómo ser educado y claro.

⚙ **Lenguaje** Imperativos, preposiciones de lugar
Aa Vocabulario Direcciones
🧩 **Habilidad** Preguntar y dar direcciones

37.1 TACHA LA PALABRA INCORRECTA DE CADA FRASE

 Go past the café and ~~turning~~ / turn left.

1 Do you know the **where** / **way** to the station?

2 The bank is **in** / **on** the corner.

3 Do you know how to **go** / **get** to the hotel?

4 The museum is **on** / **in** front of the park.

5 You should **take** / **make** the second left.

6 The library is straight ahead on **the** / **a** right.

7 Our house is just ahead **on** / **in** the left.

8 Sorry, did you **tell** / **say** it is near the school?

9 Turn right **on** / **at** the sign.

🔊

37.2 MARCA LAS FRASES QUE SEAN CORRECTAS

The office is 30 yards ahead on the right. ☑
The office is 30 yards ahead by the right. ☐

1 The entrance is in front of the factory. ☐
The entrance is on front of the factory. ☐

2 Turn right in the sign. ☐
Turn right at the sign. ☐

3 The bank is across from the school. ☐
The bank is between the school. ☐

4 Take the first road in the left. ☐
Take the first road on the left. ☐

5 Go past the movie theater. ☐
Go after the movie theater. ☐

6 The bank is on the corner. ☐
The bank is at the corner. ☐

7 The station is next in the police station. ☐
The station is next to the police station. ☐

🔊

120

37.3 VUELVE A ESCRIBIR LAS FRASES PONIENDO LAS PALABRAS EN SU ORDEN CORRECTO

| conference | the | of | The | city | is | in | hall. | front | center |

The conference center is in front of the city hall.

① | do | to | Excuse | you | the | know | way | the | hotel? | me, |

_____

② | it's | the | and | train | station. | straight | Go | opposite | on |

_____

③ | next | post | Sorry, | you | the | say | it's | office? | did | to |

_____

④ | the | yards | corner. | The | on | 40 | ahead | bank | is |

_____

🔊

37.4 ESCUCHA EL AUDIO Y MARCA LAS DIRECCIONES QUE OIGAS

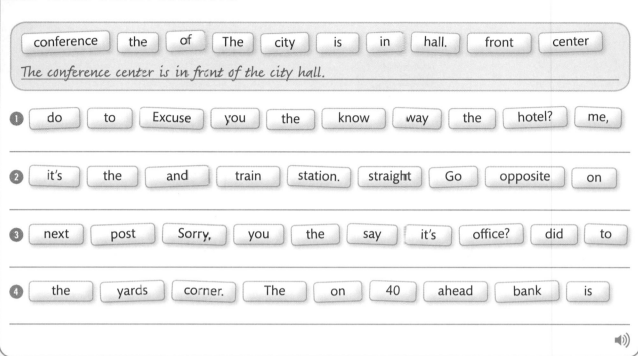

37.5 MIRA EL MAPA Y RESPONDE A LAS PREGUNTAS EN VOZ ALTA

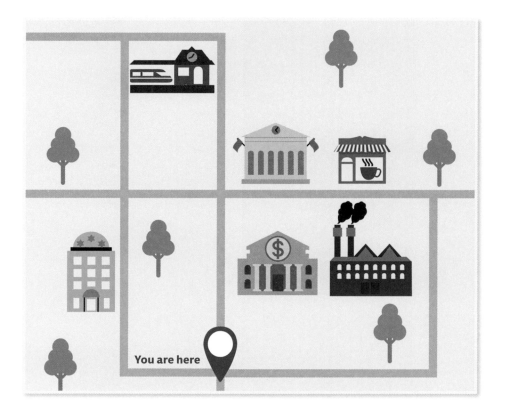

You are here

Do you know the way to the town hall?

Yes, turn right after the bank.

3 Do you know where I can find a bank?

1 How do I get to the café?

4 Do you know where the factory is?

2 Could you tell me the way to the train station?

5 Where is the closest hotel to here?

38 Describir la estancia

Puedes describir acontecimientos con frases activas o pasivas. La frase pasiva sirve para destacar la acción en lugar de lo que la ha causado.

⚙ **Lenguaje** La voz pasiva
Aa Vocabulario Hoteles y alojamiento
🧩 **Habilidad** Uso de la voz pasiva

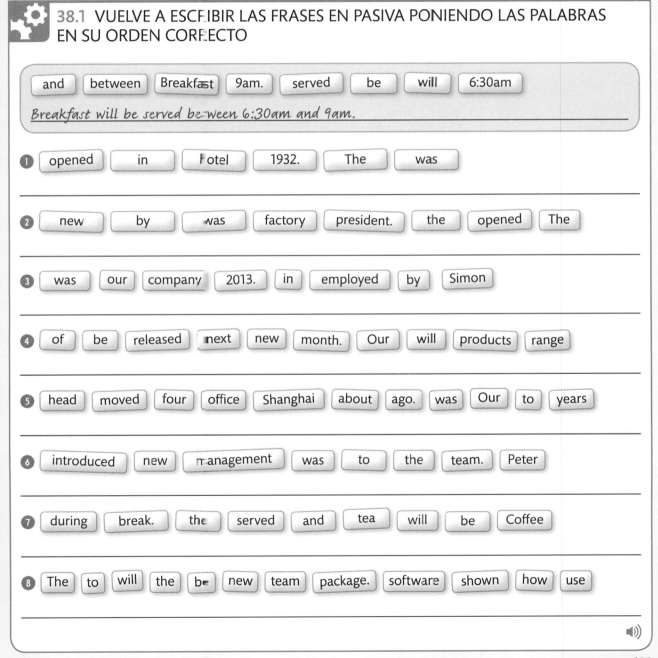

38.1 VUELVE A ESCRIBIR LAS FRASES EN PASIVA PONIENDO LAS PALABRAS EN SU ORDEN CORRECTO

and | between | Breakfast | 9am. | served | be | will | 6:30am

Breakfast will be served between 6:30am and 9am.

1. opened | in | Hotel | 1932. | The | was

2. new | by | was | factory | president. | the | opened | The

3. was | our | company | 2013. | in | employed | by | Simon

4. of | be | released | next | new | month. | Our | will | products | range

5. head | moved | four | office | Shanghai | about | ago. | was | Our | to | years

6. introduced | new | management | was | to | the | team. | Peter

7. during | break. | the | served | and | tea | will | be | Coffee

8. The | to | will | the | be | new | team | package. | software | shown | how | use

🔊

123

38.2 VUELVE A ESCRIBIR LAS FRASES EN ACTIVA COMO FRASES EN PASIVA

Someone moved the photocopier last night. = *The photocopier was moved last night.*

1 Someone met the CEO at the airport. = _____

2 Danny has redecorated the meeting room. = _____

3 My assistant booked a double room yesterday. = _____

4 Julia taught the team some Mandarin. = _____

5 Someone left the files on the train again. = _____

6 John booked the rooms on Monday. = _____

7 The hotel serves breakfast at 7:30am. = _____

8 Someone has organized the office. = _____

 38.3 ESCUCHA EL AUDIO Y NUMERA DESPUÉS LAS IMÁGENES EN EL ORDEN EN QUE LAS OIGAS

A

B 1

C

D

E

F

G

H

38.4 LEE LAS OPINIONES Y RESPONDE A LAS PREGUNTAS

The reviewer thinks Hotel Destiny is expensive.
True ☐ False ☐ Not given ☑

1 The reviewer took a taxi to Hotel Destiny.
True ☐ False ☐ Not given ☐

2 There are conference facilities at Hotel Destiny.
True ☐ False ☐ Not given ☐

3 The television at Hotel Belvedere did not work.
True ☐ False ☐ Not given ☐

4 The receptionist was helpful at Hotel Belvedere.
True ☐ False ☐ Not given ☐

Hotels etc

Hotel Destiny ★ ★ ★ ★
This hotel is comfortable and affordable. It's perfect if you're staying in Shanghai for work or a short break. My colleague and I were picked up by the hotel minibus from the airport. After checking in, we looked around the hotel: there is a small restaurant, a gym in the basement, and a karaoke bar. Great fun!

Hotel Belvedere ★
We had been told that this is one of the best hotels in the area, but what we found proved shocking. The TV didn't turn on, and the bed fell apart on the second night. When I went downstairs to complain, I was ignored by the receptionist, and finally my wife and I were forced to check out three days early.

38.5 RESPONDE AL AUDIO EN VOZ ALTA COMPLETANDO LOS ESPACIOS CON LA FORMA CORRECTA DE LAS EXPRESIONES DEL RECUADRO

How was your flight?

The flight _____ was delayed _____ by eight hours.

1 How did you get to the hotel?

We _____ at the airport by the driver.

2 How was the breakfast?

Great. It _____ at 7am each morning.

3 Was there a TV in the room?

Yes. But unfortunately it _____ .

| was broken | were picked up | ~~was delayed~~ | was served |

Aa 39.1 COMER FUERA ESCRIBE LAS PALABRAS DEL RECUADRO DEBAJO DE SU CORRESPONDIENTE DIBUJO

restaurant

1 _____

2 _____

3 _____

4 _____

5 _____

6 _____

7 _____

8 _____

9 _____

10 _____

11 _____

12 _____

13 _____

14 _____

15 _____

16 _____

17 _____

18 _____

19 _____

menu	vegan	vegetarian	boil	waitress	~~restaurant~~	roast	fry
lunch	café	food allergy / intolerance		tip		waiter	receipt
bar	chef	dessert	breakfast	make a reservation / booking			dinner

Aa 39.2 COMIDA Y BEBIDA ESCRIBE LAS PALABRAS DEL RECUADRO DEBAJO DE SU CORRESPONDIENTE DIBUJO

soup

 ❶ _____

 ❷ _____

 ❸ _____

 ❹ _____

 ❺ _____

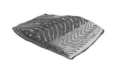 ❻ _____

 ❼ _____

 ❽ _____

 ❾ _____

 ❿ _____

 ⓫ _____

 ⓬ _____

 ⓭ _____

 ⓮ _____

 ⓯ _____

 ⓰ _____

 ⓱ _____

 ⓲ _____

 ⓳ _____

fruit	napkin	fork	tea	bread	~~soup~~	coffee
pasta	seafood	vegetables	salad	fish	milk	cake
meat	water	sandwich	knife	butter	potatoes

127

40 Congresos y visitantes

Es importante saber interactuar de manera educada en inglés, ya seas tú quien reciba visitas o el que visite otra empresa.

⚙️ **Lenguaje** "A", "some", "any"
Aa Vocabulario Hospitalidad
Habilidad Dar la bienvenida a los visitantes

40.1 MARCA LAS FRASES QUE SEAN CORRECTAS

Welcome to China, Mr. Arnold. ☑
Welcome in China, Mr. Arnold. ☐

1. Did you have any trouble getting here? ☐
   Did you have any trouble arriving here? ☐

2. Can I serve you anything? ☐
   Can I get you anything? ☐

3. It's great to meet you on person. ☐
   It's great to meet you in person. ☐

4. Have you been to Toronto before? ☐
   Have you been in Toronto before? ☐

5. Did you have a good flight? ☐
   Had you a good flight? ☐

6. Would you like something to drink? ☐
   Would you want something to drink? ☐

7. I've been looking forward to meet you. ☐
   I've been looking forward to meeting you. ☐

8. We've heard so much about you. ☐
   We're hearing so much about you. ☐

9. I'll let Mr. Song know that you arrived. ☐
   I'll inform Mr. Song know you arrived. ☐

10. Is this your first visit in India? ☐
    Is this your first visit to India? ☐

🔊

40.2 VUELVE A ESCRIBIR CORRIGIENDO LOS ERRORES

I'm eating a pasta for lunch today.
I'm eating some pasta for lunch today.

1. Is there some information about flights?
   _____

2. I need to buy any food.
   _____

3. Are there some good hotels nearby?
   _____

4. Can I get you some cup of coffee?
   _____

5. Are there some interesting talks today?
   _____

6. Do you have some luggage?
   _____

7. There is some presentation later.
   _____

8. Do you have some tea?
   _____

9. Please take some seat at the front.
   _____

🔊

40.3 CONECTA EL INICIO Y EL FINAL DE CADA FRASE

I didn't bring

information about the flight?

1 Would you like some

a glass of water?

2 Do you have any

any luggage with me.

3 Have you been

water, Mrs. Smith?

4 Can I get you

any coffee left, I'm afraid.

5 It's great to

to Los Angeles before?

6 There isn't

meet you in person.

40.4 TACHA LA PALABRA INCORRECTA DE CADA FRASE Y DI TODAS LAS FRASES EN VOZ ALTA

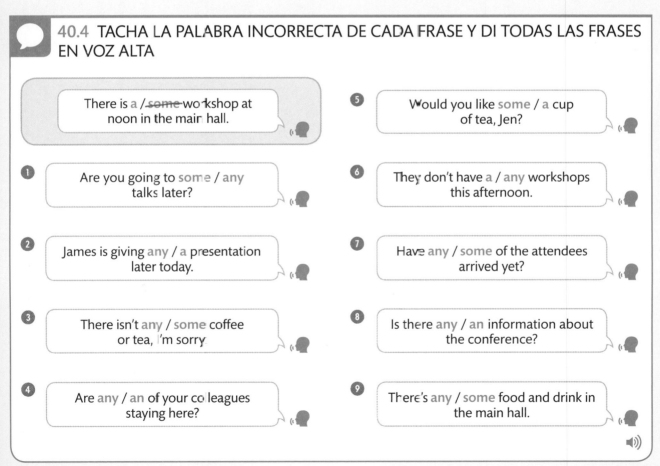

There is a / ~~some~~ workshop at noon in the main hall.

5 Would you like some / a cup of tea, Jen?

1 Are you going to some / any talks later?

6 They don't have a / any workshops this afternoon.

2 James is giving any / a presentation later today.

7 Have any / some of the attendees arrived yet?

3 There isn't any / some coffee or tea, I'm sorry.

8 Is there any / an information about the conference?

4 Are any / an of your colleagues staying here?

9 There's any / some food and drink in the main hall.

129

iTech99
Where the future is discussed today...

Welcome to our 15th annual iTech99 conference!
Guests should report to reception at the Lions Hotel, where they can collect their name badges and conference pack.
The opening plenary will be in the main hall from 3pm to 5pm, during which our keynote speaker, Doctor Arnold Smith, CEO of AstroPlus, will discuss how to develop an effective app. In the evening, there will be a reception at the Westerton Hotel. A choice of snacks and drinks will be served.

On Tuesday, AstroPlus will launch their new phone, the GH34. This will be an excellent chance for networking, during which delegates can meet some of the big stars from the world of technology.

Wednesday will see a question-and-answer session, during which attendees will have the chance to ask the some of the CEOs from the tech giants questions.

Finally on Friday, there will be talks about new developments in marketing and changes in the Asian market.

Guests should collect their conference packs from...
their hotel. ☐ **reception.** ☑ **the main hall.** ☐

① The opening plenary will take place in...
the main hall. ☐   **the Westerton Hotel.** ☐   **the reception area.** ☐

② The keynote speaker will discuss...
his company's future. ☐   **developing an app.** ☐   **building an IT team.** ☐

③ At the reception there will be...
live music. ☐   **a choice of food and drink.** ☐   **team-building exercises.** ☐

④ On Tuesday, there will be...
a product launch. ☐   **a question-and-answer session.** ☐   **a final plenary.** ☐

⑤ During the question-and-answer session, attendees will meet...
consumer focus groups. ☐   **leading CEOs.** ☐   **journalists.** ☐

⑥ The talks on Friday will discuss...
the Asian market. ☐   **networking.** ☐   **the European market.** ☐

Es importante conocer las costumbres locales en cuanto a comidas y ocio. En las comidas de negocios y congresos, sigue estas costumbres y utiliza un lenguaje adecuado.

⚙ Lenguaje "Much / many", "too / enough"
Aa Vocabulario Restaurantes
🧩 Habilidad Ofrecer y aceptar hospitalidad

41.1 MARCA LA MEJOR RESPUESTA A CADA PREGUNTA

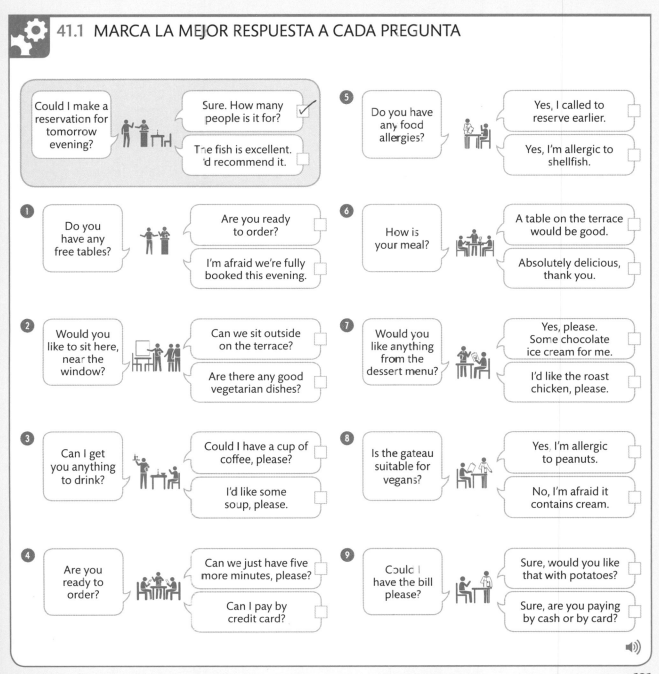

Could I make a reservation for tomorrow evening?
- Sure. How many people is it for? ✓
- The fish is excellent. I'd recommend it.

5 Do you have any food allergies?
- Yes, I called to reserve earlier.
- Yes, I'm allergic to shellfish.

1 Do you have any free tables?
- Are you ready to order?
- I'm afraid we're fully booked this evening.

6 How is your meal?
- A table on the terrace would be good.
- Absolutely delicious, thank you.

2 Would you like to sit here, near the window?
- Can we sit outside on the terrace?
- Are there any good vegetarian dishes?

7 Would you like anything from the dessert menu?
- Yes, please. Some chocolate ice cream for me.
- I'd like the roast chicken, please.

3 Can I get you anything to drink?
- Could I have a cup of coffee, please?
- I'd like some soup, please.

8 Is the gateau suitable for vegans?
- Yes, I'm allergic to peanuts.
- No, I'm afraid it contains cream.

4 Are you ready to order?
- Can we just have five more minutes, please?
- Can I pay by credit card?

9 Could I have the bill please?
- Sure, would you like that with potatoes?
- Sure, are you paying by cash or by card?

🔊

41.2 VUELVE A ESCRIBIR LAS FRASES PONIENDO LAS PALABRAS EN SU ORDEN CORRECTO

| a | I'm | wait. | 15-minute | there's | afraid |

I'm afraid there's a 15-minute wait.

1 | you | to | Are | order? | ready |

_____

2 | reserve | for | like | to | please. | I'd | table | two, | a |

_____

3 | reserved | madam? | Have | you | table, | a |

_____

4 | people | many | there | in | party? | How | are | your |

_____

5 | at | please? | dessert | I | a | the | have | menu, | Could | look |

_____

6 | the | you | would | What | for | like | entree? |

_____

7 | or | you | Do | any | allergies | intolerances? | have |

_____

8 | many | are | How | there | today? | options | vegetarian |

_____

9 | the | we | bill, | have | please? | Could |

_____

10 | you | to | cash | like | card? | or | by | Would | pay |

_____

41.3 MARCA LAS FRASES QUE SEAN CORRECTAS

How much does the steak cost? ☑
How many does the steak cost? ☐

1. How many chairs will you need? ☐
   How many chair will you need? ☐

2. I ordered too many dishes. ☐
   I ordered enough dishes. ☐

3. There's enough space here. It's tiny. ☐
   There's not enough space here. It's tiny. ☐

4. How many plates will you need? ☐
   How much plates will you need? ☐

5. There are too many chairs. ☐
   There are too much chairs. ☐

6. There's not many cake for everyone. ☐
   There's not enough cake for everyone. ☐

7. The lobster costs too much. ☐
   The lobster costs not enough. ☐

8. We haven't ordered enough dishes. ☐
   We haven't ordered too many dishes. ☐

9. How much guests are you expecting? ☐
   How many guests are you expecting? ☐

10. I don't have many cash for a tip. ☐
    I don't have enough cash for a tip. ☐

11. I've eaten too much food this evening! ☐
    I've eaten too many food this evening! ☐

12. There's enough tea for everyone. ☐
    There's much tea for everyone. ☐

🔊))

41.4 DI LAS FRASES EN VOZ ALTA COMPLETANDO LOS ESPACIOS CON LAS PALABRAS DEL RECUADRO

Tell me how ___*much*___ rice you'd like. 🔊

1. How _____ people are coming tonight? 🔊

2. Is there _____ space at the table for everyone? 🔊

3. How _____ does the meal usually cost? 🔊

4. I've eaten too _____ cake. 🔊

5. There's _____ much salt in my soup. 🔊

6. There are not _____ chairs for all of us! 🔊

7. _____ many glasses will we need this evening? 🔊

How	~~much~~	too	much
enough	much	many	enough

🔊))

133

42 Llamadas telefónicas informales

En la mayoría de empresas puedes utilizar lenguaje educado informal al hablar por teléfono con tus colegas. El inglés tiene para ello verbos de dos o tres partes.

Lenguaje Lenguaje telefónico
Aa Vocabulario Números de teléfono y etiqueta
Habilidad Llamar a los compañeros de trabajo

42.1 COMPLETA LOS ESPACIOS CON LAS PALABRAS DEL RECUADRO

Hello. Colin ____*speaking*____.

1 I'd _____ go now.

2 Can I _____ who's calling?

3 No, that's _____ , thanks.

4 OK. _____ to you soon.

5 Is there _____ else I can do?

6 Hello, Sales _____.

anything   department   Talk

ask   ~~speaking~~   better   all

42.2 ESCUCHA EL AUDIO Y NUMERA LAS FRASES EN EL ORDEN EN QUE LAS OIGAS

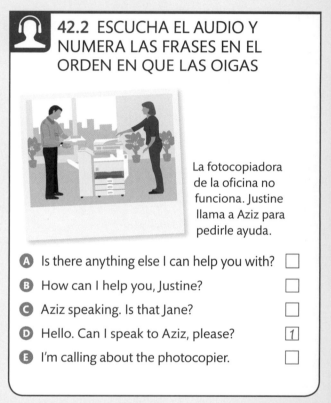

La fotocopiadora de la oficina no funciona. Justine llama a Aziz para pedirle ayuda.

A Is there anything else I can help you with? ☐

B How can I help you, Justine? ☐

C Aziz speaking. Is that Jane? ☐

D Hello. Can I speak to Aziz, please? [1]

E I'm calling about the photocopier. ☐

42.3 CONECTA LAS FRASES CON LAS RESPUESTAS CORRECTAS

Is there anything else I can help you with?

1 Hi, can I speak to Esme, please?

2 Can I ask who's calling?

3 I'd better be going.

4 Hello, Andrew speaking.

Hi, Andrew. It's José from Design.

OK. Speak to you soon.

No, that's all, thanks. Goodbye.

Esme speaking. How can I help?

Of course. It's Sergio Walker.

42.4 ESCUCHA EL AUDIO Y ANOTA LOS NÚMEROS DE TELÉFONO QUE OIGAS

0 7 3 5 8 1 3 5 2 8 8

1 _____

2 _____

3 _____

4 _____

5 _____

6 _____

7 _____

42.5 MIRA LAS TARJETAS PROFESIONALES Y RESPONDE AL AUDIO EN VOZ ALTA

What is Ben's office number?

Ben's office number is 01928 335570.

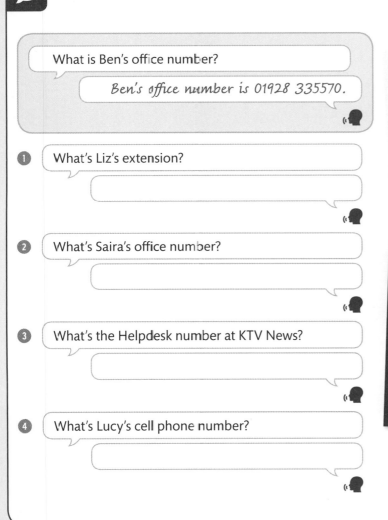

1 What's Liz's extension?

2 What's Saira's office number?

3 What's the Helpdesk number at KTV News?

4 What's Lucy's cell phone number?

Bettina's fashions

ACCOUNTS DIRECTOR: Ben Tibbs
Tel.: 01928 335570 · Ext.: 5570
Cell phone: 07327 559801

DIRECTOR'S PA: Liz Banks
Tel: 01928 333864 · Ext.: 3864

ACCOUNTANT: Saira Dhabi
Tel.: 01928 335178 · Ext.: 5178
Cell phone: 07932 358916

K TV NEWS

IT 24/7 HELPDESK:
Tel.: (616) 888-3746

DIGITAL DIRECTOR: Lucy Kehoe
Tel: (616) 885-5392 · Ext.: 8539
Cell phone: (616) 913-6205

PROGRAMMER: Sami Patel
Cell phone: (616) 561-0324

42.6 COMPLETA LOS ESPACIOS CON LAS EXPRESIONES DEL RECUADRO

 I've got a meeting in five minutes, so I have to ___*hang up*___ now.

cut you off	
~~hang up~~	
speak up	
get back	
picking up	
put you through	
breaking up	

1 I don't know why Hal's not _____ the phone.

2 I'll _____ to customer services now.

3 Can you _____ , please? I can't hear you.

4 Sorry, I'm busy now. I'll _____ to you later.

5 I'm sorry I _____ . This line is very bad.

6 You're _____ . Can I call you back?

42.7 TACHA LAS PALABRAS INCORRECTAS DE CADA FRASE

Don't hang ~~on~~ / ~~down~~ / up. I need to tell you about the China sales.

1 Could you possibly speak on / off / up, please? The line is very faint.

2 I'll call they / you / us back in ten minutes. Is that OK? I have to finish writing an email.

3 If I get cut of / on / off, call me back on the office phone. I'm back at my desk now.

4 Can I get back to / with / from you about the design later today? We're still working on it.

5 I've called Fatima three times, but she didn't pick on / up / over. Is she at work today?

6 Marc kept breaking for / up / down when I called him. The signal here is awful!

7 Katie is back at her desk now. I'll just put you through / over / up to her.

8 Mateo got back for / to / of me about the new manual. He has a few comments on it.

42.8 VUELVE A ESCRIBIR LAS FRASES PONIENDO LAS PALABRAS EN SU ORDEN CORRECTO

| hang | rude | can | on | You | customer. | up | a |

You can hang up on a rude customer.

1 | you | please? | speak | Can | up, |

---

2 | get | hope | off | cut | I | again. | don't | I |

---

3 | me | Let | Finance. | through | put | to | you |

---

4 | you | I | pick | up | didn't | called. | Sorry | when |

---

5 | back | him | you | afternoon? | to | get | this | Can |

---

6 | the | breaking | keeps | Sorry, | up. | line |

---

7 | five | I'll | you | minutes. | call | back | in |

---

8 | yesterday. | He | back | to | didn't | get | me |

---

9 | up | Don't | Dan | pick | the | calls. | phone | if |

---

43 Llamadas telefónicas formales

Cuando hables con clientes o recepcionistas, utiliza un lenguaje telefónico formal. Quizá también debas dejar o tomar un mensaje telefónico.

🔧 **Lenguaje** Orden de los adjetivos
Aa Vocabulario Lenguaje telefónico formal
🧩 **Habilidad** Dejar mensajes en el contestador

43.1 MARCA LA MEJOR RESPUESTA PARA CADA INTERVENCIÓN

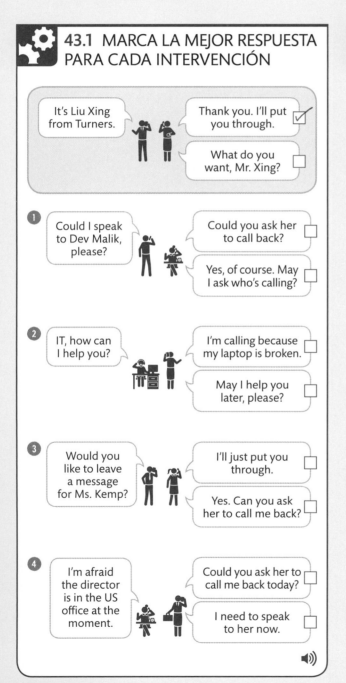

It's Liu Xing from Turners.

Thank you. I'll put you through. ✓

What do you want, Mr. Xing?

1. Could I speak to Dev Malik, please?

Could you ask her to call back?

Yes, of course. May I ask who's calling?

2. IT, how can I help you?

I'm calling because my laptop is broken.

May I help you later, please?

3. Would you like to leave a message for Ms. Kemp?

I'll just put you through.

Yes. Can you ask her to call me back?

4. I'm afraid the director is in the US office at the moment.

Could you ask her to call me back today?

I need to speak to her now.

🔊

43.2 TACHA LA PALABRA INCORRECTA DE CADA FRASE Y DI LAS FRASES EN VOZ ALTA

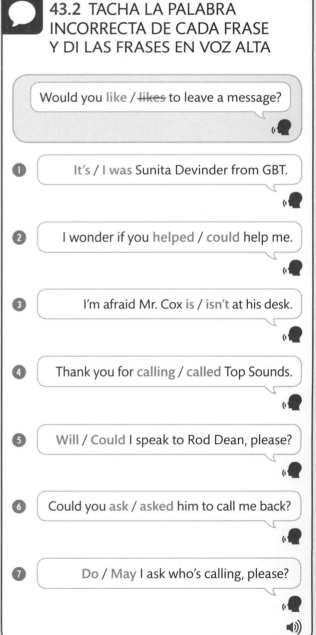

Would you like / ~~likes~~ to leave a message?

1. It's / I was Sunita Devinder from GBT.

2. I wonder if you helped / could help me.

3. I'm afraid Mr. Cox is / isn't at his desk.

4. Thank you for calling / called Top Sounds.

5. Will / Could I speak to Rod Dean, please?

6. Could you ask / asked him to call me back?

7. Do / May I ask who's calling, please?

🔊

43.3 MARCA LAS FRASES QUE SEAN CORRECTAS

I'm afraid my manager isn't here. ☑
I'm apologize my manager isn't here. ☐

1 How can I helps you? ☐
How can I help you? ☐

2 May I ask who's calling? ☐
May I ask who calls? ☐

3 I'll yet put you through. ☐
I'll just put you through. ☐

4 Will you like to leave a message? ☐
Would you like to leave a message? ☐

5 Could you ask him to call me back, please? ☐
Could you ask him call me back, please? ☐

6 How can I help you? IT department. ☐
IT department. How can I help you? ☐

7 I'll put you over to HR now. ☐
I'll put you through to HR now. ☐

8 I'm afraid he's not on his desk. ☐
I'm afraid he's not at his desk. ☐

9 Thank you for calling Quadfax. ☐
Thank you to call Quadfax. ☐

🔊

43.4 COMPLETA LOS ESPACIOS CON LAS EXPRESIONES DEL RECUADRO

Yes, of course. _____ *May I ask* _____ who's calling?

1 Savino's. How _____ you?

2 Thank you _____ Ready Solutions.

3 Hello. _____ you can help me.

4 I'm calling _____ I placed last month.

5 _____ to Becky Bradley, please?

6 I'm afraid the Accounts Manager is away _____.

7 Yes, please. _____ 20 desks?

8 _____ to leave a message?

9 Thank you. _____ you through.

I'll just put

Could I speak

can I help

~~May I ask~~

Would you like

about an order

Could I order

at the moment

for calling

I wonder if

🔊

139

Aa 43.5 ESCRIBE LAS PALABRAS DEL RECUADRO EN LOS GRUPOS CORRESPONDIENTES

OPINIÓN	TAMAÑO	EDAD	COLOR	MATERIAL
nice				

ancient   blue   leather   awful   tiny   ~~nice~~   metal   modern

purple   stylish   pink   large   plastic   antique   huge

43.6 VUELVE A ESCRIBIR LAS FRASES PONIENDO LAS PALABRAS EN SU ORDEN CORRECTO

beautiful | laptop | new | is | model. | a | My | silver

My laptop is a beautiful new silver model.

1. little | gold | lamp. | We're | a | stylish | developing

_____

2. amazing | new | has | Tom | tiny | an | smartphone. | got

_____

3. a | has | cat. | black and white | pet store | big | The | nice

_____

4. in | is | large | There | an | painting | awful | cafeteria. | modern | the

_____

5. exciting | seen | the | marketing | Have | posters? | new | you | colorful

_____

43.7 CONECTA LAS IMÁGENES CON LAS FRASES CORRECTAS

That's a stylish new design for the company logo.

1 Eco Fashion

Let's have lunch at that nice big café in the square.

2

There's a big yellow and red truck outside.

3

There's a nice big green and white plant in my office.

4

There's a huge round hole in the wall where the truck hit it.

5

Have you seen the fabulous new office chairs?

6

Have you tasted the awful new coffee?

7

There's a large rectangular parking space for motorbikes.

8

The headphones for my laptop go in a tiny round hole.

🔊

43.8 ESCUCHA EL AUDIO Y RESPONDE A LAS PREGUNTAS

Shaun llama a un hotel para acordar los detalles de una convención.

Who does Shaun want to speak to?
The receptionist ☐
The hotel manager ☑
The customer services department ☐

1 What does Shaun's company produce?
Sports cars ☐
Printed materials ☐
Cakes and cookies ☐

2 When is the conference?
Next Monday ☐
Next Thursday ☐
Next Tuesday ☐

3 What time will the conference start?
9:00 ☐
9:30 ☐
9:00–9:30 ☐

4 How many attendees will there be?
50 ☐
56 ☐
60 ☐

5 What else does Shaun ask to book?
Six taxis ☐
A minibus ☐
An extra meeting room ☐

6 What extra dietary requests does Shaun make?
Vegetarian and vegan food ☐
Vegan and gluten-free food ☐
Vegetarian and gluten-free food ☐

44 Redactar un currículum

El currículum ("résumé" en EE. UU. y también CV en el Reino Unido) es un resumen de tu carrera profesional. Los verbos de acción en past simple son útiles para describir tus logros.

⚙ **Lenguaje** Verbos de acción sobre logros
Aa Vocabulario Vocabulario de currículum
🧩 **Habilidad** Redactar un currículum

Aa 44.1 CONECTA LAS EXPRESIONES CON SUS APARTADOS DEL CURRÍCULUM

Things you enjoy doing in your free time	Career summary
① An introductory sentence about a person's skills and qualities	Professional achievements
② A list of qualifications and where they were gained	Interests
③ Important things achieved in someone's career	Personal statement
④ A list of current and previous jobs	Key skills
⑤ Important skills such as languages or IT skills	Education

🔊

⚙ 44.2 VUELVE A ESCRIBIR LAS FRASES CORRIGIENDO LOS ERRORES

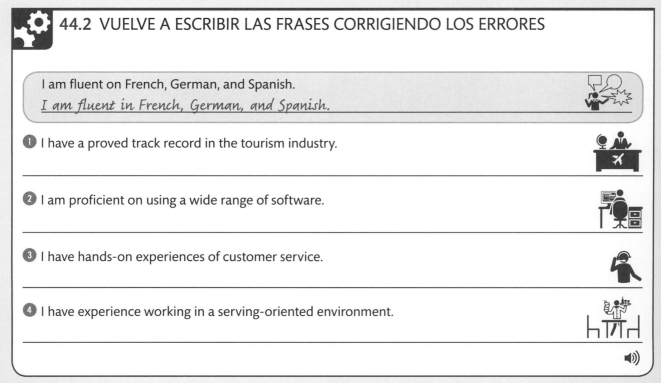

I am fluent on French, German, and Spanish.
I am fluent in French, German, and Spanish.

① I have a proved track record in the tourism industry.

② I am proficient on using a wide range of software.

③ I have hands-on experiences of customer service.

④ I have experience working in a serving-oriented environment.

🔊

44.3 VUELVE A ESCRIBIR LAS FRASES PONIENDO LAS PALABRAS EN SU ORDEN CORRECTO

| and | in | French, | I | am | German, | English. | fluent |

I am fluent in French, German, and English.

1 | in | individual | working | am | motivated | and | highly | love | I | tourism. | a |

_____

2 | construction | I | knowledge | the | gained | of | industry. | in-depth |

_____

3 | in | experience | catering | I | a | of | the | great | deal | industry. | have |

_____

4 | software. | am | in | most | types | I | accounting | of | proficient |

_____

44.4 TACHA LA PALABRA INCORRECTA DE CADA FRASE

I volunteered / ~~collaborated~~ for a local charity.

1 I managed / negotiated a large team of marketing executives.

2 Our teams collaborated / co-ordinated to create a new clothing range.

3 The company established / volunteered a new headquarters in the capital.

4 I collaborated / negotiated with our suppliers and got a good deal.

AYIDA LAMIA

123 Hills Road
Cambridge, MA 02138
ayida@lamia.com (617) 548-81313

PERSONAL STATEMENT

I am a highly motivated individual who enjoys working with others to creatively problem solve. I have a proven track record in the field of accounting.

PROFESSIONAL ACHIEVEMENTS

I oversaw the introduction of new accounting software and co-ordinated a training program for all staff in Accounts last year.

WORK EXPERIENCE

Tomkins Travel
Deputy Director of Accounts April 2013 – present
• I oversee the processing and auditing of the company's accounts
• I train staff to use a range of software packages

Kelsey Homes
Accountant September 2010 – April 2013
• I was responsible for the accounts of a construction company building new homes.

EDUCATION
• Diploma in Accounting June 2010
• BA in Business June 2009

KEY SKILLS
• Proficient in IT use, including all major accountancy software
• Fluent in Spanish and English, intermediate level Polish
• First aid qualified; I am a named first aider in the workplace

INTERESTS

Acting in the local drama group, traveling, and reading contemporary fiction

References available upon request.

How does Ayida describe herself in her personal statement?

She says she is highly motivated.

❶ What does Ayida count as a notable professional achievement?

_____

❷ What is Ayida's current job?

_____

❸ What industry did Ayida work in before her current role?

_____

❹ When did Ayida gain her diploma in Accounting?

_____

❺ What languages can Ayida speak fluently?

_____

45 Hacer planes

En inglés se utiliza el futuro con "going to" para hablar sobre planes y decisiones que ya se han tomado. Es útil para informar a los compañeros de trabajo de tus planes.

⚙ **Lenguaje** El futuro con "going to"
Aa Vocabulario Pedir cosas educadamente
🧩 **Habilidad** Hacer planes

⚙ 45.1 COMPLETA LOS ESPACIOS UTILIZANDO EL FUTURO CON "GOING TO"

I _____ am going to call _____ (call) the Miami office this afternoon.

1. He _____ (travel) to the conference by plane.

2. She _____ (not make) it to the meeting.

3. They _____ (meet) the staff from the Paris office.

4. He _____ (write) a letter to the suppliers.

5. They _____ (not sell) their shares in the company just now.

6. _____ she _____ (order) business cards with the new company logo?

7. Sergio _____ (give) a presentation about the new training course.

8. _____ you _____ (make) tea and coffee for the visitors?

9. Diana _____ (design) the new company logo.

10. They _____ (join) us for our team meeting today.

11. _____ you _____ (review) the sales data this afternoon?

🔊

45.2 MARCA LA PETICIÓN QUE SEA MÁS EDUCADA

Please could you call a taxi? ☑
You have to call a taxi now. ☐

1. Why don't we ask what Marketing think? ☐
   I want to ask Marketing what they think. ☐

2. Load the printer with paper. ☐
   Could you load the printer with paper? ☐

3. Can you help me with these files, please? ☐
   I need help with these files. ☐

4. You should send the files to production. ☐
   Could you send the files to production? ☐

5. Could we meet at 4 instead of 5? ☐
   I want to meet at 4 instead of 5. ☐

6. Can you finish the report today? ☐
   Why haven't you finished the report? ☐

7. We need to invite Jeff to the meeting. ☐
   Couldn't we invite Jeff to the meeting? ☐

8. Could you call me back later, please? ☐
   I'm too busy to talk to you now. ☐

9. Could you make coffee for the CEO? ☐
   You have to make coffee for the CEO. ☐

10. We need to cancel the meeting. ☐
    Could we possibly cancel the meeting? ☐

11. You must check this report. ☐
    Can you check this report, please? ☐

12. Could you pass round the agenda? ☐
    Pass round the agenda. ☐

13. Can we try a different approach? ☐
    Your approach to this isn't working. ☐

14. You must call the Delhi office now. ☐
    Please could you call the Delhi office? ☐

15. Could you lock up before you leave? ☐
    Why haven't you locked the door? ☐

16. Could you possibly stay late tonight? ☐
    You have to stay late tonight. ☐

17. Have you printed out these designs? ☐
    Please can you print out these designs? ☐

45.3 UTILIZA EL DIAGRAMA PARA CREAR 18 FRASES CORRECTAS Y DILAS EN VOZ ALTA

I am going to email the director.

| I / You / Kelly | am going to / are going to / is going to | email / speak to | the director. / the IT help desk. / the sales department. |

45.4 ESCUCHA EL AUDIO Y RESPONDE A LAS PREGUNTAS

Diego y Janet están
organizando un congreso

Diego is going to call the hotel.
True ☑ **False** ☐ **Not given** ☐

1 The Boston office will attend the conference.
True ☐ **False** ☐ **Not given** ☐

2 Diego doesn't like the company logo designs.
True ☐ **False** ☐ **Not given** ☐

3 Janet is going to make the name badges.
True ☐ **False** ☐ **Not given** ☐

4 Diego is going to check that the rooms have Wi-Fi.
True ☐ **False** ☐ **Not given** ☐

5 The interns won't be involved in the conference.
True ☐ **False** ☐ **Not given** ☐

45.5 LEE EL CORREO ELECTRÓNICO Y RESPONDE A LAS PREGUNTAS CON FRASES COMPLETAS

When did Jack meet Omar?
Jack met Omar on Monday.

1 Who is going to contact the presenters?

_____

2 What is Paul going to ask the printers for?

_____

3 What else are the printers going to supply?

_____

4 Who is going to meet the presenters?

_____

5 How will the presenters get to the venue?

_____

6 Why is Omar going to go to the venue?

_____

✉ ∨ ✕

To: Jack Brown

Subject: Training day preparations

Hi Jack,

Following our meeting on Monday, I have an update on the preparations for the training day. I spoke to Paul and he is going to contact the presenters. He's also going to call the printers and ask if they can print ten extra copies of the training booklets. We have asked the printers to supply name badges in the form of lanyards. They are going to assemble the name badges to save us time.

Marie is going to meet the presenters at the station and bring them to the conference center by taxi. I am going to the venue later today to talk to the catering manager. We have quite a few delegates with special dietary requirements so I want to check they will be catered for. I'll email you later with a further update.
Best wishes,
Omar

46 Vocabulario

Aa 46.1 FORMAS DE COMUNICACIÓN ESCRIBE LAS PALABRAS DEL RECUADRO DEBAJO DE SU CORRESPONDIENTE DIBUJO

switchboard

1 _____

2 _____

3 _____

4 _____

5 _____

6 _____

7 _____

8 _____

9 _____

10 _____

11 _____

12 _____

13 _____

14 _____

15 _____

---

envelope   text message   social networking   voicemail   ~~switchboard~~   stamp

bulletin board (US) / notice board (UK)   transfer a call   conference call   internal mail

web conference   mail (US) / post (UK)   presentation   letter   website   email

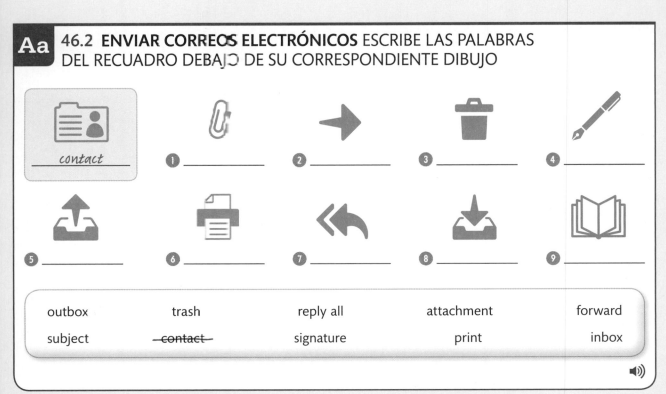

Aa 46.2 ENVIAR CORREOS ELECTRÓNICOS ESCRIBE LAS PALABRAS DEL RECUADRO DEBAJO DE SU CORRESPONDIENTE DIBUJO

contact

1 _____
2 _____
3 _____
4 _____
5 _____
6 _____
7 _____
8 _____
9 _____

| outbox | trash | reply all | attachment | forward |
| subject | ~~contact~~ | signature | print | inbox |

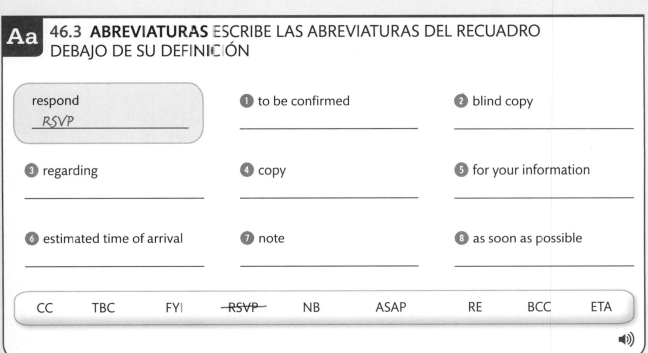

Aa 46.3 ABREVIATURAS ESCRIBE LAS ABREVIATURAS DEL RECUADRO DEBAJO DE SU DEFINICIÓN

respond
RSVP

1 to be confirmed
_____

2 blind copy
_____

3 regarding
_____

4 copy
_____

5 for your information
_____

6 estimated time of arrival
_____

7 note
_____

8 as soon as possible
_____

CC   TBC   FYI   ~~RSVP~~   NB   ASAP   RE   BCC   ETA

47 Enviar un correo electrónico

Los correos electrónicos a los clientes deben ser educados y detallar claramente los planes e intenciones de futuro. Utiliza el present continuous o "going to" al hablar de planes.

⚙ **Lenguaje** Uso de futuros para planes
Aa Vocabulario Correo electrónico formal
🧩 **Habilidad** Enviar un correo a un cliente

⚙ **47.1 VUELVE A ESCRIBIR LAS FRASES CORRIGIENDO LOS ERRORES**

> I am writing with regarding to your order.
> _I am writing with regard to your order._

1 I work at the finance department at Forrester's.

_____

2 Please confirm your availability APAS.

_____

3 Please find your attached receipt to this email.

_____

4 Please hesitate not to contact me.

_____

5 I am writing reference with invoice number 146.

_____

6 Please see the agenda attach here.

_____

7 I work in the IT department in Transtech.

_____

8 I writing to invite you to a meeting next week.

_____

9 Please hesitate to contact me.

_____

10 Please return ASAP your signed contract.

_____

11 I be grateful if you could get back to me soon.

_____

12 I am writing regard to your complaint.

_____

13 Please find the minutes attachment here.

_____

14 I would grateful if we could arrange a meeting.

_____

15 I work at the company's catering department.

_____

16 I am the new Head of Sales in Codequote.

_____

17 I am writing with regard our schedule.

_____

18 Please let me know if you any questions.

_____

19 Please finding the new designs attached here.

_____

🔊

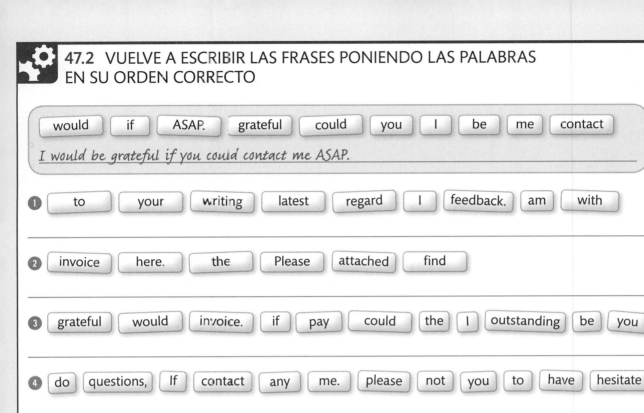

47.2 VUELVE A ESCRIBIR LAS FRASES PONIENDO LAS PALABRAS EN SU ORDEN CORRECTO

| would | if | ASAP. | grateful | could | you | I | be | me | contact |

I would be grateful if you could contact me ASAP.

1. | to | your | writing | latest | regard | I | feedback. | am | with |

2. | invoice | here. | the | Please | attached | find |

3. | grateful | would | invoice. | if | pay | could | the | I | outstanding | be | you |

4. | do | questions, | If | contact | any | me. | please | not | you | to | have | hesitate |

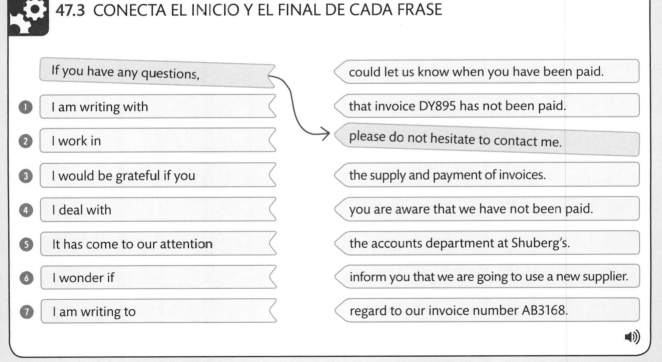

47.3 CONECTA EL INICIO Y EL FINAL DE CADA FRASE

If you have any questions, → please do not hesitate to contact me.

could let us know when you have been paid.

1. I am writing with — that invoice DY895 has not been paid.

2. I work in — the supply and payment of invoices.

3. I would be grateful if you — you are aware that we have not been paid.

4. I deal with — the accounts department at Shuberg's.

5. It has come to our attention — inform you that we are going to use a new supplier.

6. I wonder if — regard to our invoice number AB3168.

7. I am writing to

We're _____*going to send*_____ you the package you ordered ASAP.

1 He _____ all the candidates a task to do before their interview.

2 We _____ other suppliers on Tuesday.

3 Sam _____ coffee for the CEO's visitors.

4 Carlos _____ the sales figures tomorrow.

5 We _____ sales figures for the last quarter.

6 They _____ all their clients a voucher.

7 He _____ to Italy to meet the new CEO.

8 Greg _____ all the boxes into the delivery van.

9 A famous hairdresser _____ the new salon.

10 We _____ the new company logo at the sales conference.

11 The company _____ all the stationery with the old logo.

is going to pack	is giving	is going to make	is going to recycle
are going to discuss	are meeting	~~going to send~~	are launching
is going to travel	is presenting	are giving	is going to open

47.5 MARCA LAS FRASES QUE SEAN CORRECTAS

I am writing to inform you that we paying your invoice ASAP. ☐
I am writing to inform you that we are going to pay your invoice ASAP. ☑

1. I am writing with regard to the shareholders' meeting on Thursday. ☐
   I am writing with regarding the shareholders' meeting on Thursday. ☐

2. We are going to meeting new clients at the Radcliffe Hotel. ☐
   We are meeting new clients at the Radcliffe Hotel. ☐

3. The meeting is taking place in the hotel's conference center. ☐
   The meeting is going take place in the hotel's conference center. ☐

4. We is going to discuss the last quarter's sales figures. ☐
   We are going to discuss the last quarter's sales figures. ☐

5. The new CEO is go to take questions after his presentation. ☐
   The new CEO is taking questions after his presentation. ☐

6. He is going to discuss the company's future marketing strategy. ☐
   He is going to discussing the company's future marketing strategy. ☐

🔊

47.6 LEE EL CORREO ELECTRÓNICO Y MARCA EL RESUMEN CORRECTO

1. Bruno wants to meet the Head of Marketing but cannot find a suitable time. ☐

2. Bruno suggests that Ms. Moran should contact the Head of Marketing directly. ☐

3. Bruno wants to arrange a meeting. His client has not yet confirmed a suitable time for it. ☐

4. Bruno wants to arrange a conference for Mr. Jefferies. ☐

✉ ⌄ ✕

To: Laila Moran

Subject: Date for meeting

Dear Ms. Moran,
I work in the marketing department of Hailey's. I am writing with regard to the meeting you wish to have with our Head of Marketing about the launch of your new products. As you will recall, I wrote to you a week ago asking when you would be available to meet at our premises. Mr. Jefferies has availability next Wednesday afternoon and also on the morning of Friday, July 14. If you could confirm which of those slots works for you, I would be most grateful. I will then send you all the documentation ahead of your meeting with Mr. Jefferies.
Kind regards,
Bruno Martell

↩ ↩↩ 📎 🗑

Respuestas

01

1.1 🔊
1. My name's Ali Patel.
2. Hi, I'm Jeff.
3. It's good to meet you, Jane.
4. Pleased to meet you.
5. My name is Deepak Kaur.
6. Great to meet you, Tanya.
7. It's nice to meet you, too.
8. Good morning. My name is Ben Lewis.
9. It's great to meet you, Gill.
10. Good evening. My name is Karen.

1.2 🔊
1. Hello, my name's Fiona Hill.
2. Nice to meet you, too.
3. It's good to meet you, Jim.
4. Pleased to meet you.
5. It's a pleasure to meet you.
6. Good evening. My name is Roy.

1.3
1. A
2. B
3. B
4. A
5. A

1.4 🔊
1. A-L-E-X H-A-N-N
2. D-E-V S-I-N-G-H
3. F-R-A-N-C-I-S P-A-L-M-E-R
4. H-A-N-S-A S-Y-A
5. Z-A-N-D-R-A F-E-L-L-I-N-I
6. R-A-J D-H-A-B-I
7. K-A-T-Y A-D-E-N-O-V-A

1.5 🔊
1. This **is** our new designer.
2. Raj and I **work** together.
3. I **would** like you to meet our CEO. / **I'd** like you to meet our CEO.
4. Hi, **my** name's Lola. / Hi, **I'm Lola**.
5. It's great to **meet you**, Emily.
6. **May I** introduce Ewan Carlton?
7. Farah, this **is** my colleague, Leon.

1.6 🔊
1. Good morning. **My** name's Saira Khan.
2. **I'm** Harry.
3. **I'm** Andrew Shaw.
4. **It's** good to meet you.
5. Pleased **to** meet you.
6. It's a **pleasure** to meet you.
7. **May** I introduce our new HR assistant?
8. Keira, **meet** John.
9. **Great** to meet you.
10. I **would** like you to meet Dan.
11. Colin and I **work** together.

1.7
A. 5
B. 6
C. 7
D. 4
E. 1
F. 3
G. 2

02

2.1 🔊
1. I start work at 9 o'clock.
2. She has an update with her boss.
3. Mrs. Reece is a fantastic teacher.
4. I'm a firefighter.
5. Elena works late on Thursdays.
6. He drinks coffee every afternoon.
7. She leaves work at 5:30pm.

2.2 🔊
1. The IT Helpdesk **is** really good.
2. She **works** in a car factory.
3. I **eat** my lunch in the park.
4. We **take** a break at 11am.
5. John **writes** the minutes of our meetings.
6. Mrs. Rae **cleans** the meeting rooms.
7. The CEO **brings** cake on his birthday.
8. I **prepare** presentations.
9. Jomir **stops** for tea at 3pm.

2.3 🔊
1. The CEO arrives at work early.
2. We have a hot-desking policy.
3. My assistant opens my mail.
4. Shazia is an engineer.
5. Hal works for his uncle.
6. I start work at 8:30am.
7. They finish at 5pm.
8. They eat lunch in the cafeteria.
9. Kate only drinks coffee.
10. I call the US office every Monday.
11. Andrew helps me with my PC.
12. I reply to emails at 11am and 3pm.

2.4
1. The manager's PA
2. After the break
3. An hour
4. 12:30pm
5. They analyze sales
6. Twice a week

2.5 🔊
1. The director **has** an open door policy.
2. I **deal** with all his emails.
3. Gavin **leaves** work at 7pm.
4. They **work** evenings and weekends.
5. She **rides** her bike to work.
6. Tim and Pat **bring** their own lunch.
7. Deepak **turns** off his phone after work.
8. Sobek and Kurt **play** tennis after work.
9. My boss **plans** my work for the week.

2.6 🔊

1 Lulu always **gets** to work early.
2 Our reps **meet** clients at their office.
3 The CEO **talks** to all new staff.
4 He's a nurse and he **works** weekends.
5 Imran **deals** with all the contracts.
6 The printer **stops** working late in the day.
7 The staff **go** to a nearby café for lunch.
8 Raj **takes** a break at 11am.
9 Sophie **is** a travel agent.

03

3.1 🔊

1 Argentina
2 Australia
3 South America
4 China
5 Canada
6 Egypt
7 South Korea
8 France
9 Australasia
10 Japan
11 India
12 United States of America (US / USA)
13 Netherlands
14 Asia
15 Mongolia
16 Pakistan
17 New Zealand
18 Russia
19 South Africa
20 North America
21 Thailand
22 United Arab Emirates (UAE)
23 United Kingdom (UK)
24 Turkey
25 Spain
26 Africa
27 Singapore
28 Republic of Ireland (ROI)
29 Europe
30 Mexico
31 Brazil

04

4.1

1 Russia
2 India
3 Japan
4 Chile
5 Greece

4.2

PAÍSES:
South Africa, **France**, **Italy**, **Vietnam**, **Switzerland**, **China**
NACIONALIDADES:
Brazilian, **British**, **Greek**, **Canadian**, **Japanese**, **Spanish**

4.3 🔊

1 The new CEO is **from Australia**.
2 These new robots are **Japanese**.
3 We sell leather bags **from Portugal**.
4 I'm **from Argentina**, but I work in the US.
5 The designer is **British**.
6 Our sales director is **from South Korea**.
7 Our best-selling rugs are **Indian**.
8 These beautiful clothes are **from Africa**.

4.4 🔊

1 Our CEO is from America.
2 I've got a flight to Italy next Monday.
3 These sports cars are from France.
4 Most of our fabrics are from Africa.
5 My PA is from Spain.

4.5 🔊

1 We sell smartphones from **Japan**.
2 The HR manager is from **America**.
3 My team follows the **Chinese** markets.
4 Travel to the **Greek** islands with us.
5 Our products are from **Vietnam**.
6 Our CEO is **Canadian**.
7 Most of the sales team is from **Spain**.
8 I'm British, but I work in **Italy**.
9 I have a lot of **Mexican** co-workers.
10 My new assistant is from **France**.

4.6 🔊

1 **I'm not** very tall.
2 He **doesn't work** in an office.
3 We **don't sell** French cars.
4 **They're not** from Italy. / They **aren't** from Italy.
5 The fruit in the supermarket **isn't** local.
6 I **don't work** for an Asian company.
7 **You're** not happy. / You **aren't** happy.
8 She **isn't** from China. / **She's not** from China.
9 We **don't produce** robots.
10 You **don't** have any meetings today.
11 It **isn't** a steel factory. / **It's not** a steel factory.

4.7 🔊

1 These dresses **aren't** made in India.
2 She **doesn't** come from Russia.
3 The workers in this factory **aren't** American.
4 They **don't** sell energy to South Korea.
5 He **isn't** from Chile. / **He's not** from Chile.

4.8

1 IT
2 Carlos
3 Marketing
4 Tim
5 China

4.9

1. True
2. Not given
3. False
4. True
5. Not given
6. False
7. False

05

5.1 🔊

1. adhesive tape
2. calendar
3. clipboard
4. computer
5. planner (US) / diary (UK)
6. rubber bands
7. envelope
8. hole punch
9. hard drive
10. pen
11. laptop
12. pencil
13. files / folders
14. paper clips
15. eraser (US) / rubber (UK)
16. letter
17. shredder
18. cell phone (US) / mobile phone (UK)
19. printer
20. headset
21. highlighter
22. pencil sharpener
23. stapler
24. telephone / phone
25. tablet
26. notepad
27. projector
28. chair
29. ruler
30. scanner
31. lamp

06

6.1 🔊

1. Is this printer working?
2. Is this your desk?
3. Are the windows closed?
4. Is this cupboard locked?
5. Is his desk messy?
6. Is she the CEO?
7. Are you Jo's assistant?

6.2 🔊

1. Is that John's pen?
2. Is this the kitchen?
3. Is that the CEO's office?
4. Is Tina the CEO's PA?
5. Is Tom's desk organized?
6. Is the printer working?
7. Is the stationery cabinet locked?

6.3 🔊

1. **Do** you have an appointment?
2. **Does** she work with Justin?
3. **Does** your office have a scanner?
4. **Do** you go to the finance meetings?
5. **Does** Kish write the minutes?
6. **Do** you have a stapler I can borrow?
7. **Does** Saul work in your team?
8. **Do** they know what to do?
9. **Does** he know the CEO?
10. **Do** we have a meeting now?

6.4

1. False
2. True
3. False
4. False

6.5 🔊

1. Is the stationery cabinet open?
2. Do you want tea or coffee?
3. Do you know her phone number?
4. Are they free for a meeting tomorrow?

5. Do you have a laptop I can take home?
6. Do you have an appointment?
7. Are there any envelopes I can use?
8. Does he usually arrive late?

6.6 🔊

1. **How** does the scanner work?
2. **What** is on the agenda for the meeting?
3. **Why** is the stationery cabinet locked?
4. **When** do we have a break for lunch?
5. **Where** is the CEO's office?
6. **What** is the door code?
7. **Who** do I ask for ink for the printer?

6.7 🔊

1. Why is the cafeteria closed?
2. How do I scan this document?
3. When is the fire alarm tested?
4. Do you know where Faisal is?
5. Is Sandra late again?
6. What is for lunch today?
7. Does the office stay open on weekends?
8. Who do you report to?

6.8 🔊

1. **Who** buys the tea and coffee?
2. **Why** is the printer not working?
3. **When** does the office open?
4. **What** do you want for lunch?
5. **Where** is the meeting room?
6. **How** does the projector work?
7. **What** is the photocopier code?

07

7.1 🔊

1. How can I reach you?
2. Do you have many clients?
3. Do you have a website?
4. Where do you work?
5. What is your company called?

6 What's your job title?
7 This is my email address.
8 Drop me a line.
9 How can I contact you?
10 Give me a call.
11 How big is your team?

7.2
A 6
B 2
C 3
D 5
E 1
F 4

7.3 🔊
1 How can I **reach** you for more infomation?
2 Drop me a **line** when you're visiting next.
3 Does your company **have** a website?
4 Please stay in **touch**.
5 Is this your **correct** phone number?
6 **Call** me if you want further details.
7 Is this your **current** email address?
8 My job **title** is on the business card.
9 Do you **have** a portfolio with you?

7.4
1 True
2 True
3 Not given
4 Not given
5 False
6 True
7 False
8 False

7.5 🔊
1 Yes, it is.
2 No, it doesn't.
3 No, they aren't.
4 Yes, I am.
5 No, he doesn't.
6 Yes, we do.

7.6 🔊
1 No, **it isn't**.
2 No, **it doesn't**.
3 Yes, **it is**.
4 Yes, **it does**.
5 No, **they don't**.
6 No, **I'm not**.
7 Yes, **they do**.
8 Yes, **she does**.
9 Yes, **I do**.

08

8.1 🔊
1 She **has** an excellent résumé.
2 I **have** good people skills.
3 They **don't have** much time.
4 Do you **have** previous experience?
5 He's **got** excellent keyboard skills.
6 I **don't have** my own office.
7 Does he **have** any training?
8 They **have** a can-do outlook.
9 You don't **have** his number, do you?

8.2 🔊
1 Do you have a higher degree in business?
2 He has an MBA from the Boston Business School.
3 They don't have a full-time receptionist.
4 Does your assistant have an excellent résumé?

8.3
1 Travel
2 A hotel
3 Management
4 Excellent
5 In teams
6 Marketing

8.4 🔊
1 The new chef is very talented.
2 Toby is an accountant.
3 Search engines are invaluable.
4 She works for a leading company.
5 Have you seen the ad I told you about?
6 They are out of the office.
7 Did you see the new designs?
8 They hired the best candidate.
9 What skills does the job require?
10 Is there an office in India?
11 I have a certificate in sales.
12 He works for the biggest store.
13 Interns are only paid expenses.

8.5 🔊
1 I worked as **an** intern at Beales.
2 I know **the** café you mean.
3 There's **a** printer on the second floor.
4 Jon hasn't got **a** diploma.
5 The CEO is in **the** NY office this week.
6 He's **an** amazing architect.
7 I just started **a** new job.
8 I'd like to put **an** ad in the paper.
9 Have you read **the** job description?
10 I work at **the** theater next door.
11 **The** new café does great coffee.
12 Where is **the** presentation?
13 The Tate is **an** art gallery.
14 I like **the** new CEO.

8.6
A 7
B 1
C 4
D 2
E 6
F 3
G 8
H 5

157

8.7 🔊
1 I've **got three** years' experience.
2 I don't have **a** degree in business studies.
3 He has **a** diploma in economics.
4 I saw **an** ad in The Echo.
5 She has **an** excellent phone manner.
6 He works in **a** hospital.
7 I don't **like interviews**.
8 **The** agency is in the market place.
9 We are looking **for sales people**.

09

9.1 🔊
1 sales manager
2 librarian
3 doctor
4 hairdresser / stylist
5 engineer
6 train driver
7 writer
8 cleaner / janitor
9 chef
10 electrician
11 mechanic
12 pilot
13 waitress
14 vet
15 travel agent
16 plumber
17 artist
18 judge
19 sales assistant
20 musician
21 surgeon
22 receptionist
23 tour guide
24 taxi driver
25 designer
26 scientist
27 firefighter

9.2 🔊
1 shift
2 apprentice
3 full-time (F/T)
4 temporary
5 co-worker / colleague
6 part-time (P/T)

10

10.1 🔊
1 I love food, and I enjoy cooking.
2 I love working with computers.
3 I enjoy driving.
4 I enjoy traveling to different countries.
5 I don't like working on my own.

10.2 🔊
1 She loves **meeting** new clients.
2 He **doesn't** enjoy giving presentations.
3 I hate **training** big groups.
4 They like **working** in a team.
5 Jan **enjoys** working with children.
6 Ali doesn't **like** long meetings.
7 We don't **like** working weekends.
8 I love **solving** problems.
9 Jim doesn't **enjoy** business trips.

10.3
1 No le gusta
2 Le gusta
3 Le gusta
4 No le gusta
5 Le gusta
6 No le gusta
7 Le gusta

10.4 🔊
1 I **don't** enjoy work social trips.
2 They like **meeting** new people.
3 He doesn't **like** working late.
4 She hates **sitting** at a desk all day.

5 Do you enjoy **working** in a team?
6 We enjoy **giving** presentations.
7 Angus doesn't like **using** computers.

11

11.1 🔊
1 There are three printers in your department.
2 Are there ladies' toilets on the second floor?
3 There isn't a cafeteria in the building.
4 Is there a set time for lunch breaks?
5 There aren't any elevators in the office.
6 Is there a dress code at this company?
7 There's a photocopier on the first floor.
8 There aren't any trash cans in the office.
9 Are there any interns on your team?
10 There is a calendar on the notice board.

11.2 🔊
1 There is an elevator that goes to all the office floors.
2 There are some stickers in the stationery cabinet.
3 There are some men's toilets on the first and third floors.
4 There is a water cooler in the kitchen.
5 There isn't a set time for lunch breaks.

11.3
1 False
2 True
3 False
4 True
5 False
6 Not given

11.4 🔊

① There **are** two positions available at our company.

② There isn't **a** toaster in the kitchen, but there is a microwave.

③ **Is** there a spare computer I can use?

④ Are there **any** pencils in the stationery cabinet?

⑤ There **is** a big meeting room in our new office.

12

12.1 🔊

① safe
② transfer money
③ receipt
④ cash machine / ATM
⑤ bank
⑥ currency
⑦ wallet
⑧ mobile banking
⑨ bills (US) / notes (UK)
⑩ check (US) / cheque (UK)
⑪ cash register (US) / till (UK)
⑫ withdraw money
⑬ invoice
⑭ online banking
⑮ credit card

12.2 🔊

① overtime
② salary
③ benefits
④ a raise (US) / a pay rise (UK)
⑤ to earn
⑥ a bonus
⑦ annual vacation (US) / annual leave (UK)
⑧ hourly rate
⑨ a pay cut

13

13.1 🔊

① The new intern seems really bright and she is **very organized.**

② My manager doesn't ask **nervous employees** to give presentations.

③ My director **is very bossy** and she is also hardworking.

④ Sue and Robin are sometimes **rude** to our clients.

⑤ It's important to stay **calm under pressure**, even if you're very busy.

⑥ Mushira is very **intelligent**, and she will bring a great deal to the team.

⑦ It's impossible to feel relaxed when you work with **impatient people**.

⑧ The people on my team are all very **motivated**, and it's great to work with them.

⑨ We are looking for a **creative designer** to join our busy production team.

13.2 🔊

① Ian seems very hardworking.
② Kay and Jack are really polite.
③ Ben is very bossy.
④ Diane always looks well dressed.
⑤ Alex is really impatient.
⑥ Lenny is a creative chef.
⑦ This is a great team.
⑧ Jo seems very organized.
⑨ Harry seems very bright.

13.3

① creative
② organized
③ calm
④ well dressed

13.4 🔊

① **Our** team meetings are always interesting.

② Is this **your** desk? It's very messy!

③ **My** team is very motivated.

④ Is that **their** design? It's great.

⑤ Kevin is talking to **his** manager.

⑥ That's Tanya. **Her** phone manner is excellent.

⑦ The company is very proud of **its** reputation.

13.5 🔊

① Is this **his** desk?
② We don't like **their** product.
③ **My** manager is very smart.
④ This report is **yours**.
⑤ Jane does **her** job well.
⑥ They are proud of **their** reputation.
⑦ Is this tablet **hers**?
⑧ **Their** manager is never late.
⑨ Is this **your** pen?

13.6 🔊

① The interns have just finished college.
② Jorge's reputation is well deserved.
③ Nuala's assistant is very helpful.
④ Helen's manager often works late.
⑤ Maria's co-workers are really friendly.
⑥ The team members are hardworking.
⑦ Look at this ad. I like its design.
⑧ Leroy's work is very impressive.
⑨ Are there any files in the cabinet?
⑩ John's confidence has grown this year.
⑪ Sam's presentation went really well.
⑫ The CEO's new assistant is very bright.
⑬ Their products are very popular.
⑭ That's my boss's parking space.
⑮ Pablo's report is almost finished.
⑯ The company is pleased with its new logo.
⑰ Ethan's team is working on a new project.

13.7 🔊

1. You are my boss.
2. You are my co-worker.
3. You are Peter's boss.
4. You are Peter's co-worker.
5. You are very polite.
6. You are really polite.
7. They are very polite.
8. They are really polite.
9. Alex is my boss.
10. Alex is my co-worker.
11. Alex is Peter's boss.
12. Alex is Peter's co-worker.
13. Alex is very polite.
14. Alex is really polite.

14

14.1 🔊

❶ Vihaan is very **satisfied** with his office.
❷ The new login system is rather **annoying**.
❸ The quarterly results are **shocking**.
❹ The economic situation is quite **worrying**.
❺ We're **excited** about the new office.
❻ Simone was **tired** after the course.
❼ The profits were **disappointing**.
❽ John is **confused** about the schedule.
❾ We were **surprised** by the results.
❿ We thought the meeting was **boring**.
⓫ I'm often **exhausted** by Friday.

14.2 🔊

❶ boring
❷ confused
❸ exciting
❹ annoying
❺ surprising
❻ interesting
❼ disappointed
❽ worried

14.3 🔊

❶ I am very **busy** with the new project, but I'll be even **busier** next week.
❷ Our new office is **large**, but the office in Beijing is **larger**.
❸ My job is very **stressful**, but being unemployed is **more stressful**.
❹ The meeting was **long**, but last week's was even **longer**.
❺ John's flight ticket was **expensive**, but mine was **more expensive**.
❻ Our new photocopier is **fast**, but the HR department's is **faster**.
❼ Claire's news was **surprising**, but Peter resigning was **more surprising**.
❽ My current job is **interesting**, but my old one was **more interesting**.
❾ The new furniture is **comfortable**, but the furniture at G-Tech is **more comfortable**.
❿ This test is **difficult**, but the next one will be **more difficult**.
⓫ My commute is **short**; it's only 10 minutes. Pete's is even **shorter**.

14.4 🔊

❶ Your printer is **quicker** than ours.
❷ Today's meeting was **more interesting** than usual.
❸ Growth was **worse** than we had expected.
❹ Sandra has been **more successful** than last year.
❺ I'm feeling **better** after a week off work.
❻ There is **less** juice left than I thought.
❼ My new apartment is **closer** to the center.
❽ The results are **better** than in the first quarter.
❾ We will need to arrive **earlier** than usual.
❿ I start work one hour **later** than my wife.
⓫ This restaurant is **worse** than the others.
⓬ The flight was **more expensive** than I expected.

14.5 🔊

❶ The new intern is **more helpful than the old one**.
❷ Our hours are longer **than those in the German branch**.
❸ The new computers are **faster than the old ones**.
❹ I arrive at work earlier **now that the new train line has opened**.
❺ Our new office design **is more modern than the previous one**.
❻ The tickets **are more expensive than they used to be**.
❼ My raise was **smaller than last year's**.
❽ My training this year was **more interesting than last year**.
❾ The office is busier **since we merged with our competitors**.

14.6

❶ False ❷ True ❸ False
❹ Not given ❺ True ❻ True
❼ False ❽ Not given

15

15.1 🔊

❶ Karen leaves home at 7am on Fridays.
❷ Vicky usually takes notes during meetings.
❸ We don't work the week before New Year.
❹ The team always arrives before 10am.
❺ Chang arrives at 8:30am every morning.
❻ We sometimes have meetings in the evening.
❼ Terry sometimes works on the weekend.

15.2 🔊

1. Everyone arrives **by** 9:30am.
2. Peter often works **until** 11pm.
3. The office is closed **during** August.
4. The café is open **from** 6am.
5. I finish work at 4pm **on** Fridays.
6. The cafeteria is open **from** 1pm.
7. Ann sends an agenda **before** each meeting.

15.3

1. 7am
2. 1 hour
3. 8:30am
4. 2pm
5. sometimes
6. afternoon

15.4 🔊

1. I drive because it's so **convenient**.
2. Jim **takes** the bus every morning.
3. Jack travels **by** bike when he can.
4. The **rush** hour starts at 7am in my city.
5. Sam **takes** the metro home each evening.
6. Raymond **drives** his car to work.
7. I get **on** the bus near the museum.
8. I missed my **connection**.
9. Janet prefers to travel **by** train to work.
10. Karl **takes** the bus home at night.
11. There are a lot of traffic **jams** in the city.
12. You should get **off** the tram at the library.
13. It's much cheaper to **cycle** than drive.
14. I like to **walk** to work in the summer.
15. I prefer to **cycle** to my office.

15.5 🔊

1. I drive to work.
2. We take the bus.
3. Doug rides his bike to work.
4. I sometimes take a taxi home.
5. The buses run from 5am to 11pm.
6. I go by train.

7. The train arrives at 5pm.
8. Sharon gets off the bus by the station.
9. I like to go home from work on foot.
10. My train to work arrives at 7:45am.
11. Traveling by train is comfortable.
12. The train leaves at about 8pm.
13. I travel by train every day.

15.6

A. 1
B. 7
C. 2
D. 4
E. 3
F. 6
G. 5
H. 8

15.7 🔊

1. There aren't many buses **on the weekend**.
2. Hank takes the bus because **it's cheaper than the train**.
3. The office stays open **until 10 in the evening**.
4. I leave for work **between 7 and 8am**.
5. Sally often walks to work **during the summer**.
6. I take the train to work because **it's faster than the bus**.
7. Ted takes notes **during meetings**.
8. I always go to bed **before 11pm**.

16

16.1 🔊

1. Saturday
2. Monday
3. Sunday
4. Friday
5. Tuesday
6. Thursday

16.2 🔊

1. three times a week
2. hourly
3. monthly
4. daily
5. in the morning
6. in the afternoon
7. in the evening
8. before work
9. after work

16.3 🔊

1. see a play
2. do yoga
3. draw
4. meet friends
5. walk / hike
6. go out for a meal
7. play an instrument
8. watch a movie
9. stay (at) home
10. visit a museum / art gallery
11. read
12. cook
13. play sports
14. take photos
15. go shopping
16. go camping
17. write
18. go cycling
19. play board games

17

17.1 🔊

1. We often go camping on the weekend.
2. Doug sometimes meets friends after he finishes work.
3. I always go running in the morning.
4. My father never watches television.
5. She occasionally sees a play at our local theater.

6 Frank is very lazy, and he rarely does any exercise.
7 My kids sometimes play video games after school.

17.2
1 rarely 2 usually
3 often 4 never

17.3 🔊
1 Mariam usually stays **at home on weekends**.
2 I sometimes take **photos when I go on vacation**.
3 Dan rarely reads **a newspaper in the morning**.
4 She occasionally sees **a play at her local theater**.
5 Marco usually does **some exercises when he gets up**.
6 I sometimes listen to **music while I travel to work**.
7 We sometimes go out **for a meal at the Chinese restaurant**.
8 I often watch **a movie when I get home from work**.

17.4 🔊
1 The earliest flight is at 9am.
2 Sydney is the largest city in Australia.
3 Dubai is the hottest place I've visited.
4 This is the most expensive software we sell.
5 The farthest I've flown is to New Zealand.
6 Spanish is the easiest language to learn.
7 Kraków is the most beautiful city in Poland.
8 The train is the most affordable way to travel.
9 This is the most interesting gallery in town.
10 Hiroshi is the most intelligent person I know.
11 That was the scariest film I've seen.

17.5 🔊
1 The **longest** river in Brazil is the Amazon.
2 We'll have lunch at the **closest** café to the office.
3 I just watched the **worst** presentation I've ever seen.
4 I think that snowboarding is the **most exciting** sport.
5 Sean lives the **farthest / furthest** from the office.
6 Antonio is our **most loyal** employee.
7 This is the **most expensive** printer we have.

17.6
1 Dan
2 Pete
3 Pete
4 Pete
5 Dan
6 Chloe
7 Pete
8 Dan
9 Chloe
10 Dan

18

18.1 🔊
1 I didn't learn Spanish at school.
2 We walked to the conference center.
3 John lived in New York for 10 years.
4 Did the team discuss the merger?
5 He went to the conference by car.
6 My manager didn't visit the factory.
7 Selma didn't walk to work today.
8 Jimish posted the report a week ago.
9 Did Tom finish the report?

18.2 🔊
Nota: "did not" también puede escribirse en su forma contraída.
1 Akiko **finished** her presentation, then she **watched** some TV.

2 I **did not watch** the game because I **needed** to prepare for the conference.
3 Derek **wanted** to work somewhere interesting, so he **moved** to New York.
4 We **arrived** late, but we **did not miss** the meeting.
5 Sally **passed** her exams, and **decided** to go to college.

18.3 🔊
1 Fred showed me the new conference center.
2 We watched an interesting documentary about Beijing.
3 Ramon started at this company about five years ago.
4 Did you enjoy the presentation about the Indian economy?
5 It rained yesterday, so we didn't play soccer.
6 Arnold cooked me a delicious dinner last night.
7 Did Sam finish the report about the new product range?
8 I booked a table in a restaurant in the center.
9 Did Mike play tennis with the new CEO on Saturday?

18.4 🔊
1 Did Paul start working for us more than five years ago?
2 Did Sally explain how to use the new photocopier?
3 Did it rain while they were in Indonesia?
4 Did Clive pick up the guests from the railway station?
5 Did Mark join you for lunch at the Chinese restaurant?
6 Did the team attend the conference in Paris last year?
7 Did Philip play golf with the consultants last weekend?
8 Did Carl and Marie walk to work again today?
9 Did you watch the game yesterday?

⑩ Did Janet show you the new photocopier?
⑪ Did Mo study economics at Stanford University?
⑫ Did the company invest $10 million in R&D?

18.5
① False
② True
③ Not given
④ Not given
⑤ False
⑥ True
⑦ False

18.6 ◀))
① He studied for an exam.
② She visited a friend.
③ She walked to work.
④ He traveled to India.
⑤ He listened to the radio.

19

19.1
① A
② A
③ B
④ A
⑤ B

19.2 ◀))
① It's nine seventeen. / It's seventeen minutes past nine.
② It's seven o'clock. / It's seven.
③ It's half past five. / It's five thirty.
④ It's three twenty-two. / It's twenty-two minutes past three.
⑤ It's a quarter to six. / It's five forty-five.

19.3 ◀))
① The soccer tournament ends on June 20.
② American Independence Day is on the 4th of July.
③ Christmas Day is on December 25.
④ My wife's birthday is on September 5.
⑤ My daughter was born on August 3.

19.4
① 2014
② August 2015
③ July
④ Scotland
⑤ May 3

20

20.1 ◀))
① spent
② met
③ got
④ went
⑤ was / were
⑥ left
⑦ told
⑧ thought
⑨ said
⑩ began
⑪ chose

20.2 ◀))
① I **went** to Paris on a business trip last week.
② I **spent** all afternoon working on a report.
③ I **began** working at Carter's last year.
④ The CEO **told** me that my work was excellent.
⑤ I **thought** this project was very difficult.
⑥ Besim **was** off sick yesterday.
⑦ I **met** the new Sales Director this morning.

⑧ The staff **chose** the name of the company.
⑨ Kara **left** her last job because it was boring.

20.3 ◀))
① I **met** the International Marketing Director last week.
② I **had** a demanding boss.
③ I **left** my last job because it was badly paid.
④ I **got** to work very early today.
⑤ They **went** to the New York office last month.
⑥ The staff **chose** new chairs for the office.
⑦ Sally **thought** that Rohit's presentation went well.

20.4 ◀))
① I started work there after I left school.
② I worked in a bank at the start of my career.
③ I took the children to school.
④ I met many interesting people.
⑤ I worked hard and studied for an MBA.
⑥ We had a black and white uniform.

20.5
Ⓐ 7
Ⓑ 1
Ⓒ 2
Ⓓ 8
Ⓔ 3
Ⓕ 5
Ⓖ 4
Ⓗ 6

20.6 ◀))
① I **felt** very well respected by my team leader.
② The Head of Sales **taught** me to give interesting presentations.
③ My brother **made** a delicious cake, which I took to work for my birthday.

4 The staff **chose** the pictures for the meeting rooms, and they look great.

5 I **left** my last job because I didn't get along with the customers.

6 I **spent** all of yesterday writing a sales report and now I'm very tired.

21

21.1 ◀ツ

1 We **launched** a new range of apps last year.

2 At **first**, we only had four employees.

3 Two years **ago**, we opened our tenth store.

4 The company **merged** with a competitor a year ago.

5 A new Director of Marketing **started** working here last year.

21.2 ◀ツ

1 **At first**, we only had one store.

2 We **opened** a new flagship store last month.

3 We **launched** an exciting new app last year.

4 A new Director of HR started working six months **ago**.

21.3

1 Over 10,000

2 In her garage

3 50

4 Two years ago

5 At craft fairs

21.4

1 last month

2 during the first quarter

3 in the winter of 2012

4 recently

21.5 ◀ツ

1 **Last** spring, sales of umbrellas **rose** because it was wet.

2 UK sales **went up** in 2011, but **fell** in 2012.

3 **At** first, the value of shares in the company **remained** steady.

4 Online marketing costs **increased** and sales also **rose**.

22

22.1 ◀ツ

1 to accept an invitation

2 to attend a meeting

3 calendar

4 boardroom

5 to invite someone

6 office

7 conference room

8 running late

9 restaurant

10 reception

11 café

12 morning

13 afternoon

14 evening

15 appointment

16 refreshments

17 to decline an invitation

18 to miss a meeting

19 agenda

22.2 ◀ツ

1 to come up

2 to cancel

3 to be busy

4 to be unable to attend

5 to look forward to

6 to reschedule

23

23.1 ◀ツ

1 The company **is losing** money, so we **are planning** a restructure.

2 Stacy **is not working** in the office today. She **is visiting** the factory.

3 Dan **is meeting** a new client. They **are chatting** in the meeting room.

4 Colin **is starting** a new project. He **is working** with Angela.

5 The head office **is relocating** to Delhi. We **are moving** this week.

6 Profits **are falling** this year, and the team **is feeling** nervous.

7 Anika **is working** late tonight. She **is preparing** a presentation.

8 Sue and Clive **are having** lunch downtown. They **are eating** Chinese.

9 I **am going** on vacation next week. I **am missing** the training day.

10 Our company **is selling** a lot to India. We **are opening** an office in Mumbai.

11 Our secretary **is retiring**. We **are recruiting** a new one.

12 Sam and Sue **are discussing** the report. They **are planning** a meeting about it.

13 Chrissie **is choosing** a new team. She **is considering** Paul for a position.

14 Alex **is leaving** the company. He **is moving** to New York.

23.2 ◀ツ

1 Who are you meeting?

2 Is Tim writing the report?

3 Are Kim and Jo presenting today?

4 Are you printing the agenda?

5 Is the company moving?

6 When are you retiring?

7 Who are you promoting?

23.3
1. Is the conference taking place in Venice next April?
2. Is Leanne giving a presentation on the takeover plans?
3. Are our owners hoping to buy our biggest competitor?
4. Is Brendan programming the software for new machinery?
5. Are we taking time off in August this year?

23.4
1. Are you having lunch at 1pm today?
2. Tom is going to the conference today.
3. Is John working until 7pm again?
4. We are traveling to New York again.
5. Are you coming to the meeting on Friday?
6. Are you visiting the factory next month?
7. I'm not taking time off in August.
8. The head office is moving in the spring.
9. Fran isn't coming to the office tomorrow.
10. What are you doing on Tuesday?
11. Sam is meeting the client this afternoon.
12. Tim is leaving work at 5pm today.

23.5
1. On Monday morning, Frank is **visiting the factory**.
2. On Monday afternoon, Clare is **attending a course**.
3. On Tuesday, Frank is **celebrating his wedding anniversary**.
4. In the evening, he is **going to the theater**.
5. On Thursday at 2pm, Clare is **meeting Pete**.
6. They are both free at **2:30pm on Thursday**.

23.6
1. I'm having lunch with the IT team.
2. I'm meeting them at 3pm.
3. I'm flying to Edinburgh.
4. I'm returning to London at 11:30am.
5. I'm going to Sandra's leaving party.

24

24.1
1. Educada
2. No educada
3. Educada
4. Educada
5. Educada
6. No educada
7. Educada

24.2
1. True
2. False
3. True
4. False
5. Not given
6. False
7. Not given

24.3
1. I'm sorry. I'm not sure I **agree**.
2. Sorry, but in my **opinion** they will sell well.
3. I can see your **point**, but I still think senior citizens are more important.
4. If I could just **come** in here and mention the good news from France.
5. **Excuse** me, but my figures tell a different story.
6. **Could** I just say...? The budget won't cover it.
7. I'm not **sure** I agree. Sales to China are growing faster.
8. Sorry to **interrupt**, but the software is not ready yet.

24.4
1. I'm afraid Sean can't make it to the meeting and has **sent** his apologies.
2. Shall we **take** a vote on the new strategy to see what course of action to take?
3. Ramona will **take** the minutes and email them to everyone after the meeting.
4. I agree with the motion. How **about** you? What do you think about it?
5. If I could just **interrupt** for a moment. I think we need to take a vote on this.
6. That sums up most of the issues we are facing. I just have a few **closing** remarks.
7. Claude is the chair, so he has the **casting** vote if there is a tie.
8. The **chair** of our budget meetings likes to keep his closing remarks very short.
9. I read **through** the agenda before the meeting, so I know what we will be talking about.

24.5
1. footprint
2. green
3. reuse
4. resources
5. waste
6. environment
7. reduce

25

25.1
1. Me neither.
2. Neither do I.
3. So did I.
4. Neither did I.
5. Me too.
6. So do I.
7. Me neither.
8. So do I.
9. Me too.

25.2 🔊

1. I suppose so. It will be expensive though.
2. So did I. He's so entertaining.
3. I agree. The team could improve their skills.
4. I'll ask the secretary to send it again.
5. Me neither. The food's very bland.
6. So do I. It's very comfortable.
7. Exactly. I didn't understand it at all.
8. I agree. I learned some new skills.
9. Absolutely. We should promote her.

25.3 🔊

1. I'm **afraid** we'll have to cancel the meeting.
2. I'm sorry, but I **disagree** with you.
3. I **totally** disagree with you about this.
4. I'm really not **sure** about that design.
5. I'm **sorry**, Pete, but I don't agree with you.
6. I don't agree at **all**. It won't work.
7. I'm not **sure** about this. Can we talk later?
8. I'm afraid I **don't** agree with you at all.
9. I don't **agree** at all with the merger.
10. You **could** be right, but I'm not sure.
11. Sorry, but I disagree **with** this plan.

25.4

1. Greg disagrees with her.
2. Greg thinks he doesn't have enough experience.
3. Jenny strongly disagrees.
4. Greg agrees.
5. Jenny strongly agrees.

25.5 🔊

1. We **totally** agree about the redesign.
2. I can't agree with you **at** all about the downsizing.
3. We're **afraid** we totally disagree.
4. You **could** be right, but I need more evidence.
5. I'm not sure **about** the latest business plan.

26

26.1 🔊

1. Roger hurt himself when he slipped.
2. She burned herself on the coffee maker.
3. Ron blames himself for the accident.
4. Jan cut herself on the machinery.
5. We enjoyed ourselves at the office party.
6. Juan cut himself in the kitchen.
7. We need to protect ourselves from risks.

26.2 🔊

1. I hurt **myself** when I moved the photocopier.
2. They should prepare **themselves** for the course.
3. Claire's cut **herself** on the equipment.
4. Have you all signed **yourselves** up for the course?
5. Sam is teaching **himself** Japanese.

26.3

1. Not given
2. Not given
3. True
4. False
5. Not given
6. False
7. True
8. False

26.4 🔊

1. An **extinguisher** is used to stop small fires.
2. If you hear the fire alarm, go to the **assembly area**.
3. Medical equipment is kept in the **first aid kit**.
4. Each fire **escape** has a sign above the door.
5. You practice leaving the building during a **fire drill**.

27

27.1 🔊

1. How about asking Tim to write the report?
2. Why don't we ask Pete for his opinion?
3. We could have a meeting on Friday.
4. Let's ask the team for their opinions.
5. What about putting some videos online?
6. Why don't we hire another intern?
7. How about moving the meeting to 5pm?
8. Let's try calling the engineer again.

27.2 🔊

1. She should go home and rest.
2. You should ask the secretary for another.
3. You should go on a training course.
4. You should order some more.
5. He should call IT.
6. You should call the engineer.
7. You should ask for an extension.
8. You should take the bus.

27.3 🔊

1. Where have the reports gone? They've **disappeared**.
2. Pete **misunderstood** me. He thought I said 3 o'clock.
3. Cathy isn't coming in today. She's feeling **unwell**.
4. You should be **careful** crossing the road.
5. Doug is really **impatient**. He gets angry so easily.
6. I'm **unable** to come to the training because I have a meeting.
7. Don't forget to **disconnect** the machine after you've used it.
8. I'm **unfamiliar** with that program. I don't know it.
9. Jean is so **careless**. She's always making mistakes.

10 This morning is **impractical** for me. Can we meet later?

27.4 🔊
1 We should make sure no one **misunderstood** the instructions.
2 How about organizing training for everyone who is **unfamiliar** with the program?
3 Let's make sure no one on the team **spells** the name wrongly again.
4 Why don't we ask Pete to help if Laura isn't **well** tomorrow?
5 I think we should **disconnect** the machine since it's not working.
6 I don't think you should be so **impatient** with the new recruits.
7 Let's send a memo to everyone who isn't **able** to come to the meeting.
8 Let's explain to Tim that he should be more **careful** with financial information.
9 Why don't we try to find a time that is **convenient** for everyone?

28

28.1
1 young adults
2 sports wear
3 jackets
4 65%
5 80%
6 China
7 India

28.2 🔊
1 Today I'm going to talk about profit.
2 Does anyone have any questions?
3 To sum up, we are facing issues.
4 I'm happy to answer questions.
5 Last, let's look at the future.

28.3 🔊
1 I'd like to begin **by showing you this graph**.
2 I'm happy to **answer any questions**.
3 Does anyone have any more **questions or comments**?
4 Let's move **on to the next topic**.
5 After that, I would **like to talk about the merger**.
6 To sum up, it's **been an excellent quarter for the company**.

28.4 🔊
1 The **screen** is black. We can't see the graph.
2 If you use a **projector**, you can introduce graphs and visuals.
3 I'll write down the company's name on the **flipchart**.
4 There are programs to help you make professional-looking **slides**.
5 If you use a **microphone**, the people at the back will hear you.

28.5 🔊
1 I'd **like** to start with our factory in Vietnam.
2 To sum **up**, we need to invest more in infrastructure.
3 I'll **explore** the benefits of investing in web technology later.
4 Let's begin by looking at the sales figures.
5 In **short**, we need to develop new products.
6 Let's take a **look** at the second graph.
7 So we've **covered** all the topics I wanted to discuss.
8 Turning to the previous quarter's profits.
9 Then I'm going to **talk** about the situation in China.
10 **To** start, let's look at this year's performance.
11 Moving **on**, let's look at our main competitors.

12 First, I'm going to look **at** last year's results.
13 I'm happy to **answer** any questions at the end.
14 I'd like to end **by** thanking you all for your attention today.

29

29.1 🔊
1 You **don't have to** stay late tonight. It's very quiet.
2 Is your phone broken? You **can** use mine if you like.
3 We **have to** wear a jacket and tie when we meet clients.
4 You **can't** park there. It's a space for disabled drivers.

29.2 🔊
1 You can't leave early tonight. **We have an important meeting at 5pm.**
2 You don't have to pay for lunch. **Staff eat for free in the cafeteria.**
3 You can make yourself a hot drink. **There's tea and coffee in the kitchen.**
4 We have to wear business clothes. **There's a formal dress code.**
5 We have to leave the building now. **That's the fire alarm.**

29.3
1 True
2 False
3 Not given
4 True
5 False

29.4 🔊
1 I **can listen** to music at work if I use headphones.
2 He's a pilot. He **has** to wear a uniform.
3 They **don't have** to go to the training session.
4 He can't **take** more than an hour for his lunch break.
5 He **can't** leave early. It's too busy.
6 I have **to** back up my files before I turn my computer off.

29.5 🔊
1 Could you wash these cups, please?
2 Would you mind turning the light off?
3 Could you help me lift this box, please?
4 Would you mind calling me back later?
5 Could you lend me your stapler, please?

29.6 🔊
1 Could you open the window?
2 Would you mind checking this list?
3 Could you forward me Jo's email?
4 Would you mind printing the report?
5 Could you pass around the agenda?
6 Would you mind ordering more files?
7 Could you come to today's meeting?

29.7 🔊
1 Could you turn your music down?
2 Would you mind checking my report for me?
3 Could you close the window?
4 Would you mind inviting Alan to the meeting?

29.8 🔊
1 Could you check these sales figures?
2 Would you mind paying a deposit now?
3 Could you ask Ian to call me back?
4 Would you mind showing our clients around?

29.9 🔊
1 Would you mind **opening** the door? It's really hot in here.
2 Would you mind **asking** John to email me this month's sales figures?
3 Could you **take** the minutes for this afternoon's meeting?
4 Could you **remind** me who is coming to tomorrow's presentation?

30

30.1 🔊
1 to think outside the box
2 to get down to business
3 red tape
4 to take it easy
5 to be tied up with
6 to wind down
7 business as usual
8 to be out of order
9 a win-win situation
10 to be in the red
11 to work around the clock
12 the ball is in your court
13 to put something off
14 going haywire
15 throwing money down the drain
16 to be swamped
17 to pull your weight

31

31.1 🔊
1 Tanya was feeling very tired.
2 I was finishing his report.
3 Alison was talking to the CEO.
4 Was Jamie taking minutes?
5 Were you working late yesterday?
6 I was trying to call you.
7 Claire was playing very loud music.

31.2 🔊
Nota: Las respuestas negativas también pueden utilizar formas largas.
1 The train trip here was really bad. All the trains **were running** late.
2 The cleaners **were complaining** that staff left their dirty cups in the sink.
3 Harriet **wasn't listening** to the presentation.
4 Tom's manager was annoyed because Tom **wasn't meeting** his deadlines.
5 My email inbox **was getting** full, so I had to delete some messages.

31.3
1 True
2 False
3 True
4 True
5 False

31.4 🔊
1 Joshua **was giving** a talk about new markets.
2 Fiona **wasn't listening** to Bilal's new ideas for products.
3 Lucia **was taking** the minutes of the meeting.
4 They **were speaking** too loudly on the phone.
5 Helen **was eating** her lunch at her desk.

31.5
1 The windows
2 Talking
3 Her assistant
4 Her USB cable
5 Talk to a co-worker
6 Think clearly

32.1 ◀))
1 I am so sorry I was late for the meeting with our clients today.
2 I would like to apologize for not finishing the report yesterday.
3 I'm really sorry. I forgot to charge the office cell phone and it has no power.
4 I'm really sorry this line is so bad. I hope we don't get cut off.
5 I'm afraid that's not good enough. I want a full refund on my ticket.

32.2 ◀))
1 No problem. I'll help you finish it now.
2 That's not good enough. Please heat it up.
3 Never mind. We're not very busy today.
4 No problem. I'll have tea instead.
5 Don't worry. I'll print off some more.

32.3
A 4
B 3
C 1
D 5
E 2

32.4 ◀))
1 I'm really **sorry**. I forgot to send the agenda for the meeting.
2 I would like to **apologize** for the rudeness of the waitress.
3 I'm **afraid** that's not good enough You missed an important meeting.
4 That's all **right**. I'll make you a copy right now.
5 Please **make** sure it doesn't happen again.
6 Never **mind**. It's only a cup.
7 I would **like** to apologize for the delay to your train this evening.

32.5 ◀))
1 Harry **was practicing** his presentation when I **called** him.
2 Sam's cell phone **rang** when Tom **was describing** the sales for this quarter.
3 The elevator **got** stuck while they **were waiting** for it.
4 Tina **wasn't listening** when the CEO **said** all staff would get a raise.
5 The fire alarm **went** off when we **were having** our update meeting.
6 I **was working** late when I **heard** a strange noise.
7 I **was editing** the report when the fire alarm **went** off.

32.6 ◀))
1 The photocopier **broke** while I **was copying** your sales report.
2 We **were listening** to Janet's presentation when the power **went** off.
3 John **was signing** the contract when the lawyer **called** him.
4 Anna **was** furious when she found out George **was copying** her ideas.
5 Simon **was editing** the report when his computer **crashed**.
6 We **were waiting** for the bus when two buses **arrived**.

33.1 ◀))
Nota: Todas las respuestas también pueden ir en forma contraída.
1 I **have called** eight customers this morning.
2 Gareth **has made** coffee for the visitors.
3 Piotr **has cut** the hair of many famous people.
4 I **have not finished** checking my emails.
5 Carl **has not emailed** me the sales data.

33.2 ◀))
1 She hasn't sent the invoice **yet**.
2 We have **just** heard the CEO is leaving.
3 I haven't met the new director **yet**.
4 Has Tom finished fixing my laptop **yet**?
5 George has **just** called me.
6 The painters haven't finished **yet**.
7 Have you had a meeting with Ann **yet**?
8 The trainer has **just** arrived.
9 Have you **just** finished the report?

33.3 ◀))
1 I haven't ordered the stationery yet.
2 They have just introduced the new packaging.
3 Have you answered those emails yet?
4 Derinda has just written the minutes from our meeting.

33.4
1 True
2 False
3 True
4 Not given

33.5 ◀))
1 Daniel **sent** your package last Friday.
2 Jenny **showed** me the new designs yesterday.
3 Babu and Zack **haven't finished** their research yet.
4 Kate **spoke** to the HR manager last week.

33.6
1 B
2 A
3 B
4 A
5 A

33.7 🔊

1 I have done all the invoices for June.
2 He met the Chinese partners last month.
3 He hasn't sent the salaries to payroll yet.
4 They have not started the audit yet.
5 He left this morning.
6 I have just heard about your promotion.
7 She has sold the most products.
8 Have you designed that box yet?
9 They have given him a verbal warning.
10 Mark hasn't scanned it yet.
11 I have spoken to your team.

33.8 🔊

1 Yes, I've **just** scanned them.
2 No, he **hasn't** done them yet.
3 **I've** filed them all in the cabinet.
4 We've **stopped** the delivery.

34

34.1 🔊

1 We will replace your tablet free of charge.
2 The chef will cook you another pizza.
3 I'll talk to the boss about it.
4 The manager will be with you soon.
5 I'll contact our courier immediately.
6 We will give you a full refund.
7 I promise that your order will arrive today.
8 I'm afraid we won't finish the project on time.
9 I'm sorry, but we won't cancel your order.

34.2 🔊

1 We'll send it to your hotel when it gets here.
2 I'll ask the chef to cook it properly.
3 I'll refund the money to your credit card.
4 I will call the driver immediately.
5 We'll move you to another room.

34.3

1 There was no receptionist
2 They will ask receptionists to work late
3 The bathroom was dirty
4 He will speak to the cleaners' manager
5 There wasn't any hot coffee
6 Mr. Vance was kept awake
7 A full refund

34.4 🔊

1 We'll offer you a discount off your next hotel stay.
2 Will the money be refunded to my credit card?
3 The company will chase your order up for you.
4 The store manager will be with you very soon.
5 Will you replace the part on my broken washing machine?

34.5

1 No
2 Sí
3 Sí
4 No

34.6 🔊

1 I'm very sorry about that. **We'll offer** you a refund.
2 I really must apologize. I**'ll take** it back to the kitchen.
3 She**'ll be** with you in a minute.
4 I**'ll talk** to her about this.
5 It **won't happen** again.

6 I**'ll ask** the chef to make you something vegetarian.

35

35.1 🔊

1 bus
2 plane
3 helicopter
4 tram
5 bus stop
6 car
7 taxi
8 airport
9 train station
10 taxi stand (US) / taxi rank (UK)
11 bicycle

35.2 🔊

1 terminal
2 security
3 boarding pass
4 on time
5 domestic flight
6 international flight
7 connecting flight
8 delay
9 passport control
10 late
11 hotel
12 board a plane
13 check-in
14 passport
15 luggage
16 round trip ticket (US) / return ticket (UK)
17 window seat
18 aisle seat
19 seat reservation

36

36.1 🔊
Nota: Todas las respuestas también pueden ir en forma contraída.
1. If we **don't hurry**, we **will miss** the flight.
2. If we **meet** in Berlin, it **will save** us some time.
3. We **will take** on a new intern if we **win** the contract.
4. If the train **is** late, we **will miss** the meeting.
5. If the bank **is** closed, we **will not have** any money.
6. We **will pay** for your flight if you **fly** to Denver.
7. If you **work** hard, you **will pass** the exam.
8. The firm **will pay** expenses if you **are** delayed.
9. If I **go** to Rome, I **will visit** the Colosseum.
10. If I **lose** my job, I don't know what I **will do**.

36.2 🔊
1. If we don't hurry up, **we'll miss our connecting flight**.
2. We will get a discount **if we book early**.
3. Will you pay expenses **if we attend the conference**?
4. What will Samantha do if **she loses her job next month**?
5. If we lose the contract, **we will have to lay Sean off**.
6. Will you visit the factory **if you go to China**?

36.3 🔊
1. Will you have a celebration if you get the job?
2. If you buy the ticket online, it will be cheaper.

3. If we visit Paris, we will probably go sightseeing.
4. What will we do if we don't win the contract?
5. If we take on a new intern, where will they sit?
6. How will you travel to Berlin if the flight is canceled?

36.4
1. True
2. False
3. True
4. False
5. Not given
6. True

36.5 🔊
1. If it's a nice day, I walk to work.
2. If you heat water, it boils.
3. If you're late for work, isn't your boss unhappy?
4. If you press that button, the machine stops.

36.6 🔊
1. Will you visit Red Square if you **go** to Moscow?
2. People use public transportation if it **is** cheap.
3. What will we do if we **lose** the contract?
4. The ticket **will be** more expensive if we buy it later.
5. If you **pay** staff more, they work harder.
6. **Will** you pick me up from the station if I give you my details?
7. We'll miss the train if we **don't** hurry.
8. If it **rains**, the event is always moved indoors.
9. Sharon **won't** go on vacation if she loses her job.
10. **Will** Doug resign if the company loses the deal?

37

37.1 🔊
1. Do you know the **way** to the station?
2. The bank is **on** the corner.
3. Do you know how to **get** to the hotel?
4. The museum is **in** front of the park.
5. You should **take** the second left.
6. The library is straight ahead on **the** right.
7. Our house is just ahead **on** the left.
8. Sorry, did you **say** it is near the school?
9. Turn right **at** the sign.

37.2 🔊
1. The entrance is in front of the factory.
2. Turn right at the sign.
3. The bank is opposite the school.
4. Take the first road on the left.
5. Go past the movie theater.
6. The bank is on the corner.
7. The station is next to the police station.

37.3 🔊
1. Excuse me, do you know the way to the hotel?
2. Go straight on and it's opposite the train station.
3. Sorry, did you say it's next to the post office?
4. The bank is 40 yards ahead on the corner.

37.4
1. A
2. B
3. A
4. A
5. B

37.5 ◄ **Respuestas modelo**
1 Take the first right, and it's on the left after the town hall.
2 Sure, go straight ahead, and it's on the left.
3 Yes, go straight ahead, and it's on the right.
4 Yes, take the first right, and then it's on the right.
5 Turn left, then turn right, and it's on the left.

38

38.1 ◄
1 The hotel was opened in 1932.
2 The new factory was opened by the president.
3 Simon was employed by our company in 2013.
4 Our new range of products will be released next month.
5 Our head office was moved to Shanghai about four years ago.
6 Peter was introduced to the new management team.
7 Coffee and tea will be served during the break.
8 The team will be shown how to use the new software package.

38.2 ◄
Respuestas modelo
1 The CEO was met at the airport.
2 The meeting room has been redecorated.
3 A double room was booked yesterday.
4 The team was taught some Mandarin.
5 The files were left on the train again.
6 The rooms were booked on Monday.
7 Breakfast is served at 7:30am.
8 The office has been organized.

38.3
A 5
B 1
C 4
D 3
E 2
F 7
G 6
H 8

38.4
1 False 2 Not given
3 True 4 False

38.5 ◄
1 We **were picked up** at the airport by the driver.
2 Great. It **was served** at 7am each morning.
3 Yes. But unfortunately it **was broken**.

39

39.1 ◄
1 fry
2 waiter
3 vegetarian
4 chef
5 waitress
6 menu
7 make a reservation / booking
8 boil
9 receipt
10 breakfast
11 lunch
12 dinner
13 café
14 vegan
15 dessert
16 food allergy / intolerance
17 bar
18 tip
19 roast

39.2 ◄
1 fruit
2 bread
3 water
4 napkin
5 milk
6 fish
7 coffee
8 pasta
9 tea
10 meat
11 fork
12 knife
13 vegetables
14 seafood
15 salad
16 sandwich
17 potatoes
18 butter
19 cake

40

40.1 ◄
1 Did you have any trouble getting here?
2 Can I get you anything?
3 It's great to meet you in person.
4 Have you been to Toronto before?
5 Did you have a good flight?
6 Would you like something to drink?
7 I've been looking forward to meeting you.
8 We've heard so much about you.
9 I'll let Mr. Song know that you arrived.
10 Is this your first visit to India?

40.2 ◄
1 Is there **any** information about flights?
2 I need to buy **some** food.
3 Are there **any** good hotels nearby?
4 Can I get you **a** cup of coffee?
5 Are there **any** interesting talks today?
6 Do you have **any** luggage?

7 There is **a** presentation later.

8 Do you have **any** tea?

9 Please take **a** seat at the front.

40.3 🔊

1 Would you like some **water, Mrs. Smith**?

2 Do you have any **information about the flight**?

3 Have you been **to Los Angeles before**?

4 Can I get you **a glass of water**?

5 It's great to **meet you in person**.

6 There isn't **any coffee left, I'm afraid**.

40.4 🔊

1 Are you going to **any** talks later?

2 James is giving **a** presentation later today.

3 There isn't **any** coffee or tea, I'm sorry.

4 Are **any** of your colleagues staying here?

5 Would you like **a** cup of tea, Jen?

6 They don't have **any** workshops this afternoon.

7 Have **any** of the attendees arrived yet?

8 Is there **any** information about the conference?

9 There's **some** food and drink in the main hall.

40.5

1 the main hall

2 developing an app

3 a choice of food and drink

4 a product launch

5 leading CEOs

6 the Asian market

41

41.1 🔊

1 I'm afraid we're fully booked this evening.

2 Can we sit outside on the terrace?

3 Could I have a cup of coffee, please?

4 Can we just have five more minutes, please?

5 Yes, I'm allergic to shellfish.

6 Absolutely delicious, thank you.

7 Yes, please. Some chocolate ice cream for me.

8 No, I'm afraid it contains cream.

9 Sure, are you paying by cash or by card?

41.2 🔊

1 Are you ready to order?

2 I'd like to reserve a table for two, please.

3 Have you reserved a table, madam?

4 How many people are there in your party?

5 Could I have a look at the dessert menu, please?

6 What would you like for the entree?

7 Do you have any allergies or intolerances?

8 How many vegetarian options are there today?

9 Could we have the bill, please?

10 Would you like to pay by cash or card?

41.3 🔊

1 How many chairs will you need?

2 I ordered too many dishes.

3 There's not enough space here. It's tiny.

4 How many plates will you need?

5 There are too many chairs.

6 There's not enough cake for everyone.

7 The lobster costs too much.

8 We haven't ordered enough dishes.

---

9 How many guests are you expecting?

10 I don't have enough cash for a tip.

11 I've eaten too much food this evening!

12 There's enough tea for everyone.

41.4 🔊

1 How **many** people are coming tonight?

2 Is there **enough** space at the table for everyone?

3 How **much** does the meal usually cost?

4 I've eaten too **much** cake.

5 There's **too** much salt in my soup.

6 There are not **enough** chairs for all of us!

7 **How** many glasses will we need this evening?

42

42.1 🔊

1 I'd **better** go now.

2 Can I **ask** who's calling?

3 No, that's **all**, thanks.

4 OK. **Talk** to you soon.

5 Is there **anything** else I can do?

6 Hello, Sales **department**.

42.2

A 5

B 3

C 2

D 1

E 4

42.3 🔊

1 Esme speaking. How can I help?

2 Of course. It's Sergio Walker.

3 OK. Speak to you soon.

4 Hi, Andrew. It's José from Design.

42.4

1. 57336
2. 0114342190
3. 031297778
4. 0092736430
5. 2074440016
6. 00340621485
7. 8694472165

42.5 🔊

Respuestas modelo

1. Liz's extension is 3864.
2. Saira's office number is 01928 335178.
3. The Helpdesk number at KTV News is 616 888 3746.
4. Lucy's cell phone number is 616 913 6205.

42.6 🔊

1. I don't know why Hal's not **picking up** the phone.
2. I'll **put you through** to customer services now.
3. Can you **speak up**, please? I can't hear you.
4. Sorry, I'm busy now. I'll **get back** to you later.
5. I'm sorry I **cut you off**. This line is very bad.
6. You're **breaking up**. Can I call you back?

42.7 🔊

1. Could you possibly speak **up**, please? The line is very faint.
2. I'll call **you** back in ten minutes. Is that OK? I have to finish writing an email.
3. If I get cut **off**, call me back on the office phone. I'm back at my desk now.
4. Can I get back **to** you about the design later today? We're still working on it.
5. I've called Fatima three times, but she didn't pick **up**. Is she at work today?
6. Marc kept breaking **up** when I called him. The signal here is awful!

7. Katie is back at her desk now. I'll just put you **through** to her.
8. Mateo got back **to** me about the new manual. He has a few comments on it.

42.8 🔊

1. Can you speak up, please?
2. I hope I don't get cut off again.
3. Let me put you through to Finance.
4. Sorry I didn't pick up when you called.
5. Can you get back to him this afternoon?
6. Sorry, the line keeps breaking up.
7. I'll call you back in five minutes.
8. He didn't get back to me yesterday.
9. Don't pick up the phone if Dan calls.

43

43.1 🔊

1. Yes, of course. May I ask who's calling?
2. I'm calling because my laptop is broken.
3. Yes. Can you ask her to call me back?
4. Could you ask her to call me back today?

43.2 🔊

1. **It's** Sunita Devinder from GBT.
2. I wonder if you **could** help me.
3. I'm afraid Mr. Cox **isn't** at his desk.
4. Thank you for **calling** Top Sounds.
5. **Could** I speak to Rod Dean, please?
6. Could you **ask** him to call me back?
7. **May** I ask who's calling, please?

43.3 🔊

1. How can I help you?
2. May I ask who's calling?
3. I'll just put you through.
4. Would you like to leave a message?
5. Could you ask him to call me back, please?

6. IT department. How can I help you?
7. I'll put you through to HR now.
8. I'm afraid he's not at his desk.
9. Thank you for calling Quadfax.

43.4 🔊

1. Savino's. How **can I help** you?
2. Thank you **for calling** Ready Solutions.
3. Hello. **I wonder if** you can help me.
4. I'm calling **about an order** I placed last month.
5. **Could I speak** to Becky Bradley, please?
6. I'm afraid the Accounts Manager is away **at the moment**.
7. Yes, please. **Could I order** 20 desks?
8. **Would you like** to leave a message?
9. Thank you. **I'll just put** you through.

43.5

OPINIÓN:
nice, **awful**, **stylish**
TAMAÑO:
tiny, **large**, **huge**
EDAD:
ancient, **modern**, **antique**
COLOR:
blue, **purple**, **pink**
MATERIAL:
leather, **metal**, **plastic**

43.6 🔊

1. We're developing a stylish little gold lamp.
2. Tom has got an amazing tiny new smartphone.
3. The pet store has a nice big black and white cat.
4. There is an awful large modern painting in the cafeteria.
5. Have you seen the exciting new colorful marketing posters?

43.7 🔊

1 That's a stylish new design for the company logo.
2 There's a huge round hole in the wall where the truck hit it.
3 Have you seen the fabulous new office chairs?
4 There's a big yellow and red truck outside.
5 There's a nice big green and white plant in my office.
6 Have you tasted the awful new coffee?
7 The headphones for my laptop go in a tiny round hole.
8 There's a large rectangular parking space for motorbikes.

43.8

1 Printed materials
2 Next Tuesday
3 9:00
4 60
5 Six taxis
6 Vegetarian and gluten-free food

44

44.1 🔊

1 Personal statement
2 Education
3 Professional achievements
4 Career summary
5 Key skills

44.2 🔊

1 I have a **proven** track record in the tourism industry.
2 I am proficient **in** using a wide range of software.
3 I have hands-on **experience** of customer service.
4 I have experience working in a **service-oriented** environment.

44.3 🔊

1 I am a highly motivated individual and love working in tourism.
2 I gained in-depth knowledge of the construction industry.
3 I have a great deal of experience in the catering industry.
4 I am proficient in most types of accounting software.

44.4 🔊

1 I **managed** a large team of marketing executives.
2 Our teams **collaborated** to create a new clothing range.
3 The company **established** a new headquarters in the capital.
4 I **negotiated** with our suppliers and got a good deal.

44.5 Respuestas modelo

1 She oversaw the introduction of new accounting software and co-ordinated a training program.
2 She is the Deputy Director of Accounts at Tomkins Travel.
3 She worked in the construction industry.
4 She gained her diploma in Accounting in June 2010.
5 She can speak Spanish and English fluently.

45

45.1 🔊

Nota: Todas las respuestas, salvo
6, 8 y 11 también se pueden
escribir en forma contraída.

1 He **is going to travel** to the conference by plane.
2 She **is not going to make** it to the meeting.
3 They **are going to meet** the staff from the Paris office.
4 He **is going to write** a letter to the suppliers.
5 They **are not going to sell** their shares in the company just now.
6 **Is** she **going to order** business cards with the new company logo?
7 Sergio **is going to give** a presentation about the new training course.
8 **Are** you **going to make** tea and coffee for the visitors?
9 Diana **is going to design** the new company logo.
10 They **are going to join** us for our team meeting today.
11 **Are** you **going to review** the sales data this afternoon?

45.2 🔊

1 Why don't we ask what Marketing think?
2 Could you load the printer with paper?
3 Can you help me with these files, please?
4 Could you send the files to production?
5 Could we meet at 4 instead of 5?
6 Can you finish the report today?
7 Couldn't we invite Jeff to the meeting?
8 Could you call me back later, please?
9 Could you make coffee for the CEO?
10 Could we possibly cancel the meeting?
11 Can you check this report, please?
12 Could you pass round the agenda?

⑬ Can we try a different approach?
⑭ Please could you call the Delhi office?
⑮ Could you lock up before you leave?
⑯ Could you possibly stay late tonight?
⑰ Please can you print out these designs?

___

45.3 ◀))

1. I am going to email the director.
2. I am going to email the IT help desk.
3. I am going to email the sales department.
4. I am going to speak to the director.
5. I am going to speak to the IT help desk.
6. I am going to speak to the sales department.
7. You are going to email the director.
8. You are going to email the IT help desk.
9. You are going to email the sales department.
10. You are going to speak to the director.
11. You are going to speak to the IT help desk.
12. You are going to speak to the sales department.
13. Kelly is going to email the director.
14. Kelly is going to email the IT help desk.
15. Kelly is going to email the sales department.
16. Kelly is going to speak to the director.
17. Kelly is going to speak to the IT help desk.
18. Kelly is going to speak to the sales department.

___

45.4

① False
② Not given
③ False
④ True
⑤ False

45.5

Respuestas modelo
① Paul is going to contact the presenters.
② Paul is going to ask the printers for ten extra copies of the training booklets.
③ The printers are going to supply name badges in the form of lanyards.
④ Marie is going to meet the presenters.
⑤ The presenters will get to the venue by taxi.
⑥ Omar is going to check that the venue will cater for people with special dietary requirements.

46

46.1 ◀))
① text message
② website
③ stamp
④ voicemail
⑤ conference call
⑥ email
⑦ bulletin board (US) / notice board (UK)
⑧ letter
⑨ internal mail
⑩ mail (US) / post (UK)
⑪ web conference
⑫ presentation
⑬ transfer a call
⑭ envelope
⑮ social networking

___

46.2 ◀))
① attachment
② forward
③ trash
④ signature
⑤ outbox
⑥ print
⑦ reply all
⑧ inbox
⑨ subject

46.3 ◀))
① TBC
② BCC
③ RE
④ CC
⑤ FYI
⑥ ETA
⑦ NB
⑧ ASAP

47

47.1 ◀))
① I work **in** the finance department at Forrester's.
② Please confirm your availability **ASAP**.
③ Please find your **receipt attached** to this email.
④ Please **don't hesitate** to contact me.
⑤ I am writing **with reference to** invoice number 146.
⑥ Please see the agenda **attached** here.
⑦ I work in the IT department **at** Transtech.
⑧ I **am** writing to invite you to a meeting next week.
⑨ Please **don't** hesitate to contact me.
⑩ Please return your signed contract **ASAP**.
⑪ I **would** be grateful if you could get back to me soon.
⑫ I am writing **with** regard to your complaint.
⑬ Please find the minutes **attached** here.
⑭ I would **be** grateful if we could arrange a meeting.
⑮ I work **in** the company's catering department.
⑯ I am the new Head of Sales **at** Codequote.
⑰ I am writing with regard **to** our schedule.
⑱ Please let me know if you **have** any questions.

⑲ Please **find** the new designs attached here.

47.2 ◄))
① I am writing with regard to your latest feedback.
② Please find the invoice attached here.
③ I would be grateful if you could pay the outstanding invoice.
④ If you have any questions, please do not hesitate to contact me.

47.3 ◄))
① I am writing with **regard to our invoice number AB3168**.
② I work in **the accounts department at Shuberg's**.
③ I would be grateful if you **could let us know when you have been paid**.
④ I deal with **the supply and payment of invoices**.
⑤ It has come to our attention **that invoice DY895 has not been paid**.
⑥ I wonder if **you are aware that we have not been paid**.

① I am writing to **inform you that we are going to use a new supplier**.

47.4 ◄))
① He **is giving** all the candidates a task to do before their interview.
② We **are meeting** other suppliers on Tuesday.
③ Sam **is going to make** coffee for the CEO's visitors.
④ Carlos **is presenting** the sales figures tomorrow.
⑤ We **are going to discuss** sales figures for the last quarter.
⑥ They **are giving** all their clients a voucher.
⑦ He **is going to travel** to Italy to meet the new CEO.
⑧ Greg **is going to pack** all the boxes into the delivery van.
⑨ A famous hairdresser **is going to open** the new salon.
⑩ We **are launching** the new company logo at the sales conference.
⑪ The company **is going to recycle** all the stationery with the old logo.

47.5 ◄))
① I am writing with regard to the shareholders' meeting on Thursday.
② We are meeting new clients at the Radcliffe Hotel.
③ The meeting is taking place in the hotel's conference center.
④ We are going to discuss the last quarter's sales figures.
⑤ The new CEO is taking questions after his presentation.
⑥ He is going to discuss the company's future marketing strategy.

47.6
③

ENGLISH
FOR EVERYONE

LIBRO DE EJERCICIOS NIVEL ❷

BUSINESS ENGLISH

Nivel ❷ Contenidos

Presentaciones

Tienes muchas expresiones para presentarte cuando entras en una empresa. Los demás también tienen otras expresiones para presentarte.

✿ **Lenguaje** Present simple y present continuous
Aa Vocabulario Etiqueta de las presentaciones
🧩 **Habilidad** Presentarte a ti mismo y a otros

1.1 COMPLETA LOS ESPACIOS CON LAS PALABRAS DEL RECUADRO

How do you _____*do*_____ ? I'm Christophe from BlueTech.

❶ I'd like to _____ you to Marco from IT.

❷ You _____ be Paola from Madrid.

❸ Gloria, _____ Julia, our new secretary.

❹ Have you two _____ each other before?

❺ Great to _____ you again!

❻ _____ to meet you, Antonio.

❼ Sanjay has _____ me all about you.

❽ I don't _____ we've met before, have we?

❾ It's a _____ to meet you.

| pleasure | see | ~~do~~ | told | met | must | think | meet | introduce | Nice |

🔊

184

1.2 CONECTA EL INICIO Y EL FINAL DE CADA PRESENTACIÓN

Peter, Philippe, I'm not sure	Gerald, our new sales manager.
❶ Simone, I'd like to introduce you to	met. My name's Jana.
❷ Hello. I don't think we've	if you have met each other.
❸ You must be Selma from the	so much about your work.
❹ Hi, Omar. I think we	Colin, meet Liam. He's joining our team soon.
❺ My boss has told me	Chicago branch. Great to meet you.
❻ This is Colin from IT.	met at the conference in Dubai last year.

🔊

1.3 LEE EL ARTÍCULO Y RESPONDE A LAS PREGUNTAS

The author says that meeting people is easy.
True ☐ **False** ☐ **Not given** ✓

❶ Meeting people will always make you successful.
True ☐ **False** ☐ **Not given** ☐

❷ You should talk about your recent experiences.
True ☐ **False** ☐ **Not given** ☐

❸ The author thinks food is a good topic of conversation.
True ☐ **False** ☐ **Not given** ☐

❹ You shouldn't ask how much someone earns.
True ☐ **False** ☐ **Not given** ☐

❺ The author suggests talking about your education.
True ☐ **False** ☐ **Not given** ☐

❻ The author says that you shouldn't talk about clients.
True ☐ **False** ☐ **Not given** ☐

ESSENTIAL SKILLS

Meeting and greeting

Meeting new people isn't always easy, but it's an essential skill for a young business professional.

Whether you're looking for a new job, hope to grow your business, or just want to find new clients, you need to talk to the right people. It doesn't always lead to success, but it can provide a great first step. So, what's the best way to start talking?

Talk about your recent experience: "I'm working with some great software engineers at the moment" is a great way to start. You can tell them about your personal life and interests: "I play golf with my friend on the weekend" might be a good starter. But you shouldn't talk about things that are too personal. If you ask someone how much money they earn, they might be offended! Another good idea is to talk about one of your clients: "I often work with ElectroSan, an exciting new Japanese start-up." You will soon find that the person you're talking to wants to know more...

I staying at the hotel on Park Lane all this week.
I'm staying at the hotel on Park Lane all this week.

1 I am catching the train to work at 8:15am each morning.

2 We are having a new printer that is difficult to use.

3 I working at the Guangdong branch all this August.

4 Sanchez is knowing Katie because they worked together.

5 Do you enjoying this presentation? I think it's great.

6 Tim isn't knowing Anna from the Montevideo branch.

7 Marek is liking the new furniture we bought for the office.

8 How are you spelling your name?

9 The meeting usually is take only half an hour.

10 Doug is really enjoy the conference this year.

11 I'd like introduce you to my manager, José Rodriguez.

12 Clara working from 8:30 to 4:30 on Thursdays and Fridays.

1.5 TACHA LAS PALABRAS INCORRECTAS DE CADA FRASE Y DI LAS FRASES EN VOZ ALTA

Raul ~~presents~~ / is presenting at the moment.

1. Our company is having / have some difficulties at the moment.

2. Pablo, I'd like you to meet / meeting my wife, Elvira.

3. I usually hate conferences, but I enjoy / am enjoying this one a lot.

4. I have / am having two children, a son and a daughter.

5. Michael, I like / I'd like to introduce you to Michelle.

6. I don't think / am not thinking we've met before, have we?

7. It's so great to see / see you again after such a long time.

8. How do you pronounce / are you pronouncing your last name?

9. You must be / being Harold from Copenhagen. Nice to meet you.

10. Hi, I think we met in Oslo, aren't we / didn't we?

Hablar de antiguos empleos es una buena manera de conocer a los colegas. Para hacerlo se suelen utilizar el past simple y el past continuous.

⚙ **Lenguaje** Past simple y past continuous
Aa Vocabulario Compartir experiencias anteriores
🧩 **Habilidad** Hablar sobre el pasado

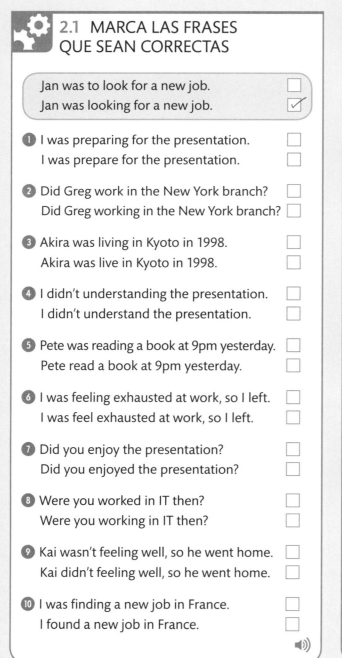

2.1 MARCA LAS FRASES QUE SEAN CORRECTAS

Jan was to look for a new job. ☐
Jan was looking for a new job. ✓

1. I was preparing for the presentation. ☐
   I was prepare for the presentation. ☐

2. Did Greg work in the New York branch? ☐
   Did Greg working in the New York branch? ☐

3. Akira was living in Kyoto in 1998. ☐
   Akira was live in Kyoto in 1998. ☐

4. I didn't understanding the presentation. ☐
   I didn't understand the presentation. ☐

5. Pete was reading a book at 9pm yesterday. ☐
   Pete read a book at 9pm yesterday. ☐

6. I was feeling exhausted at work, so I left. ☐
   I was feel exhausted at work, so I left. ☐

7. Did you enjoy the presentation? ☐
   Did you enjoyed the presentation? ☐

8. Were you worked in IT then? ☐
   Were you working in IT then? ☐

9. Kai wasn't feeling well, so he went home. ☐
   Kai didn't feeling well, so he went home. ☐

10. I was finding a new job in France. ☐
    I found a new job in France. ☐

🔊

2.2 ESCUCHA EL AUDIO Y NUMERA LAS IMÁGENES EN EL ORDEN EN QUE SE DESCRIBEN

A ☐
B 1
C ☐
D ☐
E ☐
F ☐
G ☐
H ☐

2.3 COMPLETA LOS ESPACIOS ESCRIBIENDO LOS VERBOS EN PRESENT PERFECT SIMPLE

Chloe ___*has bought*___ (buy) a new apartment in Paris.

1 Daniel _____ (work) for more than five different law firms.

2 I _____ (take) the bus to work all my working life.

3 The company _____ (employ) five new people since September.

4 Peter is a terrible waiter. He _____ (start) looking for a different job.

5 Andrea _____ (work) here since she graduated in 1999.

6 The factory _____ (produce) 15,000 machines this year.

7 Tim's really happy. He _____ (finish) his presentation for tomorrow.

8 We _____ (sell) our products in more than 25 countries.

9 I _____ (walk) to work since my car broke down.

10 I _____ (decide) that I'm going to retire next year.

11 Dave _____ (take) more time than we expected.

12 I _____ (work) at this office for more than 25 years now.

13 Chris _____ (visit) more than 50 countries so far.

2.4 CONECTA EL INICIO Y EL FINAL DE CADA FRASE

Claire was working for a bank → when she received a new job offer.

for more than ten years.

① Jim was preparing a presentation

more than an hour.

② I've worked at this company

when she received a new job offer.

③ Chris had to wait for a taxi for

before I started working here.

④ Tim moved to New York

when his boss entered the room.

⑤ I ran my own software company

bought a smaller Canadian software firm.

⑥ In 2013, our company

when he was transferred to the US office.

🔊

2.5 LEE EL ARTÍCULO Y RESPONDE A LAS PREGUNTAS

Silvia has just started work for a bank.
True ☐ False ☐ Not given ☑

① Silvia has worked for three employers so far.
True ☐ False ☐ Not given ☐

② Her first job was boring.
True ☐ False ☐ Not given ☐

③ She worked there for six months.
True ☐ False ☐ Not given ☐

④ Silvia worked in a bar while she was studying.
True ☐ False ☐ Not given ☐

⑤ She only worked in the evenings.
True ☐ False ☐ Not given ☐

⑥ She was working as an intern until recently.
True ☐ False ☐ Not given ☐

Silvia's Blog

HOME | ENTRIES | ABOUT | CONTACT

POSTED FRIDAY, 7:30AM

On the up!

I've just started my new job at Moda Fashions in Edinburgh. I've worked for three different employers so far, and I'm hoping that this job will be the best I've had.

My first job was in a local supermarket. I hated it. I was bored, I had no responsibilities, and the customers were often rude to me. I left after only three months.

After that, I worked in a bar. It was more interesting and I met some interesting people. I was studying for my business diploma while I worked there, so I had something to dream about.

Then I started to become interested in fashion. I was working as an intern for a small fashion agency when I received my job offer. I'm so excited.

2.6 TACHA LAS PALABRAS INCORRECTAS DE CADA FRASE Y DI LAS FRASES EN VOZ ALTA

My doctor told / ~~was telling~~ me that I should take a vacation.

1. At 3pm yesterday, I discussed / was discussing the new software with our IT team.

2. While Susan has eaten / was eating lunch, her team was working hard.

3. Karl moved to Berlin when he lost / has lost his job in Paris.

4. Alan traveled / was traveling to work when he received a call from his wife.

5. In 2007 I was working / have worked in the company headquarters in Geneva.

6. I have lived / was living in San Francisco since 2003.

7. Peter is sleeping / was sleeping at his desk when his phone rang.

8. They was / have been based in Frankfurt since 1994.

9. While I was living / have living in France, I worked as a waiter.

10. Derek was buying / bought his first house in 2009.

11. What were you doing / have you done at 4pm this afternoon?

12. I was studying / studied in college when I decided to work as a lawyer.

13. Who was in the meeting room when you entered / have entered?

14. We were selling / sold our first machine in China in 2003.

Aa 3.1 **DEPARTAMENTOS** ESCRIBE LAS PALABRAS DEL RECUADRO DEBAJO DE SU CORRESPONDIENTE DEFINICIÓN

Deals with buying goods and raw materials

Purchasing

1 Deals with employee relations and matters such as hiring staff

2 Ensures that all technological systems are working and maintained

3 Deals with selling a finished product to outside markets

4 Deals with maintaining a positive public image for a company

5 Ensures that all contracts and company activities are legal

6 Ensures the smooth day-to-day running of the practical aspects of a company

7 Deals with organization and internal and external communication

8 Deals with researching and developing future products for a company

9 Deals with money matters, from paying bills to projecting sales

10 Deals with promoting products

11 Ensures all manufacturing stages run smoothly

Public Relations (PR)   Administration   Research and Development (R&D)   Production

Facilities / Office Services   Accounts / Finance   Information Technology (IT)

Human Resources (HR)   Sales   ~~Purchasing~~   Legal   Marketing

Aa 3.2 **ROLES** ESCRIBE LAS PALABRAS DEL RECUADRO DEBAJO DE SU CORRESPONDIENTE DIBUJO

employer

① _____

② _____

③ _____

④ _____

⑤ _____

manager

Chief Executive Officer (CEO)

~~employer~~

Chief Financial Officer (CFO)

employee

assistant

🔊

Aa 3.3 **DESCRIBIR ROLES** ESCRIBE LAS PALABRAS DEL RECUADRO DEBAJO DE SU CORRESPONDIENTE DEFINICIÓN

To ensure something runs smoothly

to look after

① To be employed by a company

② To have a particular job or role

③ To have the duty of ensuring something is done effectively

④ To have control and author ty over something

⑤ To be employed in a department or area of an industry

to work as   ~~to look after~~   to be in charge of   to be responsible for   to work in   to work for

🔊

193

Hablar de cambios

Puedes hablar de muchas maneras sobre cambios en el trabajo en el pasado y en el presente. Muchas expresiones incluyen "used to", que tiene distintos significados.

⚙️ **Lenguaje** "Used to", "be / get used to"

Aa Vocabulario Charla informal

🧩 **Habilidad** Hablar sobre cambios en el trabajo

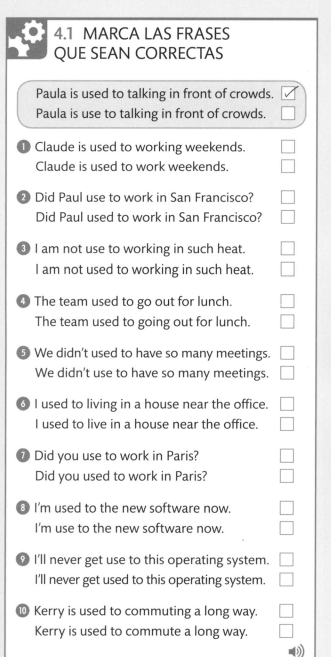

4.1 MARCA LAS FRASES QUE SEAN CORRECTAS

Paula is used to talking in front of crowds. ☑️
Paula is use to talking in front of crowds. ☐

1. Claude is used to working weekends. ☐
   Claude is used to work weekends. ☐

2. Did Paul use to work in San Francisco? ☐
   Did Paul used to work in San Francisco? ☐

3. I am not use to working in such heat. ☐
   I am not used to working in such heat. ☐

4. The team used to go out for lunch. ☐
   The team used to going out for lunch. ☐

5. We didn't used to have so many meetings. ☐
   We didn't use to have so many meetings. ☐

6. I used to living in a house near the office. ☐
   I used to live in a house near the office. ☐

7. Did you use to work in Paris? ☐
   Did you used to work in Paris? ☐

8. I'm used to the new software now. ☐
   I'm use to the new software now. ☐

9. I'll never get use to this operating system. ☐
   I'll never get used to this operating system. ☐

10. Kerry is used to commuting a long way. ☐
    Kerry is used to commute a long way. ☐

🔊

4.2 ESCUCHA EL AUDIO Y NUMERA LAS IMÁGENES EN EL ORDEN EN QUE SE DESCRIBEN

4.3 VUELVE A ESCRIBIR LAS FRASES PONIENDO LAS PALABRAS EN SU ORDEN CORRECTO

working | Peter | used | from | to | home. | is

Peter is used to working from home.

① to | time. | We | use | didn't | so | have | free | much

_____

② get | the | used | on | to | never | I'll | left. | driving

_____

③ to | branch? | use | Anthony | work | Did | in | the | Frankfurt

_____

④ get up | to | I | to | am | having | 6am. | used | at

_____

⑤ used | Derek | to | isn't | so | work. | commuting | far | to

_____

⑥ got | new | The | hasn't | to | the | team | system. | used | operating

_____

⑦ lunch | near | used | the | We | to | in | café | park. | have | the

_____

⑧ giving | Danielle | isn't | presentations. | to | used

_____

⑨ to | Pam | in | branch | used | work | the | Cologne. | in

_____

⑩ uniform | Phil | used | a | to | isn't | work. | wearing | for

_____

🔊

4.4 CONECTA LAS EXPRESIONES QUE SIGNIFICAN LO MISMO

I worked in a bank in the past.	She's not used to working long hours.
❶ She doesn't usually work long hours.	I used to work as a doctor.
❷ In the past I was a doctor.	I used to work in a bank.
❸ Dan's driven on the left for years.	She's used to getting up early.
❹ She began getting up early 10 years ago.	I'm not used to spicy food.
❺ I tried Indian food once. It's spicy!	Dan's used to driving on the left.
❻ I still hate the weather in England after 20 years.	I'm not used to working so late.
❼ I don't usually work this late.	We're getting used to the new boss.
❽ We've had our new boss for three months.	I'll never get used to English weather.

 4.5 MARCA LA MEJOR RESPUESTA PARA CADA INTERVENCIÓN

Are you getting used to your new job?

- Yes, but there's a lot to remember. ✓
- Of course I am. ☐

❸ Would you like to go for lunch?
- I'm not used to invitations. ☐
- That would be great! ☐

❶ Would you like some coffee?

- No, thanks. I'm fine. ☐
- I'm used to drinking tea. ☐

❹ Have you seen that new movie?

- I haven't yet. Is it any good? ☐
- Thanks. Tomorrow would be good. ☐

❷ You look exhausted, Jenny.

- I'm not used to this hot weather! ☐
- I will sleep later. ☐

❺ How was your commute?

- I hate public transportation. ☐
- I'm getting used to the traffic. ☐

4.6 TACHA LAS PALABRAS INCORRECTAS DE CADA FRASE Y DI LAS FRASES EN VOZ ALTA

I took a while to get used to / ~~am used~~ to the weather here.

1   Are you used to / got used to living in a tropical country yet?

2   I was used to / used to travel to work on foot before they built the metro.

3   When I lived in Berlin, we used to / get used to live in an apartment downtown.

4   Were you used to / Did you use to work in the Edinburgh branch?

5   I grew up in Japan, so I'm used to / got used to driving on the left.

6   Arnold's used to / use to waking up at 5am every morning.

7   I used to / am used to working for a demanding boss.

8   When I was a child, I didn't get used to / use to like going to school.

9   We are used to / used to go to Florida each year on vacation.

10 My father used to / getting used to work in a factory until it closed down.

05 Delegar tareas

Tal vez quieras delegar tareas a tus colegas cuando haya mucho trabajo. Para ello, en inglés se utilizan varios verbos modales para indicar el nivel de obligación.

⚙ **Lenguaje** Verbos modales de obligación
Aa Vocabulario Delegación y educación
🧩 **Habilidad** Delegar tareas a los colegas

5.1 MARCA LAS FRASES QUE SEAN CORRECTAS

Peter has to stop working during lunch. ☑
Peter has stop working during lunch. ☐

❶ Staff must not smoking in the building. ☐
Staff must not smoke in the building. ☐

❷ We don't have to go to work tomorrow. ☐
We not have to go to work tomorrow. ☐

❸ I have to go home early on Thursday. ☐
I have going home early on Thursday. ☐

❹ You have to do this assignment today. ☐
You has to do this assignment today. ☐

❺ We need increase sales this year. ☐
We need to increase sales this year. ☐

❻ Jim doesn't have to attend the meeting. ☐
Jim don't have to attend the meeting. ☐

❼ The team must not forget their timesheets. ☐
The team must forget not their timesheets. ☐

❽ Paolo has got to signing up for the course. ☐
Paolo has got to sign up for the course. ☐

❾ We will need to hire new staff this fall. ☐
We will need hiring new staff this fall. ☐

❿ We must improve our productivity. ☐
We must to improve our productivity. ☐

🔊

5.2 ESCUCHA EL AUDIO Y RESPONDE A LAS PREGUNTAS

Una jefa, Janice, encarga tareas a su asistente, James.

Janice is giving a presentation on Wednesday.
True ☐ **False** ☑ **Not given** ☐

❶ Janice's presentation is about marketing.
True ☐ **False** ☐ **Not given** ☐

❷ She hasn't reserved a meeting room yet.
True ☐ **False** ☐ **Not given** ☐

❸ Janice wants James to reserve a small room.
True ☐ **False** ☐ **Not given** ☐

❹ She doesn't need a projector or sound system.
True ☐ **False** ☐ **Not given** ☐

❺ Janice needs the room from 2:30 to 5pm.
True ☐ **False** ☐ **Not given** ☐

❻ Janice wants James to email the team.
True ☐ **False** ☐ **Not given** ☐

❼ James should order refreshments for the break.
True ☐ **False** ☐ **Not given** ☐

❽ Janice wants James to check the visuals.
True ☐ **False** ☐ **Not given** ☐

❾ Janice invites James for lunch to say thank you.
True ☐ **False** ☐ **Not given** ☐

5.3 VUELVE A ESCRIBIR LAS FRASES PONIENDO LAS PALABRAS EN SU ORDEN CORRECTO

have | before | to | the | We | presentation | 5pm. | finish

We have to finish the presentation before 5pm.

1. copy | you | minutes, | of | please? | give | the | Would | Peter | a

2. at | leave | reception. | passes | All | their | must | visitors

3. the | post | to | office, | please? | this | take | Could | letter | you

4. harder | Ramon | to | if | work | he | a promotion. | needs | wants

5. needs | the | Sharon | sign up | training | for | course. | to

6. copy | you | of | Could | on | leave a | agenda | the | please? | my desk,

7. enrolment | before | You | complete | must | the | on | Friday. | form | 5pm

8. inside | smoke | Staff | the | must | building. | not

9. everyone | Would | you | an email | to | the | send | meeting? | about

10. the | by | finish | You | project | must | evening. | Wednesday

🔊

Staff must wear → identity cards at all times in the building.

① The company must change

② I need you to finish

③ Could you keep a

④ Would you inform

⑤ The company has got to

⑥ You don't have

⑦ We need to think

if it wants to survive.

record of everything you spend this week?

the team about the recent changes, please?

the presentation by Friday.

about closing some of our branches.

invest more in training.

to finish the assignment today.

🔊

📖 5.5 LEE EL ARTÍCULO Y RESPONDE A LAS PREGUNTAS

The author says delegating is always effective.
True ☐ False ✓ Not given ☐

① You should think about who to delegate to.
True ☐ False ☐ Not given ☐

② You should follow your team's every step.
True ☐ False ☐ Not given ☐

③ You should organize team-building activities.
True ☐ False ☐ Not given ☐

④ Deadlines should always be flexible.
True ☐ False ☐ Not given ☐

⑤ Your team won't appreciate negative feedback.
True ☐ False ☐ Not given ☐

DAILY OFFICE TIPS

A problem shared... can be a problem halved

Getting your fellow team members involved in your daily tasks makes life easier for everyone, surely? But only when you know how to delegate effectively. In my experience, I've found it helps if you think about these four simple steps:

1 You need to think about who you're delegating to. Are they the best person for the job? What will they give, and what will they learn?

2 You don't have to follow your team's every step or

decision. But you should be communicative and offer advice. A supported team is an effective team.

3 You must set a clear deadline. Everyone needs to know when the project should end. Otherwise your project will lose its momentum.

4 You have to offer your team feedback. Everyone appreciates credit for success, but they also want to know what went wrong.

5.6 RESPONDE AL AUDIO EN VOZ ALTA UTILIZANDO LAS PALABRAS DEL RECUADRO PARA COMPLETAR LOS ESPACIOS

I just received Eric's memo about the conference.

Great. _____Would_____ you print me a copy, please?

1 Is this presentation high priority?

No, I _____ you to finish it today.

2 Is it OK if I hand in the report next week?

I'm sorry, Mike. We really _____ have it by Friday.

3 Can we look around the factory?

I'm sorry, but members of the public _____ enter the building.

4 The new uniforms still haven't arrived.

We need them tomorrow. _____ you call the supplier, please?

5 Do you want me to stay late tonight?

No, you _____ to. The deadline is next week.

6 I'm afraid I still haven't finished the report.

Well, I _____ it by 1pm today.

| don't have | need | ~~Would~~ | must | don't need | Could | must not |

201

06 Vocabulario

Aa 6.1 DINERO Y FINANZAS ESCRIBE LAS PALABRAS DEL RECUADRO DEBAJO DE SU CORRESPONDIENTE DEFINICIÓN

The amount of money that is available to spend on something

a budget

1 To lose money by spending more than you earn

_____

3 Extra money the bank allows you to spend

_____

4 The regular costs of running a business, such as wages

_____

6 To get into a situation where you owe people money

_____

7 To earn just enough to cover the costs of producing a product

_____

9 Money coming into a business

_____

10 An amount of money spent

_____

12 Records of money paid into and out of a business

_____

13 To fall, especially in worth or value

_____

15 To reach the highest point

_____

16 The amount of one currency that you get when you change it for another

_____

2 To charge less than others who sell the same goods or services as you

_____

5 The amount or value of total sales over a particular period

_____

8 A major decline in economic activity

_____

11 A change to more positive business conditions

_____

14 The rate at which money comes into and goes out of a business

_____

17 To no longer be able to exist as a business

_____

to make a loss   an upturn in the market

sales figures   income

an economic downturn   overheads

the exchange rate   cash flow

an overdraft   to get into debt

to go out of business   to peak

expenditure / outlay   ~~a budget~~

to undercut competitors   to drop

accounts   to break even

07 Redactar un informe

Al redactar un informe utiliza diferentes pretéritos para ilustrar el orden de los eventos. También tienes que utilizar expresiones más formales.

⚙ **Lenguaje** Past perfect y past simple
Aa Vocabulario Inglés de negocios formal
🧩 **Habilidad** Redactar informes

7.1 COMPLETA LOS ESPACIOS ESCRIBIENDO LOS VERBOS EN PAST PERFECT O PAST SIMPLE

We ___*stayed*___ **(stay)** in the hotel that our client ___*had recommended*___ **(recommend)** to us.

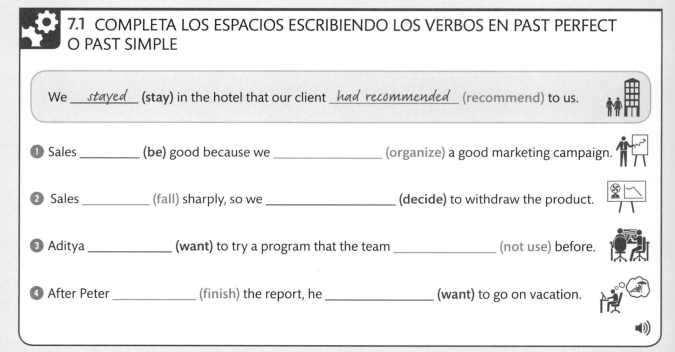

① Sales _____ **(be)** good because we _____ **(organize)** a good marketing campaign.

② Sales _____ **(fall)** sharply, so we _____ **(decide)** to withdraw the product.

③ Aditya _____ **(want)** to try a program that the team _____ **(not use)** before.

④ After Peter _____ **(finish)** the report, he _____ **(want)** to go on vacation.

🔊

7.2 TACHA LAS PALABRAS INCORRECTAS DE CADA FRASE

Sandra **gave** / ~~had given~~ a presentation that she ~~prepared~~ / **had prepared** two years ago.

① Ramon **wrote** / had written ten pages of the report when his computer **crashed** / had crashed.

② Many of our employees **did not** / had not visited the factory before and **were** / had been very impressed.

③ Bob's speech **was** / had been disappointing because he **didn't prepare** / hadn't prepared well.

④ Nobody **told** / had told the conference delegates where their hotel **was** / had been.

⑤ I **didn't delegate** / hadn't delegated tasks to Kai before, but I **thought** / had thought he did a good job.

🔊

7.3 VUELVE A ESCRIBIR LAS FRASES CORRIGIENDO LOS ERRORES

> The purpose of this report is review our advertising campaign for next year.
> *The purpose of this report is to review our advertising campaign for next year.*

1 The followed report will explore our new sales strategy.

_____

2 As can be seeing in the table, we have invested $4 million this year.

_____

3 Some of our customers have stating that they are not satisfied with the result.

_____

4 Our initial investigation suggestion that this is not true.

_____

5 Our beginning recommendation is to reduce the budget by 50 percent.

_____

6 We consulting a number of focus groups for this report.

_____

🔊

Aa 7.4 CONECTA EL INICIO Y EL FINAL DE CADA FRASE

We consulted a number	is to review our current sales strategy.
1 The purpose of our report	we should invest more in R&D.
2 The following report presents	of focus groups for this report.
3 Our clients stated that	proceed with the sale of the subsidiary.
4 Based on the initial research,	a summary of our findings.
5 Our principal recommendation is to	they were unhappy with the changes.

🔊

LOCATION REPORT

The aim of this report is to assess the advantages and disadvantages of moving the company headquarters to Alchester. The following report will look at location, transportation, housing, and the available tax breaks.

Location The site in Alchester is 20 miles from downtown. The town has two large colleges and a number of other IT companies. However, it is more than 200 miles to the nearest major city.

Transportation There is an airport and the rail connections to other cities are good. However, the airport is far (30 miles away) and the station can only be reached by taxi.

Housing Based on the initial research, we concluded that housing is much more affordable than in major cities. The proposed site is near an attractive suburb.

Tax subsidies The local government offers large grants to companies that want to move to the area. However, these are only available if the company is willing to stay in the area for more than ten years.

Conclusion Many of our employees stated that they would not be happy living so far from a city. Others stated that they found the affordable accommodation very attractive. The grants offered are attractive, but the company will need to make a big commitment.

What does the report aim to assess?

The company's profits for the year ☐

A potential new location for the company ☑

The company's current location ☐

❶ Where is the site in Alchester?

20 miles from downtown ☐

200 miles from downtown ☐

Downtown ☐

❷ What is good about the transportation links?

The location of the station ☐

The location of the airport ☐

Rail connections to other cities ☐

❸ What are the findings about housing?

It is affordable in Alchester ☐

The company is still researching it ☐

The suburbs are not attractive ☐

❹ What must companies do to get a tax subsidy?

Move to Alchester ☐

Stay in Alchester for over ten years ☐

Work with the local government ☐

❺ What is the conclusion of the report?

The company will move to Alchester ☐

The company won't move to Alchester ☐

A decision has not yet been made ☐

7.6 MARCA LAS FRASES QUE SEAN CORRECTAS

As can be see in the table, our profits have declined by 9 percent this year. ☐
As can be seen in the table, our profits have declined by 9 percent this year. ☑

1. The purpose of this report is to compare the two factories. ☐
   The purpose of this report is compare the two factories. ☐

2. Focus groups had been consulted before we implemented the policy. ☐
   Focus groups had be consulted before we implemented the policy. ☐

3. Sales of our products are fallen in comparison with the previous quarter. ☐
   Sales of our products had fallen in comparison with the previous quarter. ☐

4. Our principal recommendation is to increase investment in R&D. ☐
   Our principal recommendation is increase investment in R&D. ☐

5. Profits had risen by more than 20 percent in the first half of 2015. ☐
   Profits had risen with more than 20 percent in the first half of 2015. ☐

🔊

7.7 COMPLETA LOS ESPACIOS CON LAS PALABRAS DEL RECUADRO

CLOSED We closed the branch after our costs had _____ *risen* _____ by more than 20 percent.

1. In this report we will _____ the findings of our research.

2. The _____ of this report is to investigate the pros and cons of the new software.

3. This bar chart _____ the sales figures for the last two years.

4. Our customers _____ that they had been disappointed with the product.

| purpose | stated | compares | ~~risen~~ | present |

🔊

207

Disculparse

El present perfect continuous habla de algo en progreso del pasado que tiene efecto en el presente. Se utiliza para pedir disculpas y explicar los motivos de un problema.

☼ **Lenguaje** Present perfect continuous
Aa Vocabulario Disculpas
Habilidad Disculparse por teléfono

8.1 MARCA LA MEJOR PREGUNTA PARA CADA DECLARACIÓN

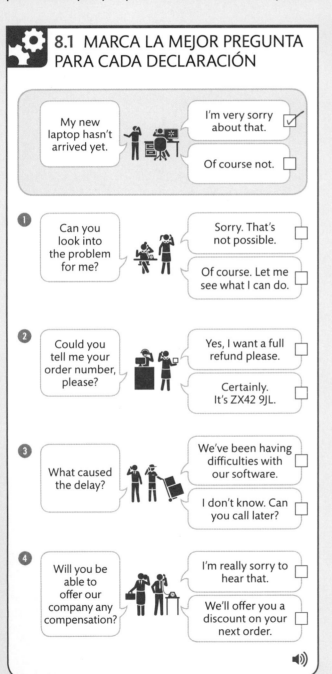

My new laptop hasn't arrived yet.

I'm very sorry about that. ✓

Of course not. ☐

1 Can you look into the problem for me?

Sorry. That's not possible. ☐

Of course. Let me see what I can do. ☐

2 Could you tell me your order number, please?

Yes, I want a full refund please. ☐

Certainly. It's ZX42 9JL. ☐

3 What caused the delay?

We've been having difficulties with our software. ☐

I don't know. Can you call later? ☐

4 Will you be able to offer our company any compensation?

I'm really sorry to hear that. ☐

We'll offer you a discount on your next order. ☐

8.2 VUELVE A ESCRIBIR LAS FRASES CORRIGIENDO LOS ERRORES

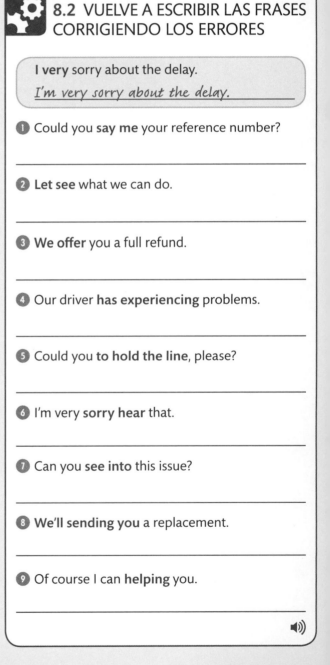

I very sorry about the delay.

I'm very sorry about the delay.

1 Could you **say me** your reference number?

_____

2 **Let see** what we can do.

_____

3 **We offer** you a full refund.

_____

4 Our driver **has experiencing** problems.

_____

5 Could you **to hold the line**, please?

_____

6 I'm very **sorry hear** that.

_____

7 Can you **see into** this issue?

_____

8 **We'll sending you** a replacement.

_____

9 Of course I can **helping** you.

_____

8.3 COMPLETA LOS ESPACIOS CON LAS PALABRAS DEL RECUADRO

Can you _____*look into*_____ the problem for me?

reference

hold

sorry

~~look into~~

offer

experiencing

discount

see

arrived

1. I'm very _____ to hear that, sir.

2. Certainly. Let's _____ what I can do.

3. Could you tell me your _____ number, please?

4. Could you please _____ the line?

5. I'm sorry. Our IT system's been _____ difficulties.

6. My order _____ dirty and broken.

7. Can you _____ any compensation?

8. Of course. We'll give you a _____ on your next order.

8.4 TACHA LA PALABRA INCORRECTA DE CADA FRASE Y DI TODAS LAS FRASES EN VOZ ALTA

I'm very **sorry** / ~~sad~~ about the delay. Let's see what we can do.

1. Could you look **through** / **into** the problem for me?

2. The company **has** / **is** been experiencing difficulties recently.

3. Please **keep** / **hold** the line for a moment.

4. I've been **wait** / **waiting** all day for my order to arrive.

209

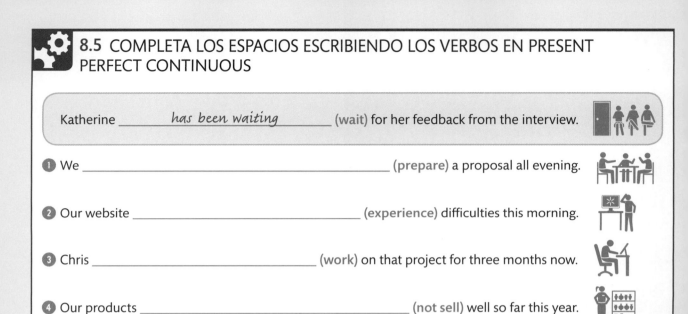

8.5 COMPLETA LOS ESPACIOS ESCRIBIENDO LOS VERBOS EN PRESENT PERFECT CONTINUOUS

Katherine _____ *has been waiting* _____ (wait) for her feedback from the interview.

① We _____ (prepare) a proposal all evening.

② Our website _____ (experience) difficulties this morning.

③ Chris _____ (work) on that project for three months now.

④ Our products _____ (not sell) well so far this year.

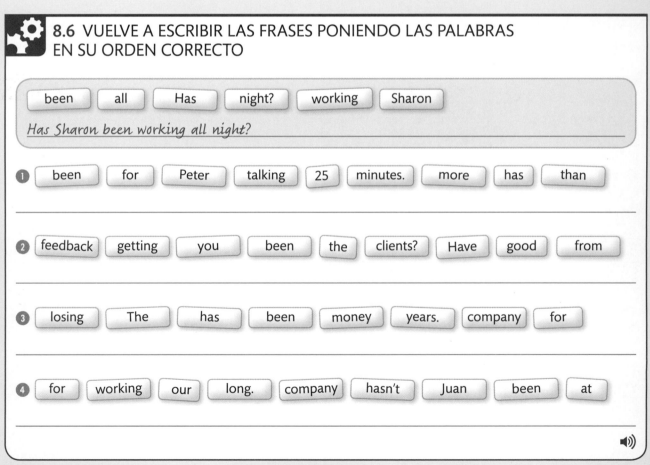

8.6 VUELVE A ESCRIBIR LAS FRASES PONIENDO LAS PALABRAS EN SU ORDEN CORRECTO

| been | all | Has | night? | working | Sharon |

Has Sharon been working all night?

① | been | for | Peter | talking | 25 | minutes. | more | has | than |

_____

② | feedback | getting | you | been | the | clients? | Have | good | from |

_____

③ | losing | The | has | been | money | years. | company | for |

_____

④ | for | working | our | long. | company | hasn't | Juan | been | at |

_____

8.7 ESCUCHA EL AUDIO Y NUMERA DESPUÉS LAS FRASES EN EL ORDEN EN QUE LAS ESCUCHES

Jock Douglas llama a sus proveedores para preguntar por un pedido que espera.

A I've been waiting for three weeks now, so I'm not at all happy. ☐

B Could you tell me your order reference number? ☐

C We would like to offer you a gift voucher worth $100. ☐

D Could you please hold the line one moment? ☐

E I'm really sorry to hear that, Mr Douglas. ☑ 1

F Your order was dispatched yesterday. ☐

8.8 LEE EL CORREO ELECTRÓNICO Y MARCA EL RESUMEN CORRECTO

❶ The wrong model of laptop arrived. This happened because of a software problem at the warehouse. The company has offered a 10 percent discount on the next order. ☐

❷ The wrong model of printer arrived. This happened because of a software problem at the warehouse. The company has offered a 40 percent discount on the next order. ☐

❸ The wrong model of software arrived. This happened because of a flood at the warehouse. The company has offered a 25 percent discount on the next order. ☐

❹ The wrong model of laptop arrived. This happened because of a software upgrade at the warehouse. The company has offered a 25 percent discount on the next order. ☐

✉ ⌄ ✕

To: Mario Grando

Subject: Your order

Dear Mario Grando,

Thank you for your email regarding your order dated August 4th. I am very sorry to hear that the wrong model of laptop arrived, and we apologize for the inconvenience this caused. I've been looking into the problem and see that you received model A147 instead of A149. We've been upgrading the software in our warehouse recently, and, unfortunately, last week we were unable to fulfill all our orders correctly. As an apology, however, we'd like to offer you a refund of 25 percent off your next order with our company. I've attached the voucher to this email.

Best regards,
Mohammed Ahmed

Aa 9.1 TECNOLOGÍA PARA COMUNICARSE ESCRIBE LAS EXPRESIONES DEL RECUADRO DEBAJO DE SU CORRESPONDIENTE DEFINICIÓN

Computer programs

software

① Internet-based tools for communicating with friends and communities

_____

③ Computerized; not operated by a human

_____

④ To enter or connect to something

_____

⑥ Current and modern

_____

⑦ Easy for the operator to use

_____

⑨ A group conversation held by phone

_____

⑩ Losing a phone or internet connection

_____

⑫ A small computing device, such as a smartphone or tablet, that is easily carried

_____

⑬ To work without an internet connection

_____

⑮ To connect a mobile device to electricity to give it more power

_____

⑯ A name and code used to access an account on a computing device

_____

2 A collection of linked pages accessed through the internet

_____

5 To work with an internet connection

_____

8 To save an extra copy of a document in case the original is lost

_____

11 To get an application from the internet onto a device or computer

_____

14 An email has been automatically returned without reaching the intended recipient

_____

17 A system of interconnected technology

_____

social media

to download an app

a username and password

to work offline

to charge   a website

to access

automated   to back up

an email has bounced

up to date

a mobile device   user-friendly

~~software~~   a network

to work online

breaking up

a conference call

10 Planear por correo electrónico

Dispones de diversas formas de hacer planes y comprobar la información por correo electrónico. Asegúrate de que incluso los mensajes informales son educados.

⚙ **Lenguaje** Lenguaje del correo electrónico
Aa Vocabulario Reuniones y talleres
Habilidad Hacer planes

10.1 CONECTA EL INICIO Y EL FINAL DE CADA FRASE

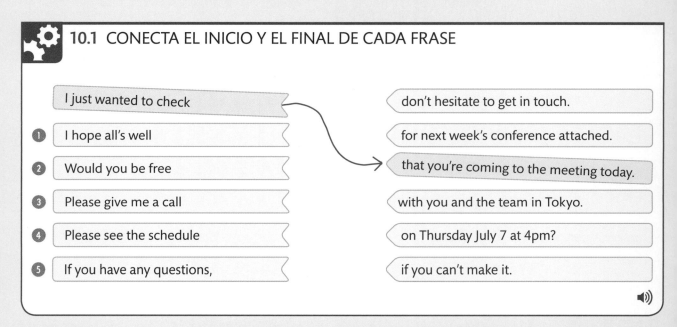

I just wanted to check — that you're coming to the meeting today.

1 I hope all's well — don't hesitate to get in touch.

2 Would you be free — for next week's conference attached.

3 Please give me a call — with you and the team in Tokyo.

4 Please see the schedule — on Thursday July 7 at 4pm?

5 If you have any questions, — if you can't make it.

🔊

10.2 COMPLETA LOS ESPACIOS CON LAS PALABRAS DEL RECUADRO

I just wanted to ___*check*___ that you're attending this week's meeting.

1 I was _____ if you could help me prepare my presentation.

2 Would you be free to _____ on Thursday evening?

3 I'm _____ Sanjay and Anita in on this email.

4 I _____ all's well with you and the team in Delhi.

5 Please see the minutes of yesterday's meeting _____ .

6 If you have any _____ , please let me know.

7 How _____ joining us at the pizza place later this evening?

about
hope
meet
questions
~~check~~
copying
wondering
attached

🔊

214

> I hope all well with you and the team.
> *I hope all's well with you and the team.*

❶ I just wanted check that you're coming to the presentation.

_____

❷ Would you free next Wednesday morning at 11:30?

_____

❸ Please find a copy of the report attach.

_____

❹ If you any questions, please let me know.

_____

❺ I'm copy Ricardo in on this.

_____

10.4 LEE EL CORREO ELECTRÓNICO Y MARCA EL RESUMEN CORRECTO

❶ Jerome wants to meet tomorrow to discuss the new software package. He has asked Claude to send him the timetable. ☐

❷ Jerome is inviting Françoise and Claude to come to software training in Room 3. ☐

❸ Jerome is emailing to check that Claude is coming to the IT meeting. Françoise has sent the agenda and a memo. ☐

❹ Jerome is inviting Françoise to a meeting with the IT team. He has sent Françoise and Claude a copy of the agenda. ☐

To: Françoise Thomas

Subject: Software package

Hi Françoise,

I hope all's well with you and the team. I just wanted to check that you got the email I sent yesterday about the new software package that goes live on Thursday. Claude and I want to meet the IT department tomorrow morning to discuss it. Would you be free to join us in meeting room 3 at 9:30am? Please find attached an agenda and memo about the software specifications. I've copied Claude in on this message. If you have any questions, please let me know.

Best regards,

Jerome

11 Informar a los clientes

Utiliza el present continuous para informar a los clientes de la situación actual y de los planes de futuro. Los tiempos continuos también suavizan las preguntas y peticiones.

⚙ **Lenguaje** Tiempos continuos
Aa Vocabulario Planes y calendarios
🧩 **Habilidad** Mantener informados a los clientes

⚙ 11.1 VUELVE A ESCRIBIR LAS FRASES EN PRESENT CONTINUOUS CORRIGIENDO LOS ERRORES

> I **are hoping** to finish my report on July's sales later today.
> _I am hoping to finish my report on July's sales later today._

❶ Mohammed **is meet** the new supplier to discuss a new deal.

_____

❷ Jola **is talk** to Sales this afternoon to agree new discounts.

_____

❸ They **is aiming** to have the presentation ready by 5:00pm.

_____

❹ I **am writeing** to inform you that there is a delay with the part you need.

_____

❺ We **still are waiting** to hear from the Chinese partners.

_____

🔊

🎧 11.2 ESCUCHA EL AUDIO Y MARCA SI LAS ACTIVIDADES DE CADA IMAGEN PASAN EN EL PRESENTE O EL FUTURO

Presente ☑ Futuro ☐

❶ Presente ☐ Futuro ☐

❷ Presente ☐ Futuro ☐

❸ Presente ☐ Futuro ☐

❹ Presente ☐ Futuro ☐

Aa 11.3 LEE LAS PISTAS Y ESCRIBE LAS PALABRAS DEL RECUADRO EN SUS LUGARES CORRESPONDIENTES EN LA PARRILLA

HORIZONTALES

1 To pause

2 To get

3 To make something definite

VERTICALES

4 To tell

5 To like more

6 To promise

Crossword across clue 1: ¹h e s i t ⁶a t e

assure   obtain   confirm   ~~hesitate~~   prefer   inform

11.4 MARCA LA FRASE MÁS EDUCADA DE CADA PAR

You need to extend the deadline. ☐
I was wondering if you would consider extending the deadline. ☑

1 Are you going to the new product launch? ☐
Will you be attending the launch of the new products? ☐

2 I was wondering if we could put our meeting back to tomorrow. ☐
Can we put our meeting back to tomorrow? ☐

3 We want to send new designs by Friday. ☐
We are aiming to send the new designs by Friday. ☐

4 Will you be paying for the order in cash or by card? ☐
Will you pay in cash or by card? ☐

5 I was wondering if you would take the clients out for dinner. ☐
Will you take the clients out for dinner? ☐

🔊

11.5 VUELVE A ESCRIBIR LAS FRASES PONIENDO LAS PALABRAS EN SU ORDEN CORRECTO

| we | laptop. | I | if | borrow | could | your | was | wondering |

I was wondering if we could borrow your laptop.

1 | final | the | We | report. | still | sales | putting | are | together |

_____

2 | tomorrow's | you | presentation | be | Will | conference? | the | giving | at |

_____

3 | postpone | were | if | We | could | meeting. | wondering | we | our |

_____

🔊

11.6 LEE EL CORREO ELECTRÓNICO Y RESPONDE A LAS PREGUNTAS

Sanjay's project is running on time.
True ☐ **False** ☑ **Not given** ☐

1 Sanjay wants to meet the suppliers.
True ☐ **False** ☐ **Not given** ☐

2 The new designs for the fabric are complex.
True ☐ **False** ☐ **Not given** ☐

3 The fabrics will be delivered in two weeks' time.
True ☐ **False** ☐ **Not given** ☐

4 Sanjay offers Fiona compensation.
True ☐ **False** ☐ **Not given** ☐

✉

To: Fiona McRae

Subject: Project update

Dear Fiona,

I was wondering if we could have a brief project update meeting as the project is running late. Unfortunately, the new designs for the fabric that we plan to launch have proved more complicated to print than we initially thought. The suppliers in Bangladesh have informed us that the final printed materials will be with us at the end of this month, not in two weeks as per our order.

The suppliers have told us they will work around the clock to minimize the delay, and they apologize for any inconvenience this may cause us.

Yours truly,
Sanjay

12 Comunicación informal

Los phrasal verbs se componen de dos o más palabras. Por lo general se utilizan en inglés informal oral y escrito, por ejemplo en mensajes y peticiones a colegas.

⚙ **Lenguaje** Phrasal verbs

Aa **Vocabulario** Planes

🧩 **Habilidad** Mantener informados a los colegas

⚙ 12.1 TACHA LAS PALABRAS INCORRECTAS DE CADA FRASE

 Is the printer jammed again? I'll ask Dave to look **into** / ~~out~~ / ~~up~~ it.

① Can you deal **with** / **at** / **out** the cleaners, please? The kitchen is a mess.

② Can we catch **on** / **up** / **off** later this morning at around 11:00?

③ Is the fridge broken again? I'll **catch** / **deal** / **look** into that now.

④ Have we run **on** / **out** / **in** of paper? There's none in the photocopier.

🔊

⚙ 12.2 COMPLETA LOS ESPACIOS CON LOS PHRASAL VERBS DEL RECUADRO

Let's _____*catch up*_____ now you're back from your vacation.

① Can we _____ a meeting with Marketing and Sales?

② Have you asked Surina to _____ all the paperwork?

③ The printer has _____ of ink again.

④ I can't _____ what Dave wants me to do.

⑤ I need to _____ the topic of punctuality with you.

figure out	bring up	fix up	~~catch up~~	fill out	run out

🔊

12.3 VUELVE A ESCRIBIR LAS FRASES CAMBIANDO LA POSICIÓN DE LA PARTÍCULA

> Can you **fill out** that form?
> _Can you fill that form out?_

1 I need to **back up** my files.

_____

2 Can you **give out** the agenda?

_____

3 Can we **call off** tomorrow's meeting?

_____

4 Can you **pass on** my message to her?

_____

5 Let me **hand out** the minutes.

_____

6 I want to **put on** my tie.

_____

7 Can you **fix up** another meeting?

_____

8 I need to **send out** an email.

_____

9 We are **taking on** new staff.

_____

10 Can you **set up** the projector?

_____

11 I'd like to **talk over** the sales plan.

_____

🔊

12.4 ESCUCHA EL AUDIO Y RESPONDE A LAS PREGUNTAS

Es el primer día de trabajo de Jack después de las vacaciones. Recibe la llamada de su colega Amanda.

> Why is Amanda calling Jack?
> **To arrange a meeting** ☐
> **To cancel a meeting** ☑
> **To place some orders** ☐

1 What is the problem with Amanda's files?
She hasn't backed them up ☐
She has deleted them ☐
Some of them are missing ☐

2 When does Jack set up a meeting with Amanda?
Thursday morning ☐
Thursday afternoon ☐
Friday morning ☐

3 What does Amanda want Jack to do?
Call customers about their feedback ☐
Deal with new customers ☐
Write a report about feedback ☐

4 What does Jack offer to do?
Delegate some of Amanda's emails ☐
Delete some of Amanda's emails ☐
Deal with some of Amanda's emails ☐

5 What does Amanda ask Jack to pass on?
A message ☐
A package ☐
A sales report ☐

6 What will Jack wear for his site visit?
His best suit ☐
His best tie ☐
His best suit and tie ☐

12.5 TACHA LAS PALABRAS INCORRECTAS DE CADA FRASE Y DI TODAS LAS FRASES EN VOZ ALTA

Can you pass a message **on** / ~~up~~ / ~~off~~ to Syed? I can't make this afternoon's meeting.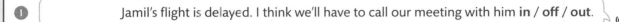

1. Jamil's flight is delayed. I think we'll have to call our meeting with him **in** / **off** / **out**.

2. All employees have to put an apron **in** / **up** / **on** before entering the kitchen.

3. We're hoping to give **off** / **out** / **in** samples of our work at the exhibition.

4. It's really important to back your files **over** / **on** / **up** every night or you could lose work.

12.6 COMPLETA LOS ESPACIOS CON LAS PALABRAS DEL RECUADRO

The paper in the printer has ___run out___ .

1. Khalil has _____ out.

2. She has just _____ on me without saying goodbye!

3. He _____ because he had an important meeting.

4. He gave _____ to everyone at the meeting.

5. They _____ up for later in the week.

his report out	~~run out~~	set a meeting
hung up	put his tie on	filled the form

221

Aa 13.1 PRODUCCIÓN ESCRIBE LAS EXPRESIONES DEL RECUADRO DEBAJO DE LA DEFINICIÓN CORRECTA

Systems that ensure that products are of a high standard

quality control

1 The external wrapping of goods before they are sold

3 Made by a person without the use of a machine

4 Something that is made or produced only once

6 Goods that a company has made but not yet sold

7 A declaration that a product meets certain standards and is suitable for sale

9 The first form of a design that can be changed, copied, or developed

10 A line of people or machinery in a factory, each making a specific part of a product

12 Moving goods from one place to another

13 Found or bought in a morally acceptable way

15 A building or group of buildings where goods are made

16 The process of making large numbers of goods, usually in a factory

2 A process to check that goods meet certain standards

_____

5 Requiring a lot of human effort to make something

_____

8 The basic substances that are used to make a product

_____

11 A place where goods are stored before being shipped to customers or sellers

_____

14 Manufacturing too much of something in relation to demand

_____

17 A company that provides or supplies another company with goods and services

_____

packaging   labor intensive

mass production   shipping

ethically sourced   handmade

raw materials   a one-off production

~~quality control~~   overproduction

stock   product approval

a factory   a prototype

a warehouse   product testing

a supplier   a production line

14 Describir un proceso

La voz pasiva es útil para describir el funcionamiento de un proceso, porque destaca la acción en lugar de la persona o la cosa que la hace.

 Lenguaje La voz pasiva
Aa Vocabulario Procesos y fabricación
Habilidad Debatir cómo se hacen las cosas

14.1 TACHA LAS PALABRAS INCORRECTAS DE CADA FRASE

Our soaps **are made** / ~~maked~~ using the finest French lavender.

1. The media **had been** / **have** told about the press launch and were out in force.

2. New models **are been** / **are being** created to coincide with the premiere of the movie.

3. The design has been **patent** / **patented** so nobody can copy it.

4. Our coffee is **producing** / **produced** using the finest coffee beans from Kenya.

5. It is thought that the sandwich **was** / **were** invented in 1762.

14.2 ESCUCHA EL AUDIO Y NUMERA LAS IMÁGENES EN EL ORDEN EN QUE SE DESCRIBEN

A

B [1]

C

D

E

F

G

H

14.3 VUELVE A ESCRIBIR LAS FRASES EN VOZ PASIVA

> Our distribution team sends out our products from our warehouse in Michigan.
> _Our products are sent out from our warehouse in Michigan by our distribution team._

1 A separate department audits our accounts every May.

_____

2 Our professional coffee tasters approve the coffee blends we produce.

_____

3 Security staff scan all passengers' luggage when they go through Departures.

_____

4 Jane designs all our marketing material for the Asia office.

_____

5 Our packing department checks all the orders before delivery.

_____

6 Stephen updates the database with customers' details.

_____

7 Our cosmetics buyer buys all our ingredients from Fair Trade suppliers.

_____

8 Nicola adds new lines to our women's fashion range on a regular basis.

_____

9 Jason invented the new product tracking app for customers.

_____

10 Our marketing team launched our new website in January.

_____

◀))

14.4 LEE EL ARTÍCULO Y RESPONDE A LAS PREGUNTAS

Bread was invented in modern times.
True ☐ **False** ✓ **Not given** ☐

① Bread is not eaten in many cultures.
True ☐ **False** ☐ **Not given** ☐

② Yeast is added to the dough after kneading.
True ☐ **False** ☐ **Not given** ☐

③ The dough is kneaded for about 10 minutes.
True ☐ **False** ☐ **Not given** ☐

④ Different countries have different shapes of bread.
True ☐ **False** ☐ **Not given** ☐

⑤ The dough is left to rise two times before it is baked.
True ☐ **False** ☐ **Not given** ☐

The stuff of life

This week we look at how bread is made throughout the world.

Bread has been made since prehistoric times and is eaten by most cultures today. But how is it made? A raising agent like yeast is added to flour with warm water. A dough is made and the gluten in the flour is activated by a process called kneading, which is when the dough is massaged for about 10 minutes. The dough is then left in a warm place to rise. Then the air is knocked out of it and it is kneaded a second time. The dough is then shaped into a loaf or rolls. Some of these are very decorative, and individual bakers often have their own special design. Finally, the dough is left to rise again and then baked in a hot oven. The result is delicious warm bread!

14.5 CONECTA LAS FRASES ACTIVAS CON LAS FRASES PASIVAS QUE SIGNIFIQUEN LO MISMO

We must beat our competitors' prices.

The order can't have been taken by her.

① They can't have checked these toys.

Our prices can't be beaten.

② She should have given them a discount.

Our competitors' prices must be beaten.

③ Freya can't have taken the order.

These toys can't have been checked.

④ We can give every customer a free bag.

Faults in the products shouldn't be ignored.

⑤ We shouldn't ignore faults in the products.

A free bag can be given to every customer.

⑥ You can't beat our prices.

His order must have been placed late.

⑦ He must have placed his order late.

A discount should have been given.

🔊

How It's Made

Learn how our cakes are baked.

First, a cake recipe _____ *is chosen* _____ by the cake-maker.

1. Next, the ingredients _____ together to make a cake mixture.

2. Then the cake mixture _____ into cake pans.

3. Next, the cakes _____ in a hot oven.

4. When the cakes are cooked, they _____ out of the oven.

5. The cakes _____ to cool on a wire cooling rack.

6. Finally, the cakes _____ and decorated with icing.

are taken	are mixed	~~is chosen~~	is poured
are assembled	are left	are put	

15 Describir un producto

Al describir un producto, lo más habitual es utilizar adjetivos. Se puede emplear más de uno, pero deben ir siempre en un orden concreto.

⚙ **Lenguaje** Orden de los adjetivos
Aa Vocabulario Adjetivos de opinión y factuales
🧩 **Habilidad** Describir un producto

15.1 ESCRIBE LAS PALABRAS DEL RECUADRO EN LOS GRUPOS CORRECTOS

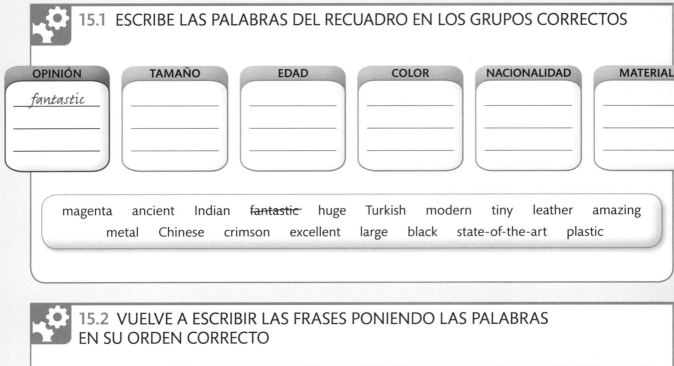

OPINIÓN	TAMAÑO	EDAD	COLOR	NACIONALIDAD	MATERIAL
fantastic					

magenta   ancient   Indian   ~~fantastic~~   huge   Turkish   modern   tiny   leather   amazing

metal   Chinese   crimson   excellent   large   black   state-of-the-art   plastic

15.2 VUELVE A ESCRIBIR LAS FRASES PONIENDO LAS PALABRAS EN SU ORDEN CORRECTO

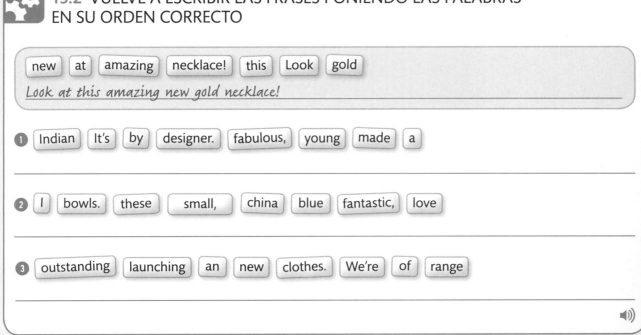

new   at   amazing   necklace!   this   Look   gold

Look at this amazing new gold necklace!

1. Indian   It's   by   designer.   fabulous,   young   made   a

_____

2. I   bowls.   these   small,   china   blue   fantastic,   love

_____

3. outstanding   launching   an   new   clothes.   We're   of   range

_____

🔊

I really like the new red /~~diamond~~ velvet sofas around the office.

1 What a lovely plastic / stylish desk you have!

2 Sam asked me to design a silver / classic brown chair.

3 I brought back some delicious china / Turkish candy from my trip.

4 Do you like this pretty / paper crimson watch for ladies?

5 Do you like our cute green / ugly teddy bear for our new children's range?

6 Our competitors are selling unfashionable / intelligent black suits.

7 Our team is developing an innovative leather / popular interior for our executive car.

8 I love buying large awesome / yellow flowers for the office.

9 Jane has bought an expensive / friendly classic car at an auction.

10 We have an amazing cotton / Italian coffee machine in our office.

11  I have ordered some of those fabulous leather / double-sided business cards.

12 We have an amazing awful / gray oven in our staff kitchen.

13 This is our new lightweight / comfortable digital camera.

15.4 ESCUCHA EL AUDIO Y MARCA LAS COSAS QUE SE DESCRIBEN

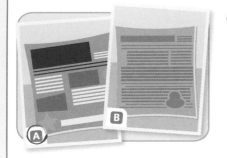

A **B**

1 **A** **B**

2 **A** **B**

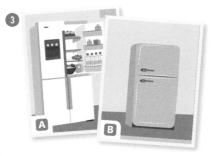

3 **A** **B**

4 **A** **B**

5 **A** **B**

15.5 LEE EL ARTÍCULO Y RESPONDE A LAS PREGUNTAS

Dress Right only sells clothes for men and women.
True ☐ **False** ☐ **Not given** ✓

1 The new range of clothing is mainly beige.
True ☐ **False** ☐ **Not given** ☐

2 Dress Right sells fashionable clothes.
True ☐ **False** ☐ **Not given** ☐

3 The new denim range is ground-breaking.
True ☐ **False** ☐ **Not given** ☐

4 Dress Right only sells uniforms in one set of colors.
True ☐ **False** ☐ **Not given** ☐

5 Dress Right is having fashion shows in all its stores.
True ☐ **False** ☐ **Not given** ☐

Dress Right for all occasions

We have everything you need to dress the family in style, whether it is for school, work, a trip or a special event. Want to know what is new? We have kept our trademark stylish, modern, and colorful style in our new range of clothing. You'll find the usual brown and red clothes as well as fashionable, new bags and shoes. In the Directions collection, there are fabulous, trend-setting styles for both men and women. In addition to this, we are also launching an innovative, modern, denim range of casual wear.

This year also sees the launch of practical, hard-wearing school clothes in a range of colors. So come and see what Dress Right can do for you in a store near you or online.

15.6 DI LAS FRASES EN VOZ ALTA COMPLETANDO LOS ESPACIOS CON LAS PALABRAS DEL RECUADRO

We offer good, _____cheap_____ food that people can afford.

7 My dad drives a _____, black truck.

1 Their website is easy to use because it has a _____ , effective style.

8 Ella makes high-quality, _____ curtains.

2 Zander's Pizzeria makes _____ , oven-baked pizzas.

9 We aim to give _____ customer service.

3 I love this _____ , leather armchair.

10 We offer a _____ , personal experience.

4 The new, _____ brochure is very bright and attractive.

11 I don't like those ugly, _____ desks. They're hideous!

5 I like the _____ , new rooms in that hotel.

12 This modern, _____ car is much faster than my old one.

6 Those small, _____ earrings are beautiful.

13 What a _____ , big photo of all the team!

huge	cotton	full-color	clean	delicious	~~cheap~~	Japanese
unique	simple	gorgeous	comfortable	diamond	excellent	wooden

🔊

16 Vocabulario

Aa **16.1 MARKETING Y PUBLICIDAD** ESCRIBE LAS PALABRAS DEL RECUADRO DEBAJO DE SU CORRESPONDIENTE DIBUJO

direct mail

1 _____

2 _____

3 _____

6 _____

7 _____

8 _____

9 _____

12 _____

13 _____

14 _____

15 _____

18 _____

19 _____

20 _____

21 _____

④ _____

⑤ _____

⑩ _____

⑪ _____

⑯ _____

⑰ _____

㉒ _____

㉓ _____

advertising agency   slogan / tagline

copywriter   online survey   leaflet / flyer

door-to-door sales   logo   brand

radio advertising   promote

merchandise   poster   consumer

television advertising   sales pitch

~~direct mail~~   billboard   word of mouth

free sample   coupons

unique selling point / USP   sponsor

market research   social media

Promocionar un producto

Se pueden utilizar diversos adjetivos y adverbios al describir las características principales de un producto o servicio para promocionarlo. No todos los adjetivos se modifican igual.

⚙ **Lenguaje** Adjetivos y adverbios

Aa Vocabulario Adjetivos descriptivos

🧩 **Habilidad** Modificar descripciones de productos

⚙ **17.1 ESCRIBE LOS ADJETIVOS DEL RECUADRO EN LAS CATEGORÍAS CORRESPONDIENTES**

EXTREMOS	ABSOLUTOS	CLASIFICADORES
enormous	*true*	*metal*

electronic   terrible   wrong   brilliant   furious   ~~enormous~~   scientific   woolen   perfect   fascinating

equal   ~~true~~   impossible   industrial   exhausted   organic   ~~metal~~   unique   empty   rural   awful

🔊

⚙ **17.2 MARCA LAS FRASES QUE SEAN CORRECTAS**

The test was absolutely impossible. ✓
The test was fairly impossible. ☐

❶ The factory was totally destroyed. ☐
The factory was very destroyed. ☐

❷ I was thoroughly tired this morning. ☐
I was thoroughly exhausted this morning. ☐

❸ The warehouse is almost empty. ☐
The warehouse is very empty. ☐

❹ Jon is an absolutely good speaker. ☐
Jon is an extremely good speaker. ☐

❺ Peter is nearly good at Spanish. ☐
Peter is fairly good at Spanish. ☐

❻ The project is largely complete. ☐
The project is very complete. ☐

❼ Sian is a fairly brilliant swimmer. ☐
Sian is an utterly brilliant swimmer. ☐

🔊

17.3 DI LAS FRASES EN VOZ ALTA COMPLETANDO LOS ESPACIOS CON LAS PALABRAS DEL RECUADRO

Where are most of our products sold?

Our customer base is ___*largely*___ Chinese.

1 Are you certain you sent the report?

_____ certain. I think I sent it yesterday.

2 Our new product range is really good!

Yeah, it's absolutely _____ . I love it.

3 Did you like Claude's presentation?

It was very impressive, but _____ identical to mine!

4 I've never seen a watch like yours before!

Yes, it's totally _____ . I have the only one.

5 Our new manager seems very popular.

That's right. _____ everyone likes him.

6 Did you enjoy the movie?

No. It was _____ awful. I almost fell asleep.

7 How was the event?

It was practically _____ . There were only a few people there.

fantastic   Nearly   almost   ~~largely~~   unique   absolutely   empty   Fairly

17.4 ESCUCHA EL AUDIO Y RESPONDE A LAS PREGUNTAS

Huong, directivo de una marca de ropa, es entrevistado por Philippa, periodista.

The employees at Huong's company are...
fairly confident. ☐
pretty happy. ☑
completely miserable. ☐

1 Philippa thought the press release was...
absolutely fantastic. ☐
fairly interesting. ☐
totally ridiculous. ☐

2 Philippa says that Huong's idea is...
utterly ordinary. ☐
largely unoriginal. ☐
utterly original. ☐

3 Huong says that jogging during the day is...
almost impossible. ☐
always possible. ☐
absolutely plausible. ☐

4 Huong says that during the day, people are...
very busy. ☐
absolutely exhausted. ☐
extremely bored. ☐

5 According to Huong, exercise is...
utterly essential. ☐
pretty important. ☐
extremely important. ☐

6 Huong developed a line that was...
very expensive. ☐
totally organic. ☐
completely new. ☐

7 The stickers on the "NightJogging" line are...
highly reflective. ☐
wholly metallic. ☐
pretty unusual. ☐

8 To begin with, promoting the line was...
pretty difficult. ☐
practically impossible. ☐
extremely easy. ☐

9 Since a sports star offered support, it has been...
absolutely amazing. ☐
absolutely exhausting. ☐
completely perfect. ☐

10 Philippa thinks the idea is...
pretty confusing. ☐
really complicated. ☐
really clever. ☐

11 Huong thinks that launching in China is...
thoroughly impractical. ☐
fairly certain. ☐
extremely unlikely. ☐

Publicidad y marca

El uso de intensificadores como "enough", "too", "so" y "such" ayudan a comunicar mejor tus ideas cuando quieras explicar cosas de tu empresa, productos o marca.

⚙️ **Lenguaje** Intensificadores

Aa **Vocabulario** "Enough", "too", "so" y "such"

🧩 **Habilidad** Añadir énfasis a las descripciones

 18.1 ESCUCHA EL AUDIO Y MARCA LAS COSAS QUE SE DESCRIBEN

 18.2 COMPLETA LOS ESPACIOS CON "SO" O "SUCH"

 I work with _*such*_ interesting people.

① There was _____ a large crowd outside.

② The results were _____ disappointing.

③ We've had _____ a fantastic year.

④ The price for the hotel was _____ high.

⑤ The week seems to pass _____ slowly.

18.3 VUELVE A ESCRIBIR LAS FRASES PONIENDO LAS PALABRAS EN SU ORDEN CORRECTO

long | It | such | was | meeting. | a

It was such a long meeting.

① so | coffee | expensive. | This | was

_____

② is | My | colleague | lazy. | so

_____

③ so | Clara's | was | interesting. | presentation

_____

④ depressing | such | That | a | book. | is

_____

⑤ The | so | sales | disappointing. | were

_____

⑥ such | It's | a | story. | strange

_____

⑦ on | It's | to | important | time. | so | be

_____

18.4 LEE EL ARTÍCULO Y RESPONDE A LAS PREGUNTAS

The ad is for an athletics club.
True ☐ False ☑ Not given ☐

① Gym members receive a free T-shirt.
True ☐ False ☐ Not given ☐

② Most adults think they don't get enough exercise.
True ☐ False ☐ Not given ☐

③ The gym offers a flexible timetable.
True ☐ False ☐ Not given ☐

④ Most people think they don't swim well enough.
True ☐ False ☐ Not given ☐

⑤ The gym offers swimming lessons for children.
True ☐ False ☐ Not given ☐

WELLNESS AND LIFESTYLE

Fellingdon Health & Sport

Feeling tired? Feeling low? Summer is here, and it's time for you to get fit, get healthy, and feel totally amazing with a free one-day pass to our gym and swimming pool in central Fellingdon.

In a recent survey 75 percent of adults said that they either don't get enough exercise, are too busy, or think that a gym would be too expensive. But our gym is affordable, and our timetable is flexible enough to fit the busiest schedule. And for those 23 percent of people who think they don't swim well enough, we offer training and expert advice. Get in touch now for a free quote!

18.5 TACHA LAS PALABRAS INCORRECTAS DE CADA FRASE Y DI TODAS LAS FRASES EN VOZ ALTA

I'd never seen ~~so~~ / such a big number of customers in the store before.

1. Our senior managers think the price of our products is **enough** / **too** high.

2. This room won't be big **enough** / **too** for this afternoon's meeting.

3. The team is **such** / **so** excited about tonight's awards ceremony.

4. I thought today's meeting was **such** / **so** a waste of time.

5. Jim doesn't speak loudly **enough** / **too**. I can barely hear him.

6. Our IT system is **enough** / **so** old. It's time we invested in a new one.

7. The new intern works **so** / **such** slowly. She prefers talking on the phone.

8. Our products were **so** / **too** expensive to appeal to middle-market customers.

9. Mary is **such** / **so** an ambitious woman. She wants to be a CEO by the age of 30.

10. You shouldn't drive **enough** / **too** quickly when you're in this part of town.

11. The strikes have caused **such** / **enough** a problem for our employees who commute.

12. The marketing campaign was **so** / **too** boring to appeal to young people.

19 Consejos y sugerencias

Los verbos modales como "could", "should" y "must" pueden utilizarse para dar consejos y sugerencias. Utilízalos para ayudar a tus colegas en situaciones complicadas o estresantes.

🔧 **Lenguaje** Verbos modales para aconsejar
Aa Vocabulario Presiones en el lugar de trabajo
🧩 **Habilidad** Aconsejar

19.1 CONECTA LAS SITUACIONES CON LOS CONSEJOS CORRECTOS

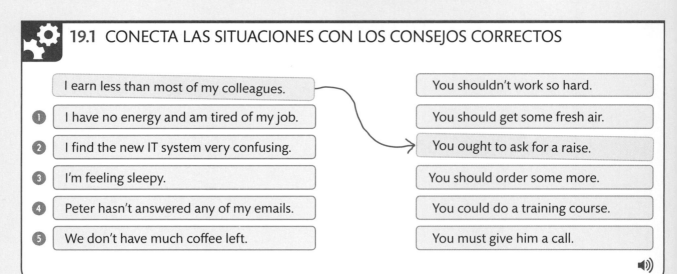

I earn less than most of my colleagues.

1 I have no energy and am tired of my job.

2 I find the new IT system very confusing.

3 I'm feeling sleepy.

4 Peter hasn't answered any of my emails.

5 We don't have much coffee left.

You shouldn't work so hard.

You should get some fresh air.

You ought to ask for a raise.

You should order some more.

You could do a training course.

You must give him a call.

🔊

19.2 TACHA LAS PALABRAS INCORRECTAS DE CADA FRASE

You really **shouldn't** / ~~doesn't should~~ eat your lunch in front of your computer.

 1 You **could** / **shouldn't** try delegating the task to your team. I'm sure they'd do a great job.

 2 Greg **ought to** / **ought** apologize to his team for his behavior. He was very rude.

 3 Antonio really **ought to** / **shouldn't** employ some new staff, or we'll never meet our deadline.

 4 We **should** / **should to** organize a training course for the interns.

 5 The secretary really **should** / **couldn't** ask her boss for a raise. She works very hard.

🔊

19.3 COMPLETA LOS ESPACIOS CON LAS PALABRAS DEL RECUADRO

Cath _____should move_____ if she lives too far from the office.

1. You _____ to work if the train is canceled.

2. You _____ the IT desk about your new password.

3. You _____ your lunch at your desk. Go to a café instead.

4. You _____ your manager when you want to book time off.

5. Clare _____ a break if she's tired of her job.

6. You _____ an English course if you want to learn English.

7. Dave _____ home if he's not feeling well.

8. Pete _____ to the public about company secrets.

could do

must tell

~~should move~~

ought to call

shouldn't eat

ought to go

shouldn't talk

should walk

ought to take

19.4 LEE EL CORREO ELECTRÓNICO Y MARCA EL RESUMEN CORRECTO

1. Vikram strongly advises Clara to make a list of her most important tasks. He suggests she might take a break from work for a week. ☐

2. Vikram says Clara must delegate her tasks to her team, and suggests she might ask another manager to help her complete her work. ☐

3. Vikram strongly advises Clara to list all her duties, and suggests she might ask a team member to complete half her work. ☐

4. Vikram strongly advises Clara to make a list of all her tasks, and suggests that she might ask her clients for more time. ☐

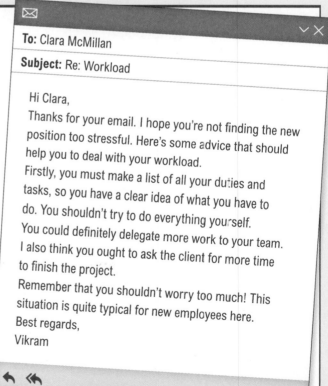

To: Clara McMillan

Subject: Re: Workload

Hi Clara,

Thanks for your email. I hope you're not finding the new position too stressful. Here's some advice that should help you to deal with your workload.

Firstly, you must make a list of all your duties and tasks, so you have a clear idea of what you have to do. You shouldn't try to do everything yourself.

You could definitely delegate more work to your team.

I also think you ought to ask the client for more time to finish the project.

Remember that you shouldn't worry too much! This situation is quite typical for new employees here.

Best regards,

Vikram

19.5 VUELVE A ESCRIBIR LAS FRASES CORRIGIENDO LOS ERRORES

> What about work at home on Friday?
> _What about working at home on Friday?_

1 Why don't we organizing a feedback session?

_____

2 What about ask Pedro to do it?

_____

3 Why don't you hiring some new staff?

_____

4 What about buy a new printer?

_____

5 Why doesn't Mabel going on vacation?

_____

6 Why not they close the Mumbai branch?

_____

7 What about invite the clients to dinner?

_____

🔊

19.6 ESCUCHA EL AUDIO Y CONECTA LAS IMÁGENES CON LAS EXPRESIONES CORRECTAS

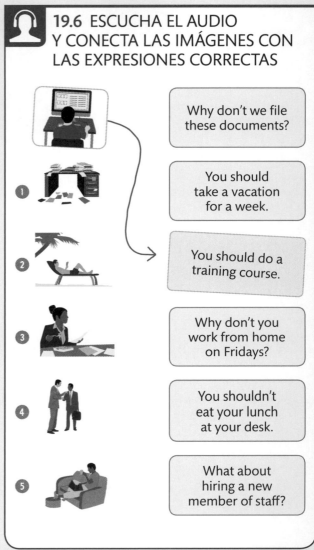

Why don't we file these documents?

You should take a vacation for a week.

You should do a training course.

Why don't you work from home on Fridays?

You shouldn't eat your lunch at your desk.

What about hiring a new member of staff?

19.7 UTILIZA EL DIAGRAMA PARA CREAR SEIS FRASES CORRECTAS Y DILAS EN VOZ ALTA

What about asking Pete to do it?

| What / Why | about / don't we | asking / ask / organize / organizing / sell / selling | Pete to do it? / a workshop? / our products online? |

🔊

19.8 MARCA LAS FRASES QUE SEAN CORRECTAS

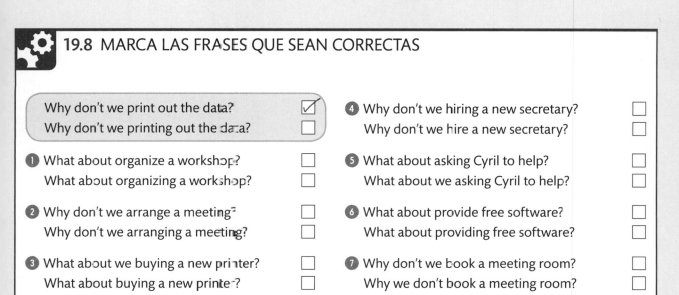

Why don't we print out the data? ☑
Why don't we printing out the data? ☐

1 What about organize a workshop? ☐
What about organizing a workshop? ☐

2 Why don't we arrange a meeting? ☐
Why don't we arranging a meeting? ☐

3 What about we buying a new printer? ☐
What about buying a new printer? ☐

4 Why don't we hiring a new secretary? ☐
Why don't we hire a new secretary? ☐

5 What about asking Cyril to help? ☐
What about we asking Cyril to help? ☐

6 What about provide free software? ☐
What about providing free software? ☐

7 Why don't we book a meeting room? ☐
Why we don't book a meeting room? ☐

🔊

19.9 VUELVE A ESCRIBIR LAS FRASES PONIENDO LAS PALABRAS EN SU ORDEN CORRECTO

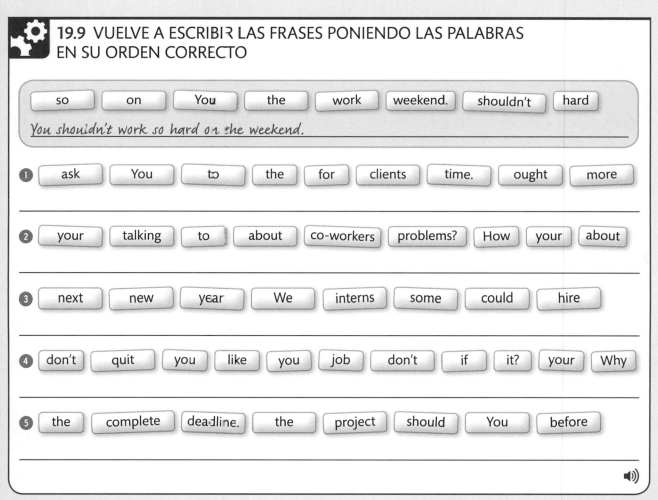

| so | on | You | the | work | weekend. | shouldn't | hard |

You shouldn't work so hard on the weekend.

1 | ask | You | to | the | for | clients | time. | ought | more |

2 | your | talking | to | about | co-workers | problems? | How | your | about |

3 | next | new | year | We | interns | some | could | hire |

4 | don't | quit | you | like | you | job | don't | if | it? | your | Why |

5 | the | complete | deadline. | the | project | should | You | before |

🔊

20 Vocabulario

Aa 20.1 DIRECCIÓN Y LIDERAZGO ESCRIBE LAS EXPRESIONES DEL RECUADRO DEBAJO DE SU CORRESPONDIENTE DEFINICIÓN

To give a task to somebody

to allocate a task

❶ Money added to a person's wages as a reward for good performance

❹ To give work or tasks to a person in a position junior to you

❺ How well a person carries out tasks

Aa 20.2 CAPACIDADES Y HABILIDADES ESCRIBE LAS EXPRESIONES DEL RECUADRO DEBAJO DE SU CORRESPONDIENTE DIBUJO

initiative

❶ _____

❷ _____

❸ _____

❻ _____

❼ _____

❽ _____

❾ _____

⓬ _____

⓭ _____

⓮ _____

⓯ _____

2 An interview to discuss an employee's performance

_____

3 To officially confirm something meets the required standards

_____

6 To be given a more senior position within a company

_____

to delegate   to approve   to be promoted

an appraisal / a performance review

performance   a bonus   ~~to allocate a task~~

4 _____

5 _____

10 _____

11 _____

16 _____

17 _____

IT / computing   written communication

data analysis   research   able to drive

fast learner   ~~initiative~~   teamwork

work well under pressure   organization

decision-making   numeracy

public speaking   problem-solving

leadership   telephone manner

attention to detail   time management

21 Hablar sobre capacidades

Para hablar sobre las capacidades de otros, por ejemplo en una evaluación de rendimiento, utiliza verbos modales para expresar capacidades pasadas, presentes y futuras.

🔧 **Lenguaje** Verbos modales de capacidades
Aa Vocabulario Capacidades del lugar de trabajo
🧩 **Habilidad** Describir capacidades

21.1 COMPLETA LOS ESPACIOS CON "CAN" O "CAN'T"

Jenny has great people skills. She _____ *can* _____ talk to all sorts of people.

① Tom _____ fix your car this afternoon. It will be ready at 5:00.

② Karl _____ drive. He failed his driving test again.

③ Jon used to be really nervous, but now he _____ give presentations.

④ She _____ type really quickly. She types over 60 words per minute.

⑤ I _____ work the new photocopier. It's too difficult.

⑥ Hansa is a really good cook. She _____ cook really nice Indian food.

⑦ Ali _____ read my handwriting. He says it's really messy.

⑧ Ania _____ speak French. She learned it in college.

⑨ Petra _____ manage her staff any more. They do what they like.

⑩ Parvesh _____ write clear reports. They are easy to read.

🔊

21.2 ESCUCHA EL AUDIO Y MARCA SI LAS IMÁGENES CORRESPONDEN A UNA CAPACIDAD PRESENTE O PASADA

Presente ✓
Pasada ☐

1 Presente ☐
Pasada ☐

2 Presente ☐
Pasada ☐

3 Presente ☐
Pasada ☐

4 Presente ☐
Pasada ☐

21.3 VUELVE A ESCRIBIR LAS FRASES CORRIGIENDO LOS ERRORES

George can't understand the old CEO because she had a strong accent.
George couldn't understand the old CEO because she had a strong accent.

1 Janice can tell me if sales are up until she gets the final reports in.

_____

2 Phil loves meeting new people, so he can't work in the HR department.

_____

3 Saira can't type fast, but now she can type 60 words a minute.

_____

4 Ed can't write reports very well. I'm going to ask him to help me write mine.

_____

5 Keira could use the database, but now she trains people in how to use it.

_____

6 For years Alex can't speak Arabic but now he has done a beginners' course.

_____

◀))

21.4 LEE LA EVALUACIÓN DE RENDIMIENTO Y RESPONDE A LAS PREGUNTAS

> Matt has worked for Pietro's for four years and has made good progress in that time. He joined us as an assistant chef and was rather unconfident in his cooking abilities then.
>
> He didn't feel he could reach the standards required of a professional kitchen, but soon showed he was a very competent chef.
>
> He was promoted two years ago to the position of head chef after proving he can create interesting and exciting menus with new dishes. His manager and I think he could be an excellent trainer of young chefs. We believe he would make a great mentor to talented young chefs.

Matt has worked at Pietro's for five years.
True ☐ **False** ☐ **Not given** ☑

❶ Matt has made little progress in his time at Pietro's.
True ☐ **False** ☐ **Not given** ☐

❷ He was a confident assistant chef.
True ☐ **False** ☐ **Not given** ☐

❸ He particularly enjoys cooking Italian food.
True ☐ **False** ☐ **Not given** ☐

❹ Matt has worked as head chef for four years.
True ☐ **False** ☐ **Not given** ☐

❺ He can create exciting menus.
True ☐ **False** ☐ **Not given** ☐

❻ He could be an excellent trainer of young chefs.
True ☐ **False** ☐ **Not given** ☐

 21.5 CONECTA LOS PARES DE FRASES QUE VAN JUNTAS

Carrie is a great team member.	She could train staff to do them.
❶ Jim is quite shy.	He could be head of the department.
❷ Clare couldn't manage her old team.	She would work well in any team.
❸ Carl is more confident now.	She can manage her new team much better.
❹ Bea is good at giving presentations.	She wouldn't be a good trainer.
❺ Jola is very impatient.	Before, he wouldn't talk in public.
❻ Sam is very talented.	He would do well in a smaller team.

🔊

21.6 MARCA LAS FRASES QUE SEAN CORRECTAS

You're an excellent team member and you would do well on the sales team. ☑
You're an excellent team member and you can't do well on the sales team. ☐

1 David has given his team excellent training. Now they can't do anything. ☐
David has given his team excellent training. Now they can do anything. ☐

2 Have you seen his brilliant designs? He can create our banners. ☐
Have you seen his brilliant designs? He couldn't create our banners. ☐

3 No one couldn't read the boss's handwriting. It was terrible. ☐
No one could read the boss's handwriting. It was terrible. ☐

4 Sebastian is a very proactive person and would do well in marketing. ☐
Sebastian is a very proactive person and couldn't do well in marketing. ☐

21.7 TACHA LA PALABRA INCORRECTA DE CADA FRASE Y DI TODAS LAS FRASES EN VOZ ALTA

If Jorge keeps on working hard, he ~~would~~ / **could** be area manager one day.

1 We think you are very talented and **would** / **couldn't** be a great addition to our department.

2 I don't know what is wrong with the coffee machine. I **can** / **can't** get it working.

3 My confidence is much better now. Before, I **couldn't** / **could** give presentations.

4 Laila couldn't negotiate with her old boss, but she **can't** / **can** with her new boss.

249

22 Comparar y contrastar

En las discusiones de equipo, los marcadores del discurso facilitan la conversación, pues ayudan a unir ideas similares u opuestas, o conectan una acción con su resultado.

⚙ **Lenguaje** Marcadores del discurso
Aa Vocabulario Trabajo en equipo y cohesión
🧩 **Habilidad** Expresar tus ideas

⚙ 22.1 TACHA LAS PALABRAS INCORRECTAS DE CADA FRASE

 Team A enjoyed the task a lot. Team B found it very rewarding **as well** / ~~however~~.

① This training is really interesting. It is a lot of fun, **also** / **too**.

② Team-building days are useful. They are **also** / **too** fun.

③ Some people always wash their coffee cups, **while** / **as well** others don't.

④ **However** / **Although** Team A did the task quickly, Team B didn't finish it.

⑤ Team A built the bridge very quickly. Team B was **as well** / **equally** successful.

⑥ Team A helped each other, **while** / **as well** Team B disagreed with each other.

⑦ Hard work is an excellent trait in a team, **equally** / **whereas** laziness is terrible.

⑧ Yesterday's training was useful. **However** / **Although**, this morning's task was pointless.

⑨ Some people want to lead a team, **as well** / **while** others are happy to be team members.

⑩ It is important to say what we all think. We should listen to each other **as well** / **equally**.

⑪ This training is very useful. It is **equally** / **as well** a good way to get to know people.

🔊

22.2 MARCA LAS FRASES QUE SEAN CORRECTAS

> We learned a lot from that training session, whereas it was a lot of fun. ☐
> We learned a lot from that training session. It was a lot of fun, too. ☑

1 However, Sam went to the training day, he didn't learn anything new. ☐
Although Sam went to the training day, he didn't learn anything new. ☐

2 Team A solved the problem really quickly. Team B was equally successful. ☐
Team A solved the problem really quickly. Team B was as well successful. ☐

3 This training is useful for managers. It is too useful for team members. ☐
This training is useful for managers. It is also useful for team members. ☐

4 Some people want to be managers, while others want to be team members. ☐
Some people want to be managers, as well others want to be team members. ☐

5 Laziness is a terrible trait for a team member, whereas honesty is excellent. ☐
Laziness is a terrible trait for a team member, also honesty is excellent. ☐

6 We'd like all staff to follow our usual dress code for the training. Please be on time, however. ☐
We'd like all staff to follow our usual dress code for the training. Please be on time, too. ☐

🔊

22.3 ESCUCHA EL AUDIO Y NUMERA DESPUÉS LAS FRASES EN EL ORDEN EN QUE LAS ESCUCHES

La líder de un equipo evalúa
el desempeño de su equipo
en una determinada tarea.

A Team A was the first to complete the task. ☐

B This was a very challenging task. ☐ 1

C Creative thinking can be equally useful. ☐

D It is important to read instructions carefully. ☐

E However, Team B worked well together, too. ☐

F We hope you also found it very rewarding. ☐

22.4 VUELVE A ESCRIBIR LAS FRASES PONIENDO LAS PALABRAS EN SU ORDEN CORRECTO

people | in | Some | prefer | while | team, | others | working | enjoy | alone. | a | working

Some people enjoy working in a team, while others prefer working alone.

① was | The | and | it | useful | lot | task | also | of | was | team-building | fun. | a

_____

② to | pizza. | had | Team A | a | build | make | had | a | Team B | bridge, | whereas | to

_____

③ some | had | the | Team B | completed | While | task | problems. | first, | they

_____

④ often | as well. | really | they | are | courses | and | fun | are | Training | useful

_____

⑤ was | Team A | cooperative. | equally | together | Team B | worked | as | well. | very

_____

⑥ identify | This | your | task | weaknesses, | also | strengths. | will | your | but

_____

⑦ a | team | However, | didn't | cake. | the | activity | baked | matter. | Our

_____

⑧ worked | other | Although | we | came | first, | together. | the | team | well

_____

⑨ easy, | today's | Yesterday's | difficult. | more | task | was | task | was | while

_____

⑩ the | finished | its | took | Team A | whereas | task | time. | quickly, | Team B

_____

22.5 CONECTA LOS PARES DE FRASES QUE VAN JUNTAS

The team worked well together.	Consequently, they all won a medal.
❶ The course taught me how to manage people.	As a result, everyone attends them.
❷ Team Orange completed the challenge first.	As a result, they completed the task.
❸ I'd never driven a forklift truck before.	Consequently, she was promoted last week.
❹ The training days are useful.	As a consequence, I am now a team leader.
❺ Jess learned a lot from the training.	For this reason, I was very nervous.

◀))

22.6 DI LAS FRASES EN VOZ ALTA COMPLETANDO LOS ESPACIOS CON LAS PALABRAS DEL RECUADRO

The task taught us how to run a team. As a _____result_____ , I now lead a team of ten.

❶ Team-building days are great for morale. _____ , the atmosphere in our office is good.

❷ We have regular IT training sessions. For this _____ , everyone has good computer skills.

❸ We do team building every year. As a _____ , we work really well together.

❹ During team building we meet new staff. _____ reason, we know our co-workers well.

For this	consequence	Consequently	~~result~~	reason

◀))

253

23 Planear eventos

Muchos verbos ingleses que se utilizan para dar opiniones o hablar sobre planes e intenciones van seguidos por un gerundio o un infinitivo.

⚙ **Lenguaje** Patrones verbales
Aa Vocabulario Ocio corporativo
Habilidad Hablar sobre eventos de la empresa

23.1 TACHA LAS PALABRAS INCORRECTAS DE CADA FRASE

We must keep ~~to remind~~ / **reminding** customers of our new product range.

1. We plan **to launch** / **launching** our new product range at the conference.

2. Would you consider **to organize** / **organizing** the accommodation for the visitors?

3. I really enjoy **to take** / **taking** clients out for dinner at famous restaurants.

4. Jenny has offered **to meet** / **meeting** our visitors at the airport.

5. I keep **to suggest** / **suggesting** that we should have a staff training session.

🔊

23.2 VUELVE A ESCRIBIR LAS FRASES CORRIGIENDO LOS ERRORES

I really enjoy to give presentations.
I really enjoy giving presentations.

1. Our clients expect receive good customer service.

_____

2. Would you consider to make the name badges for the delegates?

_____

3. Colin has offered organizing the training program for the new staff.

_____

4. I hope impressing our clients when I show them around the new office.

_____

🔊

CORPORATE EVENTS

RED GIRAFFE EVENTS PLANNING

How we can plan the ideal event for your company

Kayaking is one of the team-building events that Red Giraffe will offer soon.

Red Giraffe is an international events management business. We are one of the biggest events organizers in the US, and our clients range from start-up businesses to large corporations. We enjoy all aspects of the job, but the most enjoyable is entertaining clients. Our clients expect to receive excellent service and we pride ourselves on meeting their every requirement. We often take clients out for lunch during the planning phase to talk about their requirements. It's good to do this over a meal as they say what they really want when they are relaxed and enjoying the food.

After lunch, we have a brainstorming session in groups. When all the clients have arrived, we serve coffee as it helps to get the ideas flowing. All kinds of things come up in these sessions. For instance, when we planned a launch for a media company, the employees kept saying we should have a boat trip on the river. But some people didn't like this idea because their competitors had done the same, so we went for a covered venue in a converted warehouse. Next year, we plan to start offering team-building events, such as sports days and treasure hunts. We expect these to be very popular with our clients.

What clients does Red Giraffe work with?

Small start-up businesses ☐

Only big corporate clients ☐

All sizes of business ☑

1 What do the company's employees enjoy?

Entertaining clients ☐

Organizing refreshments ☐

Having great accommodation ☐

2 What do the company's clients expect?

To have a free lunch ☐

To receive good customer service ☐

To eat a planned dinner ☐

3 Why should you go out for a meal with clients?

They like eating great food ☐

They like talking about the food ☐

They give their honest opinion ☐

4 Why didn't one client want to have a boat trip?

They wanted an outdoor venue ☐

Their competitors had had one ☐

Their CEO didn't like boats ☐

5 What does Red Giraffe plan to do next year?

Offer team-building events ☐

Go on a treasure hunt ☐

Become popular with clients ☐

23.4 COMPLETA LOS ESPACIOS CON LAS PALABRAS DEL RECUADRO

Did you remember _____*to call*_____ the hotel about the catering?

1 I regret _____ you that I can't take the clients out for dinner. I'm very sorry.

2 Do you remember _____ Dan last month? He has a question about a discount you offered.

3 Sue stopped _____ the program for the launch event. It looked really interesting!

4 He regrets _____ her his idea for the event because she copied it.

5 David gave his presentation, and went on _____ about new events.

6 I stopped _____ my presentation because the CEO had a question.

| to talk | giving | telling | calling | to read | ~~to call~~ | to tell |

23.5 ESCUCHA EL AUDIO Y NUMERA LAS IMÁGENES EN EL ORDEN EN QUE SE DESCRIBEN

A ☐

B 1

C ☐

D ☐

E ☐

F ☐

G ☐

H ☐

23.6 VUELVE A ESCRIBIR LAS FRASES PONIENDO LAS PALABRAS EN SU ORDEN CORRECTO

| visitors | at | has | the | to | our | offered | airport. | Kelly | meet |

Kelly has offered to meet our visitors at the airport.

1 | entertaining | I | clients. | enjoy | really | new |

_____

2 | invited | the | Sandra | overseas | to | conference. | re | sales | attend |

_____

3 | book | My | the | asked | to | accommodation. | manager | me |

_____

4 | him | Tom | manager | a | soon. | expects | promotion | his | to | give |

_____

5 | me | recent | My | to | give | sales. | him | asked | an | on | boss | update |

_____

6 | our | come | We | to | all | to | party. | invited | customers | our |

_____

🔊

23.7 UTILIZA EL DIAGRAMA PARA CREAR 16 FRASES CORRECTAS Y DILAS EN VOZ ALTA

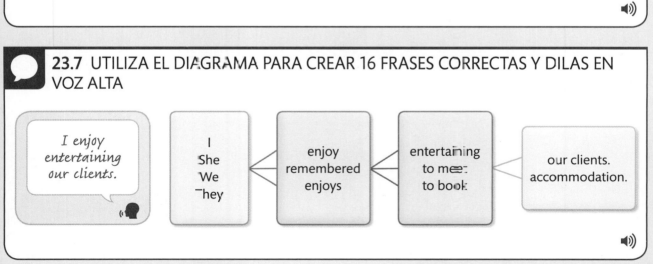

| I enjoy entertaining our clients. | I She We They | enjoy remembered enjoys | entertaining to meet to book | our clients. accommodation. |

🔊

257

24 Vocabulario

Aa **24.1 REUNIONES** ESCRIBE LAS PALABRAS DEL RECUADRO DEBAJO DE SU CORRESPONDIENTE DEFINICIÓN

To conclude

to sum up

1 To write a record of what was said during a meeting

_____

3 To answer questions

_____

4 To be not present

_____

6 To have no more time left to do something

_____

7 A plan for achieving a particular goal

_____

9 Proposals for specific action to be taken

_____

10 To present information to a group of people

_____

12 To say something before someone else has finished speaking

_____

13 People who have been to or are going to a meeting

_____

15 When everyone agrees

_____

16 To look again at the written record of a past meeting

_____

2 To consider or focus on something

_____

5 To come to an agreement about an issue

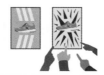

_____

8 The primary aim

_____

11 To send a plan for what will be discussed

_____

14 To put forward an idea or plan for others to discuss

_____

17 A vote made by raising hands in the air to show agreement

_____

a show of hands   attendees

action points   to give a presentation

to take minutes   to suggest / propose

to send out an agenda   to look at

~~to sum up~~   to review the minutes

main objective   to interrupt

to be absent   unanimous agreement

a strategy   to reach a consensus

to run out of time   to take questions

259

25 Lo que han dicho otros

Cuando expliques a los colegas lo que alguien ha dicho, puedes tomar sus palabras (direct speech) y referirlas con claridad y precisión: es lo que se llama reported speech.

🕸 **Lenguaje** Reported speech
Aa Vocabulario Reuniones
🧩 **Habilidad** Decir lo que dijo alguien

25.1 CONECTA EL DIRECT SPEECH CON SU REPORTED SPEECH

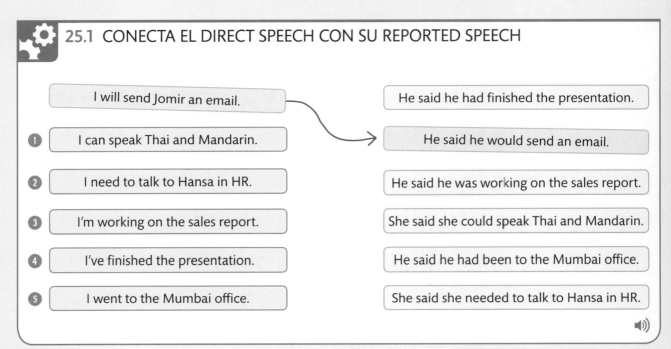

I will send Jomir an email.

① I can speak Thai and Mandarin.

② I need to talk to Hansa in HR.

③ I'm working on the sales report.

④ I've finished the presentation.

⑤ I went to the Mumbai office.

He said he had finished the presentation.

He said he would send an email.

He said he was working on the sales report.

She said she could speak Thai and Mandarin.

He said he had been to the Mumbai office.

She said she needed to talk to Hansa in HR.

25.2 VUELVE A ESCRIBIR LAS FRASES COMO REPORTED SPEECH CON "SAID"

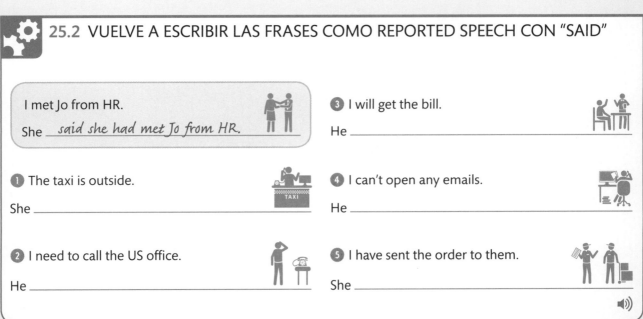

I met Jo from HR.
She _said she had met Jo from HR._

③ I will get the bill.
He _____

① The taxi is outside.
She _____

④ I can't open any emails.
He _____

② I need to call the US office.
He _____

⑤ I have sent the order to them.
She _____

25.3 VUELVE A ESCRIBIR LAS FRASES PONIENDO LAS PALABRAS EN SU ORDEN CORRECTO

| said | He | figures! | couldn't | those | believe | he |

He said he couldn't believe those figures!

1 | busy | she | that | was | She | afternoon. | said |

_____

2 | his | like | He | that | he | didn't | boss. | said | new |

_____

3 | received | said | hadn't | the | they | delivery. | They |

_____

4 | was | He | to | in | week. | Tokyo | that | going | said | be | he |

_____

5 | to | new | had | product | They | been | the | said | launch. | they |

_____

6 | invoice | She | away. | right | would | she | an | said | issue |

_____

7 | give | company | said | 5 percent | the | could | discount. | a | He |

_____

8 | said | she | the | had | well | gotten | interviewer. | along | She | with |

_____

9 | said | They | were | they | range. | a | new | designing |

_____

25.4 ESCUCHA EL AUDIO Y NUMERA LAS FRASES EN REPORTED SPEECH EN EL ORDEN EN QUE LAS HAYAS OÍDO EN EL CORRESPONDIENTE DIRECT SPEECH

 Suzanne habla con una colega a lo largo del día.

A Suzanne said she'd send him the report the following day. ☐

B Suzanne said she had met the new CEO in the Miami office that week. ☑ 1

C Suzanne said her laptop wasn't working that day. ☐

D Suzanne said she could help Alemay prepare her presentation that afternoon. ☐

E Suzanne said she had come into work early that morning. ☐

F Suzanne said she had to stay late and call the Mexico office that evening. ☐

G Suzanne said she was going to design a new app with Tim the week after. ☐

25.5 TACHA LAS PALABRAS INCORRECTAS DE CADA FRASE

 Jake ~~told~~ / said that he wanted a promotion before the end of the year.

1 He said / told me that he'd been to China twice.

2 She suggested / said that she was going to Montreal.

3 He promised / told that he wouldn't be late for the train.

4 He explained / promised that he didn't know how to use the photocopier.

5 He denied / told that he had broken the coffee machine.

6 She promised / complained that the food was cold when the waiter brought it.

7 He confirmed / announced that the tickets had been booked.

I am not the person in charge of this project.

He _____ denied _____ that he was the person in charge of that project.

1 I'll definitely call you back after 2:00 this afternoon.

She _____ to call me back after 2:30 that afternoon.

2 I need a printout, and I will also need a copy of Simon's report about the year-end accounts.

He _____ that he needed a copy of Simon's report about the year-end accounts.

3 The new all-in-one printer isn't difficult to use.

She _____ that the new all-in-one printer wasn't difficult to use.

4 Yes, that's right. I'd like to buy 100 units of the new product.

He _____ that he'd like to buy 100 units of the new product.

5 I'm not happy with the customer service I have experienced.

He _____ that he wasn't happy with the customer service he had experienced.

6 How about asking Ameera what she thinks?

She _____ that we should ask Ameera what she thought.

| explained | promised | suggested | complained | added | ~~denied~~ | confirmed |

26 Lo que han preguntado otros

El reported speech se utiliza a veces para citar lo que preguntó alguien. Las preguntas en direct y en reported speech ordenan las palabras de maneras diferentes.

⚙ **Lenguaje** Preguntas en reported speech
Aa Vocabulario "Have", "make", "get", "do"
Habilidad Decir lc que preguntó alguien

26.1 VUELVE A ESCRIBIR LAS FRASES PONIENDO LAS PALABRAS EN SU ORDEN CORRECTO

how · Kevin · gone. · asked · negotiations · me · the · had

Kevin asked me how the negotiations had gone.

❶ where · Selma · put · me · you · annual · the · report. · asked · had

_____

❷ wanted · Krishnan · why · was · know · I · late · again. · to · for · work

_____

❸ asked · My · what · I · the · IT · new · about · me · system. · boss · thought

_____

❹ me · asked · Hans · would · where · we · have · the · afternoon. · presentation · this

_____

❺ wasn't · he · Sophie · Claude · why · at · meeting. · asked · the

_____

❻ me · Tabitha · who · cell · taken · her · phone. · asked · had

_____

❼ the · Fiona · to · had · know · who · minutes. · wanted · taken

_____

🔊

26.2 ESCUCHA EL AUDIO Y RESPONDE A LAS PREGUNTAS

Sam le cuenta a Shelly una conversación que ha tenido con Doug.

Doug is feeling confident about the conference.
True ☐ **False** ☑ **Not given** ☐

5 There are meeting facilities at the Classic Inn.
True ☐ **False** ☐ **Not given** ☐

1 Shelly has booked the flights for Monday.
True ☐ **False** ☐ **Not given** ☐

6 Doug is planning to bring his family.
True ☐ **False** ☐ **Not given** ☐

2 The Hotel Belle Vue is fully booked.
True ☐ **False** ☐ **Not given** ☐

7 Shelly has finished the promotional materials.
True ☐ **False** ☐ **Not given** ☐

3 Shelly has booked the rooms for three nights.
True ☐ **False** ☐ **Not given** ☐

8 Shelly also has to prepare a presentation.
True ☐ **False** ☐ **Not given** ☐

4 The Classic Inn includes breakfast.
True ☐ **False** ☐ **Not given** ☐

9 Ted can help Shelly with her work.
True ☐ **False** ☐ **Not given** ☐

26.3 CONECTA CADA DEFINICIÓN CON LA COLOCACIÓN CORRESPONDIENTE

explain to someone what they have done wrong

1 offer advice or ideas

2 lose your job because of misconduct

3 misunderstand, or do something incorrectly

4 try as hard as you can

5 help someone without thought of reward

6 find work

7 investigate a topic, or discover information

8 write down information during a meeting

make a suggestion

make a mistake

have a word

get fired

do someone a favor

make notes

do research

do your best

get a job

265

26.4 VUELVE A ESCRIBIR LAS FRASES EN FORMA DE PREGUNTAS EN REPORTED SPEECH

Who took the minutes yesterday?
She *asked me who had taken the minutes yesterday.*

❶ How many people work in the company?

She _____

❷ Why did you hand in the report so late?

He _____

❸ Who got promoted?

He _____

❹ Who is the new senior manager?

He _____

❺ Which candidate did you choose?

She _____

❻ How long have you worked here?

He _____

❼ Why were you so late this morning?

She _____

❽ What time do you get home?

He _____

❾ Where did you have the appointment?

He _____

❿ Which printer do you prefer?

She _____

26.5 DI LAS FRASES EN VOZ ALTA COMO PREGUNTAS EN REPORTED SPEECH

Did you make notes during the meeting?

He _asked me if I had made notes during the meeting._

1 Did the package arrive safely?

He _____.

2 Can you do me a favor?

She _____.

3 Can I have a word with you later?

He _____.

4 Have you finished writing the report yet?

She _____.

5 Can I make a suggestion?

He _____.

6 Did you read last year's report?

She _____.

7 Are you coming to the awards ceremony on Saturday?

He _____.

8 Did you enjoy the presentation?

She _____.

9 Have you booked a table at the restaurant?

He _____.

27 Informar de cantidades

En presentaciones e informes, quizá tengas que hablar sobre qué cantidad hay de algo. Las palabras que utilices dependen de lo que describas.

⚙ **Lenguaje** "Few", "little" y "all"
Aa Vocabulario Reuniones
Habilidad Hablar sobre cantidades

📖 **27.1 LEE EL INFORME Y RESPONDE A LAS PREGUNTAS**

Sales have grown fast in the last year.
True ☐ **False** ☑ **Not given** ☐

❶ China has been a strong competitor over the last year.
True ☐ **False** ☐ **Not given** ☐

❷ There is not much chance of a quick solution.
True ☐ **False** ☐ **Not given** ☐

❸ The company should reduce its prices dramatically.
True ☐ **False** ☐ **Not given** ☐

❹ The most expensive product made in China costs $25.
True ☐ **False** ☐ **Not given** ☐

❺ The brand is well known among older people.
True ☐ **False** ☐ **Not given** ☐

❻ The brand is unpopular with teenagers.
True ☐ **False** ☐ **Not given** ☐

❼ The company's advertising campaign is old.
True ☐ **False** ☐ **Not given** ☐

❽ The company needs to open more stores in Asia.
True ☐ **False** ☐ **Not given** ☐

❾ It costs less to open stores in Asia than Europe.
True ☐ **False** ☐ **Not given** ☐

❿ Asia is not a very valuable market for the company.
True ☐ **False** ☐ **Not given** ☐

REPORT

Problem:
Over the past 12 months, our overseas sales have fallen dramatically. Competition from Asia, particularly China, is intense.

Proposed solutions:
There is little we can do to turn this situation around in the next couple of months. However, if we take a long-term view, there are a few solutions.

1) We can lower our prices a little. This will make our products more price-competitive. Currently, our products are 15–25% more expensive than China-made products.

2) We can launch a new advertising campaign. Our research suggests that few people over the age of 50 have heard of our brand. This is a big market we can access if we get our advertising message right. At the other end of the market, very few teenagers seem interested in our products. We need to position our advertising to make our brand appear current and fashionable.

3) We have very few stores in Asia. We can consider opening a few more stores in Asia so that we can become a more familiar brand in this important market.

27.2 MARCA LAS FRASES QUE SEAN CORRECTAS

There's little bit of money left in the budget to redesign the website. ☐
There's a little bit of money left in the budget to redesign the website. ☑

1. Unfortunately, we have few problems with our production line. ☐
   Unfortunately, we have a few problems with our production line. ☐

2. Regrettably, few people have the skills necessary to run a multinational company. ☐
   Regrettably, a few people have the skills necessary to run a multinational company. ☐

3. So few of our customer reviews are positive that it's becoming a problem. ☐
   So a few of our customer reviews are positive that it's becoming a problem. ☐

4. I have a little doubt that the conference will be a success. ☐
   I have little doubt that the conference will be a success. ☐

27.3 TACHA LAS PALABRAS INCORRECTAS DE CADA FRASE Y DI TODAS LAS FRASES EN VOZ ALTA

We have very **few** / ~~little~~ rooms left on the 12th of December.

1. **A little** / **Few** employees have worked for the company for as long as Sofia.

2. We have **little** / **a little** bit of time before the meeting ends.

3. So **few** / **a few** companies offer this service that demand is sure to be high.

4. Very **few** / **little** can be done to improve facilities in the short term.

5. We can expect **a few** / **a little** increase in profits over the summer season.

6. It's great that you have **few** / **a few** ideas about how we can improve sales.

269

27.4 VUELVE A ESCRIBIR LAS FRASES PONIENDO LAS PALABRAS EN SU ORDEN CORRECTO

well · in · goes · the · all · boss. · your · I · meeting · hope · with

I hope all goes well in your meeting with the boss.

1 will · customer. · be · sure · to · all · you've · spoken · I'm · well · once · the

_____

2 know · late. · that · the · All · I · order · is · is

_____

3 that · need? · all · Is · you

_____

4 is · for · wait · we · do · a · the · can · client. · response · All · from

_____

27.5 CONECTA LOS PARES DE FRASES QUE SIGNIFICAN LO MISMO

Some people can afford our luxury vacations. ──────→ A few people can afford our luxury vacations.

Little can be done to improve staff morale.

1 I have some suggestions about how we can improve staff morale.

2 People are not interested in our new app.

There are a few things we can do to improve staff morale.

3 There is not much we can do to improve staff morale.

So few people have money to spend on our luxury vacations.

4 Not many people can afford our luxury vacations.

We've had little interest in our new app.

5 There has been a lot of interest in our new app.

Our new app is very popular.

28 Comprobar la información

A veces es necesario aclarar si se ha entendido un punto. Hay diversas maneras de comprobar educadamente la información en una conversación.

⚙ **Lenguaje** Preguntas de sujeto, question tags
Aa Vocabulario Comprobaciones y preguntas eco
🧩 **Habilidad** Comprobar la información

28.1 VUELVE A ESCRIBIR LAS FRASES PONIENDO LAS PALABRAS EN SU ORDEN CORRECTO

| is | price? | the | What | sale |

What is the sale price?

① | year? | is | target | our | this | What |

_____

② | account? | is | Who | the | handling |

_____

③ | in | Who | is | charge? |

_____

④ | your | target? | sales | is | What |

_____

⑤ | complaints? | Who | to | responds |

_____

⑥ | Jones? | Who | Mr. | spoke | to |

_____

⑦ | action? | plan | is | What | our | of |

_____

🔊

28.2 MARCA LA MEJOR PREGUNTA PARA CADA RESPUESTA

✓ Who made the most sales?

Did Yousef make the most sales?

Yousef made the most sales.

① Do I need to dress formally?

What is the dress code?

Yes, you do.

② Did you quote this price?

Who quoted this price?

No, I didn't.

③ What should I tell the client?

Should I tell the client the truth?

You should tell them the truth.

④ Does he want to work in New York?

Who wants to work in New York?

Ian would love to work in New York.

🔊

271

28.3 CONECTA EL INICIO Y EL FINAL DE CADA FRASE

Joel is our best negotiator,   →   isn't he?

① We should increase our margins,   am I?

② I didn't send you the report,   did I?

③ She'll be a great manager,   isn't he?

④ I'm not getting a raise,   didn't he?

⑤ We haven't made a loss,   aren't we?

⑥ We're going to win the award,   shouldn't we?

⑦ Louis has worked here since 2012,   have we?

⑧ Brett worked late last night,   won't she?

                                                           hasn't he?

🔊

 28.4 COMPLETA LOS ESPACIOS CON LAS QUESTION TAGS CORRECTAS

I've made a mistake, _____*haven't I?*_____

⑥ We're not ready for the meeting, _____

① We could launch our product early, _____

⑦ They are opening a new store, _____

② Jakob ordered the samples, _____

⑧ You weren't in London last week, _____

③ We can't cut prices any further, _____

⑨ You traveled to Paris by train, _____

④ We haven't achieved our target, _____

⑩ I'm writing the proposal, _____

⑤ We need to improve product quality, _____

⑪ I emailed the right person, _____

🔊

28.5 ESCUCHA EL AUDIO Y RESPONDE A LAS PREGUNTAS

Una agente de ventas llama a su superior para comprobar unos detalles y confirmar la información.

> Anya is very busy when Mike calls.
> **True** ☐ **False** ☑ **Not given** ☐

❶ The conference takes place every year.
True ☐ **False** ☐ **Not given** ☐

❷ Mike's plan is to put out 100 seats.
True ☐ **False** ☐ **Not given** ☐

❸ Only five people have replied to the invitation.
True ☐ **False** ☐ **Not given** ☐

❹ Anya thinks they should put out 140 seats.
True ☐ **False** ☐ **Not given** ☐

❺ Pauline is dealing with the food and drink.
True ☐ **False** ☐ **Not given** ☐

❻ Anya wants her guests to feel welcome.
True ☐ **False** ☐ **Not given** ☐

❼ Anya will contact Francesca about catering.
True ☐ **False** ☐ **Not given** ☐

28.6 TACHA LAS PALABRAS INCORRECTAS DE CADA FRASE Y DI TODAS LAS FRASES EN VOZ ALTA

> They received government funding, **didn't they** / ~~did they~~?

❶ What was her name? I didn't **listen** / **hear** it.

❷ **Who** / **What** is responsible for training?

❸ You're not worried about the meeting, **aren't you** / **are you**?

❹ **What** / **Who** is our timetable for this project?

❺ Sales are better than expected, **aren't they** / **are they**?

❻ Sorry, I **lost** / **missed** that.

273

Aa 29.1 SECTORES ESCRIBE LAS PALABRAS DEL RECUADRO DEBAJO DE SU CORRESPONDIENTE DIBUJO

shipping

1 _____

2 _____

3 _____

4 _____

5 _____

6 _____

7 _____

8 _____

9 _____

10 _____

11 _____

12 _____

13 _____

14 _____

15 _____

16 _____

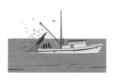

17 _____

18 _____

19 _____

fashion   catering / food   tourism   recycling   transportation   hospitality   energy

manufacturing   finance   agriculture / farming   electronics   ~~shipping~~   chemical   healthcare

real estate (US) / property (UK)   fishing   education   pharmaceutical   mining   entertainment

Aa 29.2 **ATRIBUTOS PROFESIONALES** ESCRIBE LAS PALABRAS DEL RECUADRO DEBAJO DE SU CORRESPONDIENTE DIBUJO

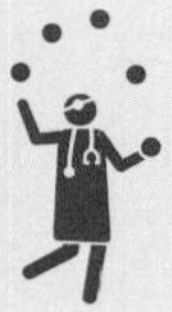

flexible

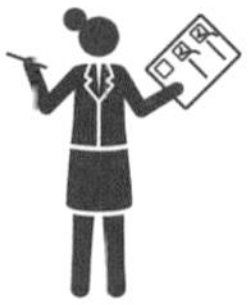

1 ______

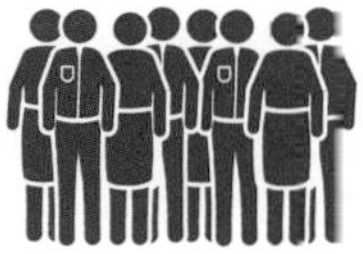

2 ______

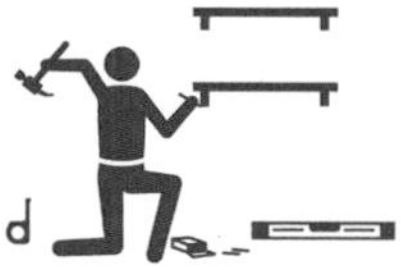

3 ______

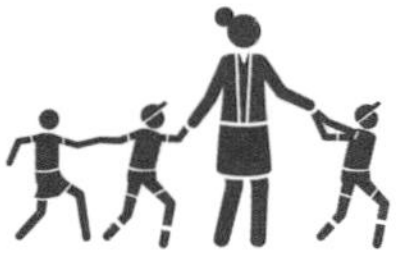

4 ______

5 ______

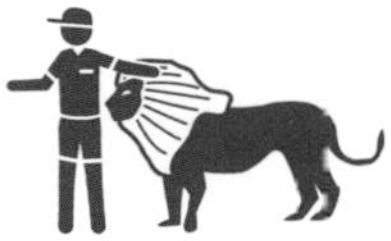

6 ______

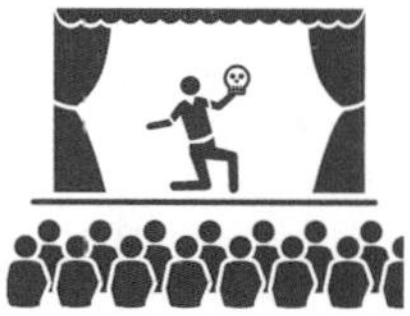

7 ______

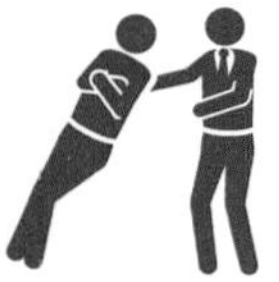

8 ______

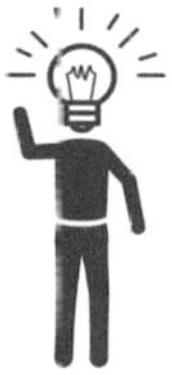

9 ______

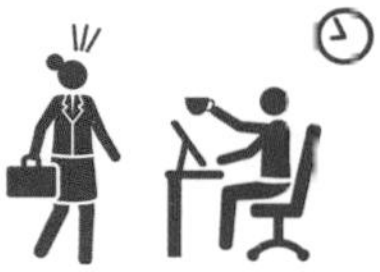

10 ______

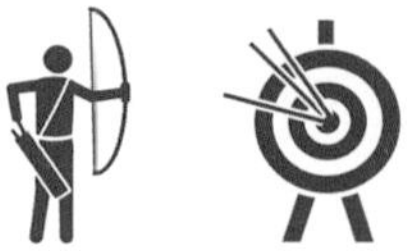

11 ______

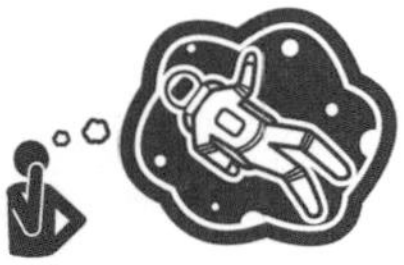

12 ______

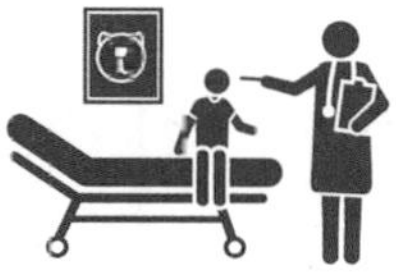

13 ______

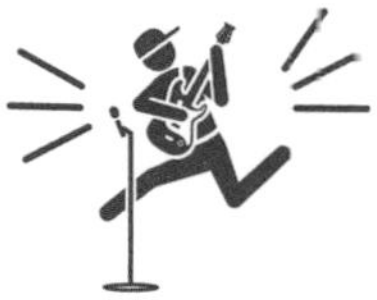

14 ______

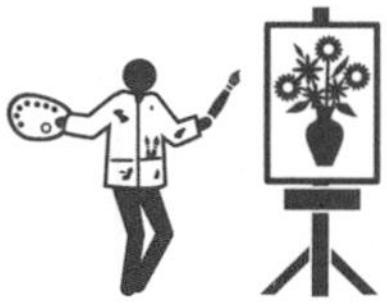

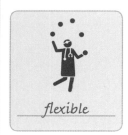

15 ______

creative reliable practical professional ~~flexible~~
motivated confident ambitious accurate team player
organized energetic responsible punctual innovative calm

30 Describir un puesto

Utiliza "a" o "an" en las descripciones de trabajo y para nueva información. No utilices artículo cuando hables de cosas generales; utiliza "the" para referirte a cosas concretas.

⚙ **Lenguaje** Artículos
Aa Vocabulario Describir y solicitar un puesto
🧩 **Habilidad** Describir un puesto

 30.1 TACHA LAS PALABRAS INCORRECTAS DE CADA FRASE

> I applied for a job as ~~a/an~~ / ~~the~~ IT engineer. ~~A~~ / ~~An~~ / The salary is really good.

❶ I want to apply for **a** / **an** / **the** job in **a** / **an** / **the** office.

❷ I've got **a** / **an** / **the** interview next week for **a** / **an** / **the** job I told you about.

❸ **A** / **An** / **The** ideal candidate enjoys working in **a** / **an** / **the** team

❹ **A** / **An** / **The** deadline for applications for **a** / **an** / **the** job in IT is next Monday.

❺ Please complete **a** / **an** / **the** form on **a** / **an** / **the** job page on our website.

🔊

 30.2 ESCUCHA EL AUDIO Y NUMERA LAS IMÁGENES EN EL ORDEN EN QUE SE DESCRIBEN

30.3 MARCA LAS FRASES QUE SEAN CORRECTAS

> Mark loves teaching students. The students he teaches at the college are all adults. ✓
> Mark loves teaching the students. Students he teaches at the college are all adults. ☐

1 The nurses often have to work very long hours. They are the very important people. ☐
Nurses often have to work very long hours. They are very important people. ☐

2 Working hours are from 8:30 to 5:00. Lunch is from 1:00 to 2:00. ☐
The working hours are from 8:30 to 5:00. The lunch is from 1:00 to 2:00. ☐

3 Vale loves giving training sessions. The training sessions she gave yesterday were amazing. ☐
Vale loves giving the training sessions. Training sessions she gave yesterday were amazing. ☐

4 Job I applied for is based in Madrid. It's in the sales and marketing. ☐
The job I applied for is based in Madrid. It's in sales and marketing. ☐

5 The people who interviewed me for the job were really nice. They were managers. ☐
People who interviewed me for the job were really nice. They were the managers. ☐

6 I have just applied for a job in finance department at your company. ☐
I have just applied for a job in the finance department at your company. ☐

7 The salary for this job is not very good. I don't think I'll apply for it. ☐
Salary for this job is not very good. I don't think I'll apply for it. ☐

8 The successful candidate will have three years' experience branding new products. ☐
Successful candidate will have three years' experience branding the new products. ☐

9 Our company is currently recruiting more the staff for Paris office. ☐
Our company is currently recruiting more staff for the Paris office. ☐

10 I have the meetings with CEO and some of our new clients today. ☐
I have meetings with the CEO and some of our new clients today. ☐

11 Marisha is good at pitching products. It's the thing she enjoys most about her job. ☐
Marisha is good at pitching the products. It's thing she enjoys most about her job. ☐

12 This job requires in-depth knowledge of business trends in the wider world. ☐
This job requires the in-depth knowledge of the business trends in wider world. ☐

🔊

30.4 LEE LA DESCRIPCIÓN DEL PUESTO Y RESPONDE A LAS PREGUNTAS

VACANCIES

Arctic Foods
Sales and Marketing Manager

The job is a sales and marketing role.
True ✓　**False** ☐

Do you have a passion for selling new ideas? Then we could have the job for you.

Arctic Foods is looking for a dynamic sales and marketing manager. You will have previous experience in a sales and marketing role, preferably in the frozen food sector. You will be good at giving presentations and fully up to date with market trends. Previous experience leading a sizeable team is essential.

Full product training will be given to the successful candidate.

1 No previous experience is needed.
True ☐　**False** ☐

2 The job involves giving presentations.
True ☐　**False** ☐

3 The job requires market-specific knowledge.
True ☐　**False** ☐

4 No leadership experience is needed.
True ☐　**False** ☐

5 The successful candidate will have training.
True ☐　**False** ☐

30.5 TACHA LAS PALABRAS INCORRECTAS DE CADA FRASE Y DI TODAS LAS FRASES EN VOZ ALTA

At the second-round interview, you will meet ~~HR manager~~ / the HR manager.

1 We need someone who is willing to travel, and can speak the Spanish / Spanish.

2 Tara works in the finance department / finance department of an advertising agency.

3 Marc and Samantha often travel to China on business / on the business.

4 The company is based in the UK, but it does business throughout EU / the EU.

5 I started looking for a job as an engineer / the engineer after I finished college.

31 Solicitar un puesto

Una carta de presentación para solicitar un puesto debe mostrar naturalidad y confianza. Utiliza las preposiciones adecuadas detrás de cada verbo, sustantivo y adjetivo.

🔧 **Lenguaje** Preposiciones dependientes
Aa Vocabulario Léxico de cartas de presentación
🧩 **Habilidad** Redactar una carta de presentación

 31.1 CONECTA LAS IMÁGENES CON LAS FRASES CORRECTAS

❶

❷

❸

❹

I am fully trained in all aspects of health and safety.

I have several years of experience in the catering industry.

I graduated from college in June 2016 with a degree in chemistry.

I am writing to apply for the role of head chef.

I heard about the job on your website.

31.2 TACHA LAS PALABRAS INCORRECTAS DE CADA FRASE

> At college, I focused ~~in~~ / on / ~~at~~ business studies. It has been very useful in my career.

1 Jim graduated **from** / **at** / **out** college with a degree in physics. Now he is a research scientist.

2 He is fully trained **to** / **with** / **in** all aspects of sales and marketing. I think he'll do a great job.

3 In my role as Senior Program Developer, I reported **in** / **on** / **to** the Director of IT.

4 Tanya has applied **at** / **for** / **on** a job in the marketing department of our company.

5 I worked **at** / **of** / **for** the owner of a leading hairdressing salon. I learned a lot from him.

31.3 LEE LA CARTA DE PRESENTACIÓN Y RESPONDE CON ORACIONES COMPLETAS

> Why is Ellie writing the letter?
> _To apply for the role of Head of Marketing._

1 How long has Ellie worked in marketing?

_____

2 What did she develop in her previous jobs?

_____

3 What did she introduce last year?

_____

4 What is she responsible for in her current job?

_____

5 Which region does she look after?

_____

6 How does she describe herself?

_____

Dear Ms. Jenkins,

I am writing to apply for the position of Head of Marketing as advertised on your company website.

I have more than ten years' experience in marketing, and I have worked in the marketing departments of several big companies, where I developed award-winning campaigns in key markets. Last year I was responsible for introducing a new customer-focused branding initiative.

In my current position, I am responsible for training junior members of staff. I run the sales and marketing operations for the Europe region. This includes setting the sales and marketing strategy for the region.

I would welcome the opportunity to learn new skills. I am also energetic, dynamic, and extremely reliable.

Please find attached my résumé and references. I look forward to hearing from you.

Yours sincerely,

Ellie Abrahams

Aa 31.4 CONECTA LAS DEFINICIONES Y LAS EXPRESIONES CORRECTAS

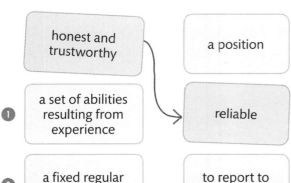

honest and trustworthy	a position
① a set of abilities resulting from experience	reliable
② a fixed regular payment	to report to someone
③ a job	skills
④ to make an official request for a job	salary
⑤ to have someone in charge of you	a team
⑥ the group of people you work with	a résumé
⑦ a document detailing your skills	an opportunity
⑧ a chance to do something	to amount to
⑨ to equal a total number	to apply for a job

🔊

31.5 LEE LA CARTA DE PRESENTACIÓN Y TACHA LAS PALABRAS INCORRECTAS

3257 Gateway Drive
Portland, OR
March 29, 2014

Dear Mr. Chang,

I am writing to ~~apply to~~ / **apply for** the position of Senior Sales Consultant, as advertised on your website.

I have **worked on** / **worked in** the sales industry for more than eight years, and am **trained in** / **trained of** selling a range of products to varied markets. In my current position, I am **responsible of** / **responsible for** sales to Asian markets, and last year I **looked up** / **looked after** the new market of China, where sales **amounted to** / **amounted on** more than $10 million.

I am **passionate for** / **passionate about** working in the sales industry and welcome the opportunity to learn new skills. I run the training program for new staff members and ten of the junior sales consultants **report to** / **report on** me. In their training, I **focus in** / **focus on** developing awareness of the most effective sales strategies.

Please find my résumé and references attached. I look **forward at** / **forward to** hearing from you.

Yours sincerely,
Deepak Singh

32 Entrevistas de trabajo

En una entrevista de trabajo es importante que describas tus logros de una manera concreta y detallada. Utiliza cláusulas relativas para hacerlo.

⚙ Lenguaje Cláusulas relativas
Aa Vocabulario Entrevistas de trabajo
🧩 Habilidad Describir detalladamente tus logros

32.1 TACHA LAS PALABRAS INCORRECTAS DE CADA FRASE

 This is the app ~~who~~ / that / ~~what~~ I designed for the new client.

① The person who / what / which I admire the most in the company is the Sales Manager.

② The office that / which / where I work is a tall, modern building.

③ The customers what / who / why gave us feedback were all very positive.

④ The team that / what / where I lead is fully qualified and highly motivated.

32.2 CONECTA EL INICIO Y EL FINAL DE CADA FRASE

We work with clients ——→ who want innovative products.

① We sell apps — that are designed by IT specialists.

② We are based in an office — who have high standards.

③ I work with clients — where we sell the most.

④ This is the reason — that is in the business park.

⑤ Spain and Italy are the countries — that I applied for this job.

282

32.3 VUELVE A ESCRIBIR LAS FRASES CORRIGIENDO LOS ERRORES

> In my previous job, what was in sales, I learned a lot from my boss.
> *In my previous job, which was in sales, I learned a lot from my boss.*

1 Training staff, that is my favorite part of the job, is really interesting.

_____

2 In my current job, who I serve lots of customers, I have learned how to deal with complaints.

_____

3 My boss, which is very understanding, encourages me to leave the office on time.

_____

4 While I was in college I worked in a café, what taught me a lot about customer service.

_____

32.4 ESCUCHA EL AUDIO Y NUMERA LAS IMÁGENES EN EL ORDEN EN QUE SE DESCRIBEN

A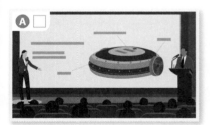

B

C 1

D

E

F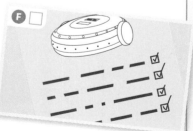

32.5 COMPLETA LOS ESPACIOS CON LAS PALABRAS DEL RECUADRO

The sales team, _____*whose*_____ staff work very hard, always meet their targets.

❶ Last summer, _____ I had just graduated, I worked as an intern in a bank.

❷ My teacher, _____ was an amazing person, inspired me to study law.

❸ My apprenticeship, _____ I completed in 2016, was in IT.

❹ The place _____ I want to work as a tour guide is New York.

who	where	~~whose~~	which	when

32.6 MARCA LAS FRASES QUE SEAN CORRECTAS

In 2014, when I had just graduated, I worked as an intern. ☑
In 2014, which I had just graduated, I worked as an intern. ☐

❶ Tom's team, who staff are hard-working, hit their sales targets last month. ☐
Tom's team, whose staff are hard-working, hit their sales targets last month. ☐

❷ In my previous job, which was in sales, I learned to give presentations. ☐
In my previous job, what was in sales, I learned to give presentations. ☐

❸ I sometimes work from home as it is the place which I can concentrate best. ☐
I sometimes work from home as it is the place where I can concentrate best. ☐

❹ My clients, who expect good customer service, said my work was excellent. ☐
My clients, whose expect good customer service, said my work was excellent. ☐

32.7 DI LAS FRASES EN VOZ ALTA COMPLETANDO LOS ESPACIOS CON LAS PALABRAS DEL RECUADRO

What experience do you have of customer service?

I work with clients _____ *who expect* _____ excellent service at all times.

1. What do you like most about your job?

The thing _____ me excited is when we hit our sales targets.

2. What would you say is your biggest strength?

People _____ me well say I am customer-focused and give good customer service.

3. What do you think you would bring to our company?

I have a can-do attitude, _____ that I get things done.

4. What are your salary expectations?

I would hope to receive more than my current salary, _____ $45,000 a year.

5. How soon can you start, supposing we offer you the job?

My boss, _____ quite understanding, would allow me to leave after a month's notice.

| that gets | who know | ~~who expect~~ | which is | who is | which means |

Aa 33.1 MODISMOS DE EMPRESA ESCRIBE LAS EXPRESIONES DEL RECUADRO DEBAJO DE LAS DEFINICIONES CORRECTAS

To agree totally

to see eye to eye

1 To talk to someone briefly in order to catch up or get an update

3 A strategy worked out beforehand

4 To be in agreement about something

6 Operating properly

7 Simply and succinctly

9 To start doing a job or role that someone else has just left

10 Original and a big departure from what was there before

12 To stop the current activity

13 To do something in a cheaper or easier way, at the expense of high standards

15 A rough estimate

16 To do something strictly according to the rules

2 An increase or decrease in speed from what is normal

_____

5 Uncertain and undecided

_____

8 To make more effort than is usually expected

_____

11 To confirm or settle an agreement or contract

_____

14 To be ahead of your competitors in a certain field

_____

17 To have control of a particular market

_____

a ballpark figure   to touch base

in a nutshell   to go the extra mile

a change of pace   to corner the market

to be ahead of the game   to cut corners

~~to see eye to eye~~   to clinch the deal

to fill someone's shoes   groundbreaking

to do something by the book

a game plan   up in the air

to be on the same page   up and running

to call it a day

34 Relaciones laborales

A menudo se utilizan phrasal verbs para hablar de la relación con los colegas y los clientes. Es importante utilizar el orden adecuado de las palabras con los phrasal verbs.

⚙ **Lenguaje** Phrasal verbs de tres palabras
Aa Vocabulario Redes sociales
🧩 **Habilidad** Redes sociales y contactos

34.1 COMPLETA LOS ESPACIOS CON LAS PALABRAS DEL RECUADRO

My team looks _____*up*_____ to me.

1 Alex comes up _____ great ideas.

2 Hal looks down _____ his co-workers.

3 I'm _____ forward to the launch.

4 Fred _____ up with a lot of noise.

5 She comes _____ as rather superior.

6 The printer has run _____ of paper.

7 Jim's staff get _____ with being late.

8 Shona has to _____ up to poor sales.

9 We need to _____ up with the schedule.

across	face	with
puts	~~up~~	on	keep
away	looking	out	

🔊

34.2 VUELVE A ESCRIBIR LAS FRASES PONIENDO LAS PALABRAS EN SU ORDEN CORRECTO

them. | down | looks | on | John
John looks down on them.

1 my | team. | get | with | I | along
_____

2 friendly. | across | She | as | comes
_____

3 with | I | put | music! | up | can't | his
_____

4 with | good | comes | ideas. | He | up
_____

5 gets | with | lot. | Tom | away | a
_____

6 out | We | run | have | of | coffee.
_____

7 to | We | facts. | must | up | face
_____

🔊

288

34.3 LEE LA PÁGINA WEB Y RESPONDE A LAS PREGUNTAS CON ORACIONES COMPLETAS

Business Tips

HOME | ENTRIES | ABOUT | CONTACT

Keeping up with competitors

Some companies have been slow to get up to speed with using social media to strengthen their brand. Some even look down on using social media as trivial and having no value in the business world, but they do so at their own risk. With social media you can reach out to a wider audience and keep up with the latest trends.

Here at ABC Foods we use social media to tell our customers our news. We have previews of our TV ads, so subscribers feel they are keeping up with our news and developments.

We also run competitions that make us stand out from our competitors. Last month, we asked our subscribers to post recipes they had come up with using their favorite ABC foods. We then had customers like their favorite recipes and the best three won prizes.

Using social media in such ways allows us to build loyal customer relationships. Customer loyalty is key to us as loyal customers make repeat purchases. We have to constantly be coming up with new features for our social media activity. Perhaps you have an idea for our next competition!

RECIPE OF THE WEEK

What can social media help you do?

It can help you strengthen your brand.

❶ Why don't some companies like social media?

_____

❷ Why is it a risk to ignore social media?

_____

❸ Why does ABC Foods use social media?

_____

❹ What does ABC Foods have previews of?

_____

❺ Why does the company do this?

_____

❻ Why does ABC Foods run competitions?

_____

❼ Why is customer loyalty so important?

_____

34.4 REESCRIBE LAS FRASES CON PRONOMBRES DE OBJETO

> You must check out their website.
> *You must check it out.*

❶ I'll look up our competitors online.
_____

❷ Can you fill in this form?
_____

❸ I'd like you to take on this task.
_____

❹ I can't let down our clients.
_____

❺ Can we talk over your problem?
_____

❻ Could you look over my résumé?
_____

❼ We are giving away free books.
_____

❽ I need to call off our meeting.
_____

❾ I can't figure out these sales figures.
_____

❿ The taxi will pick up Tom.
_____

⓫ I keep putting off writing my report.
_____

⓬ Yola turned down the job offer.
_____

◀))

34.5 ESCUCHA EL AUDIO Y RESPONDE A LAS PREGUNTAS

Bilal hace una presentación sobre el uso de las redes sociales en la empresa.

What should you encourage clients to do?
Look at your website ☑
Take on difficult tasks ☐
Sell your products ☐

❶ What do you need to do regularly?
Be in the news ☐
Update your website ☐
Focus on selling ☐

❷ What do customers expect from business social media sites?
To find new ideas for your product ☐
To buy more of your products ☐
To read old news stories ☐

❸ What is vital for small businesses?
Missing out on opportunities ☐
Translating social media use into sales ☐
Advertising on social media ☐

❹ How do successful businesses engage with their target customers?
Uploading photos of their products ☐
Entering competitions ☐
Sharing users' questions and answers ☐

34.6 CONECTA LOS DIBUJOS CON LAS FRASES CORRECTAS

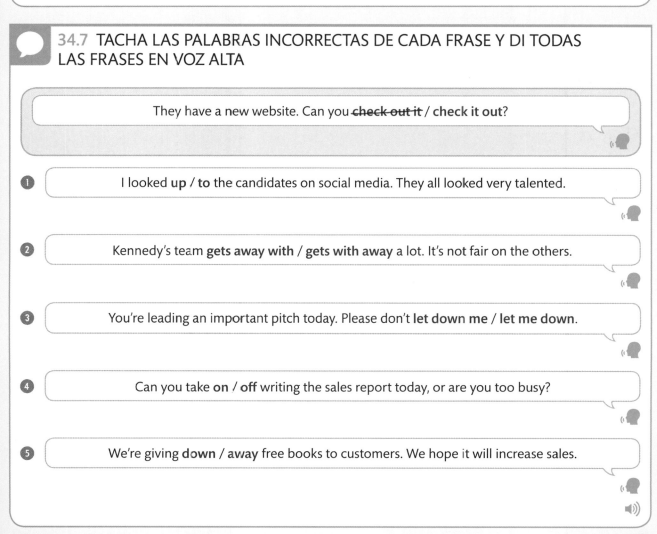

① 💡

②

③

④

⑤

The copier has run out of paper.

I can't put up with his music!

Cev always comes up with great ideas.

Rohit keeps up with the business news.

Dan and Sam don't get along with each other.

Here's a form. Can you fill it in?

34.7 TACHA LAS PALABRAS INCORRECTAS DE CADA FRASE Y DI TODAS LAS FRASES EN VOZ ALTA

They have a new website. Can you ~~check out it~~ / **check it out**?

① I looked **up** / **to** the candidates on social media. They all looked very talented.

② Kennedy's team **gets away with** / **gets with away** a lot. It's not fair on the others.

③ You're leading an important pitch today. Please don't **let down me** / **let me down**.

④ Can you take **on** / **off** writing the sales report today, or are you too busy?

⑤ We're giving **down** / **away** free books to customers. We hope it will increase sales.

35 Futuro profesional

Para hablar de posibles acontecimientos futuros, como el desarrollo profesional, utiliza "will", "might" y "won't" para indicar qué probabilidad existe de que algo se produzca.

⚙ **Lenguaje** Verbos modales de posibilidad
Aa Vocabulario Desarrollo profesional
🧩 **Habilidad** Hablar del futuro

35.1 CONECTA LAS FRASES QUE VAN JUNTAS

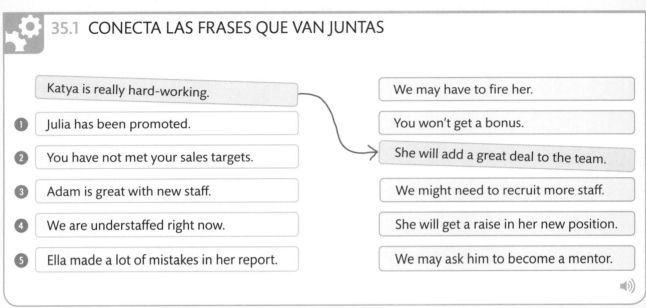

Katya is really hard-working. → She will add a great deal to the team.

We may have to fire her.

You won't get a bonus.

1 Julia has been promoted.

2 You have not met your sales targets.

3 Adam is great with new staff.

4 We are understaffed right now.

5 Ella made a lot of mistakes in her report.

We might need to recruit more staff.

She will get a raise in her new position.

We may ask him to become a mentor.

35.2 ESCUCHA EL AUDIO Y RESPONDE A LAS PREGUNTAS

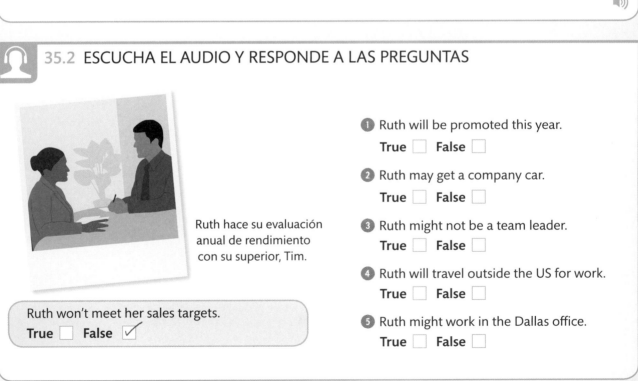

Ruth hace su evaluación anual de rendimiento con su superior, Tim.

Ruth won't meet her sales targets.
True ☐ **False** ✓

1 Ruth will be promoted this year.
True ☐ **False** ☐

2 Ruth may get a company car.
True ☐ **False** ☐

3 Ruth might not be a team leader.
True ☐ **False** ☐

4 Ruth will travel outside the US for work.
True ☐ **False** ☐

5 Ruth might work in the Dallas office.
True ☐ **False** ☐

35.3 MARCA LAS FRASES QUE SEAN CORRECTAS

The company has made a loss this year. You will get a bonus. ☐
The company has made a loss this year. You might not get a bonus. ☑

1 Our staff can't use the new database. We might have to provide more training. ☐
Our staff can't use the new database. We won't have to provide more training. ☐

2 David has over 15 years' experience and he will lead our marketing department. ☐
David has over 15 years' experience and he won't lead our marketing department. ☐

3 I need your report by Thursday. You need might to work overtime. ☐
I need your report by Thursday. You might need to work overtime. ☐

4 Anna's laptop is broken. She wills get a new one this week. ☐
Anna's laptop is broken. She will get a new one this week. ☐

5 There is a pay freeze at the moment, so you won't get a raise. ☐
There is a pay freeze at the moment, so you will get a raise. ☐

6 If Rita's work doesn't get better, we won't have to fire her. ☐
If Rita's work doesn't get better, we may have to fire her. ☐

7 We have some meetings in France. You may have to go to Paris. ☐
We have some meetings in France. You don't may have to go to Paris. ☐

8 We can't hire any staff at the moment, so you don't might get an assistant until March. ☐
We can't hire any staff at the moment, so you might not get an assistant until March. ☐

9 If your presentation goes well, the CEO might ask you to give it to the board. ☐
If your presentation goes well, the CEO won't ask you to give it to the board. ☐

10 Tanya has been promoted. She will lead a team next year. ☐
Tanya has been promoted. She will to lead a team next year. ☐

11 Dev has had a bad trading year. He will meet his sales targets. ☐
Dev has had a bad trading year. He won't meet his sales targets. ☐

12 Paula always goes the extra mile. She will make a great addition to the team. ☐
Paula always goes the extra mile. She won't make a great addition to the team. ☐

🔊

35.4 VUELVE A ESCRIBIR LAS FRASES PONIENDO LAS PALABRAS EN SU ORDEN CORRECTO

will   bonus   probably.   You   a   get

You will probably get a bonus.

---

1 promoted.   will   definitely   He   be

_____

2 probably   raise.   You   a   will   get

_____

3 need   She   training.   probably   won't

_____

4 bonus.   They'll   a   get   definitely

_____

5 I   go   won't   vacation.   probably   on

_____

6 I   jobs.   definitely   change   won't

_____

7 We   intern.   hire   an   probably   will

_____

8 He   meet   probably   clients.   won't

_____

9 sell   It   definitely   well.   will

_____

🔊

35.5 DI LAS FRASES EN VOZ ALTA PONIENDO EL MODIFICADOR EN EL LUGAR CORRECTO

You won't be promoted. [definitely]

You definitely won't be promoted.

1 You will be promoted. [probably]

2 He will get the job. [definitely]

3 She won't get a raise. [definitely]

4 They will get a bonus. [probably]

5 I won't get a new laptop. [probably]

6 You will get a company car. [definitely]

7 I will move to the head office. [probably]

8 You won't need much training. [probably]

9 We will hire a new assistant soon. [definitely]

🔊

35.6 TACHA LAS PALABRAS INCORRECTAS DE CADA FRASE

> Everything's up in the air right now. We **might not** / ~~will definitely~~ meet our deadline.

1. Katrina doesn't have much experience. She **will probably** / **definitely won't** need more training.

2. Meliz has to travel to see clients. She **definitely won't** / **will probably** get a company car.

3. Mr. Cox has complained about our service. He **probably won't** / **definitely will** use us again.

4. The negotiations are going quite well. We **definitely won't** / **might** clinch the deal tomorrow.

5. You're doing a great job, but our profits are down. You **might not** / **definitely will** get a raise.

35.7 LEE LA EVALUACIÓN DE RENDIMIENTO Y RESPONDE A LAS PREGUNTAS CON ORACIONES COMPLETAS

> What is Isaac's work like?
> _Isaac's work is very thorough._

1. What did Isaac do this year?

_____

2. What might happen to Isaac next year?

_____

3. Who will Isaac mentor from next month?

_____

4. Where will Isaac start selling products?

_____

5. What might Isaac need in his new role?

_____

6. How does the company think he will perform?

_____

Name: Isaac Hawkins
Position: Sales adviser
Subject: Performance review

Isaac has worked in our sales department for four years and has a positive attitude. His work is very thorough and he never cuts corners. He met all his sales targets this year, so he will be considered for promotion next year. He is great with new staff and will mentor two new employees from next month. Isaac has shown himself to be a confident and competent sales adviser and from next month will take on sales to Asia after working in the European department for two years. We may need to give Isaac additional training in this field and I am confident he will perform well in this role.

36 Vocabulario

Aa 36.1 EQUIPO DE OFICINA Y PRESENTACIONES ESCRIBE LAS PALABRAS DEL RECUADRO DEBAJO DE SU CORRESPONDIENTE DIBUJO

projector screen

① _____

② _____

③ _____

④ _____

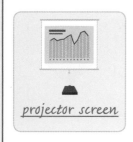

⑥ _____

⑦ _____

⑧ _____

⑨ _____

⑩ _____

⑫ _____

⑬ _____

⑭ _____

⑮ _____

⑯ _____

⑱ _____

⑲ _____

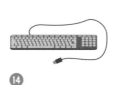

⑳ _____

㉑ _____

㉒ _____

5 _____

printer

handout   projector

USB drive / flash drive

keyboard   speakers

router   voice recorder

low battery   cue cards

pointer   webcam

~~projector screen~~   lectern

video camera   cursor

touch screen   laptop

computer   mouse

microphone   laminator

power cable   chairs

11 _____

17 _____

23 _____

🔊

36.2 PRESENTAR DATOS
ESCRIBE LAS PALABRAS DEL RECUADRO DEBAJO DE SU CORRESPONDIENTE DIBUJO

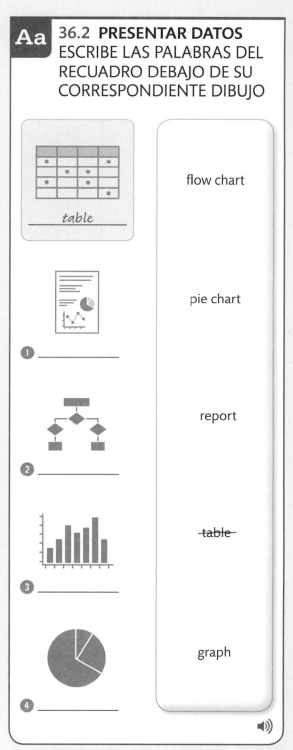

table

flow chart

pie chart

report

~~table~~

graph

1 _____

2 _____

3 _____

4 _____

🔊

297

37 Estructurar una presentación

Cuando hables ante un público, es importante estructurar el discurso para que sea claro y fácil de entender. Existen diversas expresiones que te ayudarán a conseguirlo.

🔧 **Lenguaje** Lenguaje orientador
Aa Vocabulario Material para presentaciones
🧩 **Habilidad** Estructurar una presentación

37.1 VUELVE A ESCRIBIR LAS FRASES PONIENDO LAS PALABRAS EN SU ORDEN CORRECTO

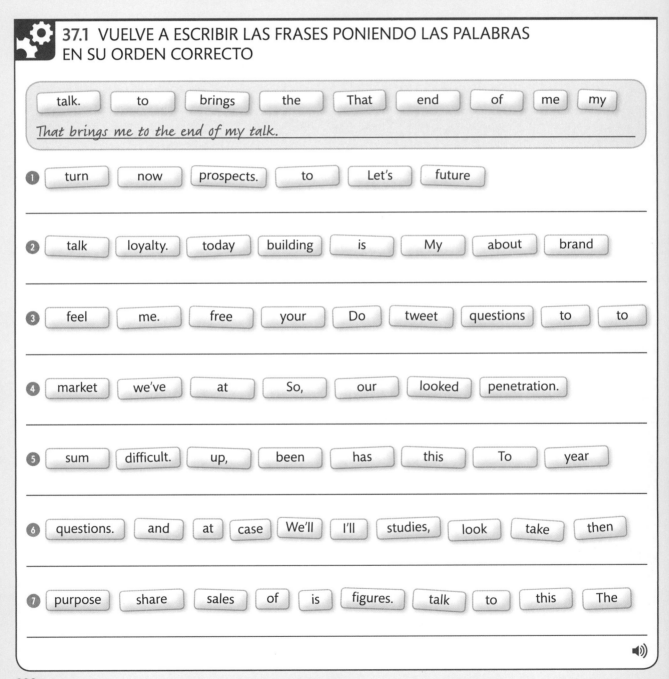

talk. | to | brings | the | That | end | of | me | my

That brings me to the end of my talk.

1 turn | now | prospects. | to | Let's | future

2 talk | loyalty. | today | building | is | My | about | brand

3 feel | me. | free | your | Do | tweet | questions | to | to

4 market | we've | at | So, | our | looked | penetration.

5 sum | difficult. | up, | been | has | this | To | year

6 questions. | and | at | case | We'll | I'll | studies, | look | take | then

7 purpose | share | sales | of | is | figures. | talk | to | this | The

🔊

37.2 DI LAS FRASES EN VOZ ALTA COMPLETANDO LOS ESPACIOS CON LAS PALABRAS DEL RECUADRO

I'll quickly explain the latest proposal, and ___*then*___ I'll go through some case studies.

1. To _____ up, it's been a very successful year for us.

2. We'll _____ at the competitor's products, then I'll introduce our new product.

3. Do _____ free to interrupt if you'd like to comment.

4. So, we've _____ at problems we need to overcome.

5. Now let's _____ to the solutions to those problems.

| feel | look | ~~then~~ | looked | sum | turn |

Aa 37.3 CONECTA LAS DEFINICIONES CON EL MATERIAL

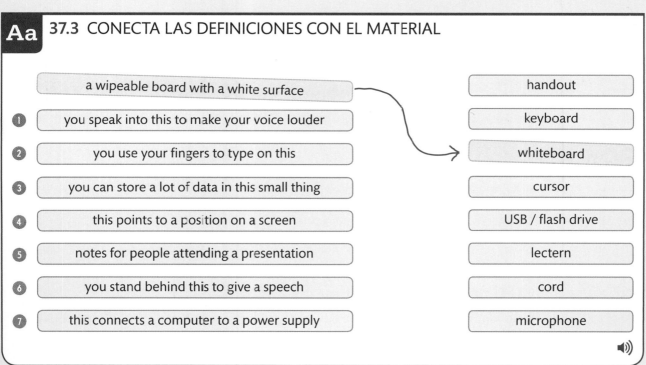

a wipeable board with a white surface → whiteboard

handout

1. you speak into this to make your voice louder — keyboard

2. you use your fingers to type on this — whiteboard

3. you can store a lot of data in this small thing — cursor

4. this points to a position on a screen — USB / flash drive

5. notes for people attending a presentation — lectern

6. you stand behind this to give a speech — cord

7. this connects a computer to a power supply — microphone

299

37.4 LEE EL ARTÍCULO Y RESPONDE A LAS PREGUNTAS

> Presentation equipment is always a good idea.
> **True** ☐ **False** ☑ **Not given** ☐

① Most people do not practice their presentations.
True ☐ **False** ☐ **Not given** ☐

② It is not important to practice your presentation.
True ☐ **False** ☐ **Not given** ☐

③ It doesn't take long to check your equipment.
True ☐ **False** ☐ **Not given** ☐

④ You should not use built-in cameras too often.
True ☐ **False** ☐ **Not given** ☐

⑤ The aim of a presentation is to convey a message.
True ☐ **False** ☐ **Not given** ☐

⑥ It is not always necessary to use lots of equipment.
True ☐ **False** ☐ **Not given** ☐

WELL PRESENTED

Using equipment in presentations can be useful, but it can also make you look unprofessional if you don't know how to use it correctly.

• Practice! Don't leave it until the day to work out how to use the projector screen. Have two or three dry runs to resolve any problems so that your presentation is smooth and professional.

• Make sure equipment is working! Charge any batteries, make sure cords are plugged into sockets and test built-in cameras to make sure they are working, especially if you only use them now and again.

• Don't forget the handouts. High-tech equipment may be great, but the most important thing is that your audience understands the message.

• Sometimes, less is more. If you're not familiar with presentation software, and you fumble when using the remote and pointers, you may be better off not using any visual aids at all. Make your presentation interesting, and whatever you use should be enough.

37.5 ESCUCHA EL AUDIO Y NUMERA DESPUÉS LAS FRASES EN EL ORDEN EN QUE LAS ESCUCHES

Un responsable de recursos humanos habla al personal sobre los cambios en la política de la empresa en materia de tecnología.

Ⓐ They're small, they're light, and they have a built-in camera. ☐

Ⓑ Many of you need to respond to emails out of the office. ☐

Ⓒ That's the end of my talk. Do feel free to ask any questions. ☐

Ⓓ Let's now turn to how this will happen. You will receive an email with a time allocation. ☐

Ⓔ Good morning, everyone. On your chairs, you should have a handout. ☐ 1

Ⓕ Now, all of you already have company laptops. Next month you'll also be issued with tablets. ☐

Ⓖ To sum up, we want to make it as easy and efficient as possible for you to do your jobs. ☐

38 Desarrollar un argumento

Durante una presentación dispones de expresiones concretas para desarrollar tu argumento y hacer que el público sepa qué va a pasar.

⚙ **Lenguaje** Lenguaje útil para presentaciones
Aa Vocabulario Presentaciones
🧩 **Habilidad** Desarrollar un argumento

38.1 VUELVE A ESCRIBIR LAS FRASES PONIENDO LAS PALABRAS EN SU ORDEN CORRECTO

| customers. | and | key | teenagers | large, | are | By | our |

By and large, teenagers are our key customers.

1 we | successful. | Barcelona store, | can | If | on | see | our | is | we | it | home in

_____

2 regions | from | Southwest. | sales | All | achieved | their | aside | targets, | the

_____

3 has | Eastern | positive, | Europe. | excepting | response | Customer | been

_____

4 America. | products | are | South | in | speaking, | our | Generally | popular

_____

5 are | up. | the | February, | sales | exception | With | of

_____

6 is | social | focusing | year | the | company | media | This | campaign. | on | its

_____

7 we | sales | have | focus | on | we | dropped. | can | If | chart, | see | this

_____

🔊

301

38.2 CONECTA EL INICIO Y EL FINAL DE CADA FRASE

If we focus on these results	to our magazines is falling.
① Excepting East Asia, our sales	as dealing with customers.
② In actual fact, the consumer group said	we can see a general trend downward.
③ As a matter of fact, I don't think	they really liked our prototype.
④ For instance, we've had a lot of positive	many areas where we can improve.
⑤ In general, the number of subscribers	have grown by more than 10 percent.
⑥ Concentrating on the basics, there are	feedback about our menswear.
⑦ Jorge needs to improve key skills such	Alyssa is suitable for the role.

🔊

38.3 TACHA LAS PALABRAS INCORRECTAS DE CADA FRASE Y DI TODAS LAS FRASES EN VOZ ALTA

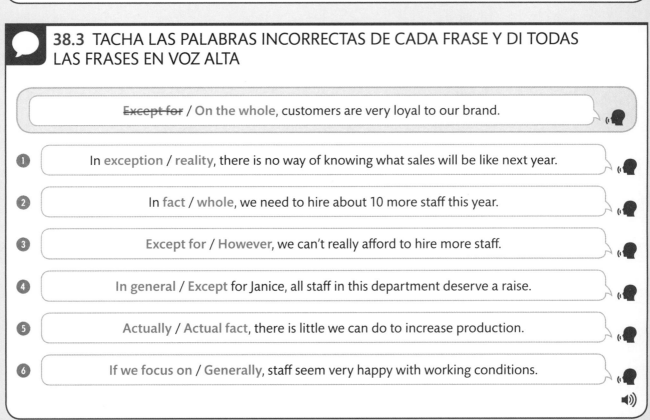

~~Except for~~ / On the whole, customers are very loyal to our brand.

① In exception / reality, there is no way of knowing what sales will be like next year.

② In fact / whole, we need to hire about 10 more staff this year.

③ Except for / However, we can't really afford to hire more staff.

④ In general / Except for Janice, all staff in this department deserve a raise.

⑤ Actually / Actual fact, there is little we can do to increase production.

⑥ If we focus on / Generally, staff seem very happy with working conditions.

🔊

38.4 LEE EL ARTÍCULO Y RESPONDE A LAS PREGUNTAS

At the start of a presentation, give a summary.
True ☑ **False** ☐ **Not given** ☐

① It's important to pack your talk full of details.
True ☐ **False** ☐ **Not given** ☐

② It's best to speak in a dramatic way.
True ☐ **False** ☐ **Not given** ☐

③ You can end your presentation by giving advice.
True ☐ **False** ☐ **Not given** ☐

④ You should invite the audience to ask questions.
True ☐ **False** ☐ **Not given** ☐

⑤ The ideal length for a presentation is 5 minutes.
True ☐ **False** ☐ **Not given** ☐

⑥ Quality is more important than quantity.
True ☐ **False** ☐ **Not given** ☐

PRESENTING PROFESSIONALLY

Your boss asks you to give a presentation, but you don't know where to start. Here are our top tips.

✓ On the whole, you should begin your presentation with a summary statement: explain what issue you are addressing and what your presentation will contain.

✓ Home in on key trends. By and large, you don't need to talk about every single detail of an issue. In fact, it's much better to summarize the most important information, or the most dramatic results.

✓ In general, you should end with a recommendation or conclusion. What do you think your company should do in the future? How can they solve a problem or work more efficiently? You can also ask your audience a question: give them something to think about.

✓ Keep it brief. It's much better to give an excellent 5-minute presentation than to give a boring talk for 30 minutes.

38.5 COMPLETA LOS ESPACIOS CON LAS PALABRAS DEL RECUADRO

In actual _fact_ , Simone has never been late.

① If we _____ in on profits, we can see growth.

② If we focus _____ prices, it's clear they're too high.

③ _____ and large, our T-shirts are our bestseller.

④ In _____ , there's no way we can recover.

⑤ As a _____ of fact, I am very disappointed.

⑥ Except _____ Korea, I've been to most of Asia.

⑦ _____ general, China is our biggest market.

| reality | matter | In | home | ~~fact~~ | on | for | By |

🔊

39 Promocionar un producto

Al describir un producto a un cliente potencial, es útil compararlo con los de la competencia mediante adjetivos comparativos y superlativos.

⚙ **Lenguaje** Comparativos y superlativos
Aa Vocabulario Marketing de productos
🧩 **Habilidad** Comparar productos

⚙ 39.1 TACHA LAS PALABRAS INCORRECTAS DE CADA FRASE

 Our new tablet is **slimmer** / ~~more slim~~ than any other tablet on the market.

① This sports car is **the fastest** / **the most fast** car on sale today.

② Our leather jackets are **fashionable** / **more fashionable** than our competitors' jackets.

③ This digital camera is **the best** / **best** model ever.

④ Our new microwave oven is more efficient **than** / **then** any other model.

⑤ This ice cream maker is **easyer** / **easier** to use than any other on the market.

⑥ Our customers said our sofa is **more comfortable** / **comfortabler** than other models.

⑦ Our organic vegetables are **more fresher** / **fresher** than supermarket vegetables.

⑧ Book a train trip with us in advance to get **the most cheapest** / **the cheapest** fares.

⑨ Our cake range was voted **the tastiest** / **tastiest** on the market in a recent survey.

⑩ These batteries last **more long** / **longer** than the leading brand.

⑪ We think our new winter coat is **the most warm** / **the warmest** on the market.

🔊

39.2 ESCUCHA EL AUDIO Y CONECTA LOS PRODUCTOS CON LAS EXPRESIONES QUE LOS DESCRIBEN

more energy-efficient

the biggest

cheaper

the most comfortable

more stylish

39.3 DI LAS FRASES EN VOZ ALTA COMPLETANDO LOS ESPACIOS CON LAS PALABRAS DEL RECUADRO

We think it is _____ *the best* _____ tablet on the market today.

1 We will create _____ flowers for the tables and the bride's bouquet.

2 Our drink is _____ than that brand because it has a natural caffeine substitute.

3 Our fitness tracker is _____ more expensive models, but is cheaper.

4 We offer _____ other cell phone companies do.

just as effective as   healthier   the most beautiful   ~~the best~~   better technical support than

39.4 VUELVE A ESCRIBIR LAS FRASES PONIENDO LAS PALABRAS EN SU ORDEN CORRECTO

> detergent | as | effective | expensive | just | is | Our | as | brands. | more | laundry
>
> *Our laundry detergent is just as effective as more expensive brands.*

① tasty | cheaper. | is | as | much | the | This | leading | pizza | but | brand, | as

_____

② other | budget | is | as | the | brands | Our | market. | stylish | on | clothing | as

_____

③ are | good | leader. | dishwasher | the | tablets | These | as | market | as | store-brand

_____

④ is | seen. | action | movie | as | Our | anything | you've | as | exciting | latest | ever

_____

⑤ not | eco-friendly | good | brand. | liquid | This | is | as | the | leading | dishwashing | as

_____

🔊

 39.5 VUELVE A ESCRIBIR LAS EXPRESIONES MARCADAS CORRIGIENDO LOS ERRORES

> *more exciting*

① _____

② _____

③ _____

④ _____

⑤ _____

⑥ _____

FOOD MONTHLY

SALAD BOX

Receive delicious vegetables, dressings, and a recipe to make excitinger salads each week!

In our boxes, you'll find all you need to make salads as exciting they can be. We also provide you with a recipe card that tells you how to make five different salads. What could be more simpler? Enjoy a convenienter way to dine in at home.

Our salads are among the healthyest on the market. Every box comes with a nutritional information leaflet so you know you are enjoying the most good food. Our recipe boxes are just as cheaper than shopping in your local supermarket. So what are you waiting for? Place your order today.

40 Proporcionar datos y cifras

Al hacer una presentación o redactar un informe, es importante describir los cambios y las tendencias con un lenguaje preciso y que suene natural.

⚙ **Lenguaje** Colocaciones
Aa Vocabulario Tendencias del negocio
🧩 **Habilidad** Describir datos y cifras

40.1 ESCUCHA EL AUDIO Y LUEGO NUMERA LAS TENDENCIAS EN EL ORDEN EN QUE SE DESCRIBEN

40.2 CONECTA LAS FRASES QUE SIGNIFICAN LO MISMO

There are fewer customer complaints.

We expect a considerable drop in prices.

① Customer complaints are more common.

The share value has rallied slightly.

② Prices peaked, then fell.

Customer complaints have fallen steadily.

③ The price is going up and down a lot.

There was a sharp rise in the share value.

④ Prices are likely to fall significantly.

The price is fluctuating wildly.

⑤ The share value increased dramatically.

There has been an increase in complaints.

⑥ The share value has improved a bit.

There was a dramatic spike last year.

🔊

40.3 TACHA LA PALABRA INCORRECTA DE CADA FRASE

There was a fall **of** / ~~on~~ more than 13 percent.

❶ Staff numbers went **for** / **from** 120 to 150.

❷ **Between** / **To** 15 and 18 percent of stock is unsold.

❸ We've experienced a boom **of** / **at** 56 percent.

❹ Profits have fallen **by** / **at** 11 percent.

❺ The share price peaked **on** / **at** $22.

❻ Complaints doubled **in** / **on** the last quarter.

❼ Our sale was **from** / **between** May and June.

🔊

40.4 LEE EL INFORME Y RESPONDE A LAS PREGUNTAS

Profits have fallen because of the political situation.
True ✓ **False** ☐ **Not given** ☐

❶ Mayvis Homes was established 12 years ago.
True ☐ **False** ☐ **Not given** ☐

❷ Mayvis Homes' share price dropped in the first quarter.
True ☐ **False** ☐ **Not given** ☐

❸ People think Mayvis Homes' share price will climb in the next few months.
True ☐ **False** ☐ **Not given** ☐

❹ Customers do not like the latest houses built by Mayvis Homes.
True ☐ **False** ☐ **Not given** ☐

❺ Last year, there was a sharp rise in Rushington Construction's share price.
True ☐ **False** ☐ **Not given** ☐

❻ Most of Rushington Construction's work comes from the government.
True ☐ **False** ☐ **Not given** ☐

INDUSTRY AND TECHNOLOGY

Gloom in construction sector

The construction sector experienced a difficult first quarter, with share prices in the leading construction companies declining considerably. It is believed that worries about recent political events have contributed to a considerable drop in profits in the sector.

Mayvis Homes, which specializes in residential property for the over-60s, saw its share price fall by 12 percent in the first quarter, and there are fears that it could fall further before the end of the year. CEO Stan Gilmore said that customers are adopting a "wait and see" approach before making the decision to buy.

Going against the general trend is Rushington Construction PLC, which focuses on the education and healthcare sectors. Although the company's share price fluctuated slightly last year, the first quarter saw a return to stability, with the company's share price rallying slightly in the first quarter. The company relies on government contracts for between 60 and 85 percent of its work, and therefore is not so affected by short-term market trends.

40.5 RESPONDE AL AUDIO COMPLETANDO LOS ESPACIOS CON LAS PALABRAS DEL RECUADRO

What are you doing about customer service staff?

We are increasing our customer service staff from ___10 to 15___ .

1 What's happening to the price of rice?

There's been a _____ because of a poor harvest.

2 When was your best sales period last year?

Our sales _____ $200,000 a day in December.

3 Your production facility seems very efficient.

Yes, malfunctions have _____ since last year.

4 How much of the stock is on sale?

Between _____ percent of our stock is on sale.

5 Are you happy with our profits this year?

Yes, they've _____ since last year.

6 Why have our costs gone up?

There was an _____ 10 percent in the cost of electricity.

~~10 to 15~~	20 and 30	dramatic spike	fallen steadily
increase of	peaked at	rallied slightly	

41 Planes y sugerencias

Utilizamos los verbos modales para hacer sugerencias y las preguntas indirectas o la voz pasiva para solicitar información o avisar de un error de manera educada.

⚙️ **Lenguaje** Preguntas indirectas
Aa Vocabulario Negociación empresarial
🧩 **Habilidad** Negociar educadamente

Aa 41.1 CONECTA EL INICIO Y EL FINAL DE CADA FRASE

Would you mind bringing — our fee in installments?

1 Are you able to pay — as soon as possible.

2 We might move forward with the contract — the delivery date forward by a week?

3 I would like to resolve this issue — that you could design our new logo.

4 Maybe we could discuss some — if you would consider buying in bulk.

5 We were thinking — something more innovative.

6 I'm afraid I was hoping for — alternative options for the design.

🔊

41.2 ESCUCHA EL AUDIO Y NUMERA DESPUÉS LAS IMÁGENES EN EL ORDEN EN QUE LAS ESCUCHES

Pippa negocia con un cliente sobre su contrato para redecorar su tienda.

Ⓐ Well, we were hoping for something more modern. ☐

Ⓑ I'm afraid we need it sooner. ☐

Ⓒ I was wondering what sort of look you want. 1

Ⓓ Would you mind waiting until next month for payment? ☐

Ⓔ I was thinking we could use the company colors. ☐

Ⓕ Are you able to pay in installments? ☐

41.3 VUELVE A ESCRIBIR LAS FRASES COMO PREGUNTAS INDIRECTAS PONIENDO LAS PALABRAS EN SU ORDEN CORRECTO

tell | Could | expect | me | you | deliver | order? | to | you | our | when

Could you tell me when you expect to deliver our order?

① try | wondering | I | these | on. | was | where | clothes | I | can

_____

② me | sample | you | tell | will | when | ready? | designs | be | the | Could

_____

③ I | to | Samia's | I | about | if | you | was | talk | performance. | could | wondering

_____

④ tell | store? | product | you | me | I | order | Could | this | in | whether | can

_____

⑤ have | whether | invoice | was | my | you | wondering | paid | yet. | I

_____

⑥ tell | the | Could | is? | me | warranty | you | period | what

_____

⑦ how | new | from | was | the | I | product | is | one. | wondering | old | different | the

_____

⑧ when | you | price | available? | will | me | the | Could | be | tell | list

_____

⑨ able | be | I | offer | if | was | a | wondering | to | me | discount. | would | you

_____

🔊

41.4 VUELVE A ESCRIBIR LAS FRASES EN VOZ PASIVA

> I'm afraid you didn't pay our invoice on time.
> *I'm afraid our invoice wasn't paid on time.*

1 I'm afraid you missed our deadline.

_____

2 It looks as if you sent the wrong size.

_____

3 It seems that you did not apply the discount.

_____

4 I'm afraid you delivered our order to the wrong address.

_____

5 It looks as if you calculated the price incorrectly.

_____

6 It seems that you do not train your employees very well.

_____

7 I'm afraid you did not satisfy our customers.

_____

8 It seems that you lost my order while it was being delivered.

_____

9 I'm afraid you did not cook my steak properly.

_____

10 It looks as if you have made a mistake.

_____

11 It seems that you still haven't fixed the printer.

_____

12 I'm afraid you did not check the document thoroughly enough.

_____

41.5 TACHA LAS PALABRAS INCORRECTAS DE CADA FRASE Y DI TODAS LAS FRASES EN VOZ ALTA

Could / ~~Do~~ you tell me when my order will be ready?

1. I was wondering if **you could** / **could you** look at my presentation.

2. Could you **tell** / **telling** me when my order will be dispatched?

3. I was wondering if you **do** / **would** be free to meet tomorrow.

4. Could you tell me when **can we** / **we can** expect our invoice to be paid?

5. I was wondering what time **does the store open** / **the store opens**.

6. Could you **tell me** / **know** how much the new product should retail for?

41.6 LEE EL CORREO ELECTRÓNICO Y MARCA EL RESUMEN CORRECTO

1. Juanita has only paid 25 percent of Brendan's invoice because she is not happy with the service she received. She wants the staff to receive training. ☐

2. Juanita has not paid Brendan's invoice because she is unhappy with the service that she received. She does not think Brendan has trained his staff well. ☐

3. Brendan has not invoiced Juanita for the bikes because his staff were rude to Juanita. He is going to give them training in customer service. ☐

4. Brendan has sent a revised invoice for the bikes because the order was delivered two weeks late. He is going to look into training his staff. ☐

To: Brendan Schultz

Subject: Late delivery

Dear Mr. Schultz,

I am writing to complain about the poor service we received from your company. We placed an order for 25 bikes, which were due to be delivered on December 2. However, nothing was delivered from you on that date. Your staff did not appear to know anything about our order, which makes me think they must not have been trained properly. The order was delivered two weeks later, which led to us losing sales. We are therefore withholding payment until the situation can be resolved.

Kind regards,

Juanita Estevez

42 Destacar tu opinión

Existen muchas expresiones en inglés para destacar educadamente tu punto de vista. Son útiles cuando hay desacuerdos en el lugar de trabajo.

⚙️ **Lenguaje** Marcadores de énfasis
Aa Vocabulario Desacuerdos en el trabajo
🧩 **Habilidad** Destacar tu opinión

⚙️ 42.1 MARCA LAS FRASES QUE SEAN CORRECTAS

What we need is an up-to-date delivery schedule from you. ☑
What need is an up-to-date delivery schedule from you. ☐

① If I ask you, you won't find a better deal ☐
If you ask me, you won't find a better deal. ☐

② Actually, we are waiting for the factory to send us more of that product. ☐
We are waiting actually for the factory to send us more of that product. ☐

③ The most thing is that we agree on schedule dates. ☐
The main thing is that we agree on schedule dates. ☐

④ What I'm saying is that I can offer free delivery on orders over a hundred. ☐
What I say is that I can offer free delivery on orders over a hundred. ☐

🔊

🎧 42.2 ESCUCHA EL AUDIO Y RESPONDE A LAS PREGUNTAS

Tia negocia con un responsable de tienda, Roger, que espera que venda su nuevo producto.

① The raincoats sell for $30 in the store.
True ☐ **False** ☐ **Not given** ☐

② Roger is happy with Tia's revised deal.
True ☐ **False** ☐ **Not given** ☐

③ Roger places an order for 200 raincoats.
True ☐ **False** ☐ **Not given** ☐

④ The raincoats are the cheapest on the market.
True ☐ **False** ☐ **Not given** ☐

⑤ Tia would sell the raincoats in another store.
True ☐ **False** ☐ **Not given** ☐

Roger is happy with Tia's asking price.
True ☐ **False** ☑ **Not given** ☐

42.3 RESPONDE AL AUDIO EN VOZ ALTA COMPLETANDO LOS ESPACIOS CON LAS EXPRESIONES DEL RECUADRO

Unfortunately, I can't do the job until next month.

That's OK. _The main thing is_ that we have the right person to do the job.

① Could you send some sample designs for us to look at?

_____ , we sent you an email with them this morning.

② Is there any way you could offer a reduced asking price?

I'm afraid not. If _____ , this is a great deal.

③ We'd like to sign the contract today if that is possible.

What _____ an assurance that you can meet our schedule dates.

④ Would you consider offering us a discount?

The _____ that we agree on a price that allows enough profit.

⑤ Can we say a price of $50 per unit?

_____ your asking price is too high. Can we say $40 a unit?

I'm afraid	Actually	~~The main thing is~~
you ask me	main thing is	we need is

315

Debatir condiciones

Se suele utilizar el first conditional y el second conditional para negociar con clientes y colegas, mientras que el zero conditional sirve para hablar de verdades generales.

⚙ **Lenguaje** Condicionales
Aa Vocabulario Negociar y regatear
🧩 **Habilidad** Debatir posibilidades

43.1 COMPLETA LOS ESPACIOS CON LOS VERBOS EN LOS TIEMPOS CORRECTOS PARA FORMAR ORACIONES EN SECOND CONDITIONAL

If the contract _____was_____ (be) clearer, we _____would sign_____ (sign) it now.

1. If they _____ (give) us a discount, we _____ (place) an order.

2. If the product _____ (be) cheaper, we _____ (buy) it.

3. If they _____ (move) the deadline, we _____ (meet) it.

4. I _____ (reply) to the email now if I _____ (have) more time.

5. We _____ (sell) more online if our website _____ (be) faster.

6. We _____ (send) the package tomorrow if you _____ (order) before 9 tonight.

7. If the agency _____ (send) us better temps, we _____ (use) them again.

8. If I _____ (work) late every night, I _____ (finish) my report for Friday.

9. I _____ (apply) for the job if the hours _____ (not be) so long.

◀))

43.2 ESCUCHA EL AUDIO Y RESPONDE A LAS PREGUNTAS

Andrés negocia con una empresa de decoración y pintura las reformas que quiere hacer en su casa.

The team can start in December.
True ☐ False ☐ Not given ☑

1 The team might finish by the end of January.
True ☐ False ☐ Not given ☐

2 There are six painters on the team.
True ☐ False ☐ Not given ☐

3 Andrés asks the team to repaint all the rooms.
True ☐ False ☐ Not given ☐

4 Andrés knows what colors he wants.
True ☐ False ☐ Not given ☐

5 Andrés wants to see more wallpaper samples.
True ☐ False ☐ Not given ☐

6 Andrés won't see new designs until next week.
True ☐ False ☐ Not given ☐

43.3 VUELVE A ESCRIBIR LAS FRASES EN ZERO CONDITIONAL PONIENDO LAS PALABRAS EN SU ORDEN CORRECTO

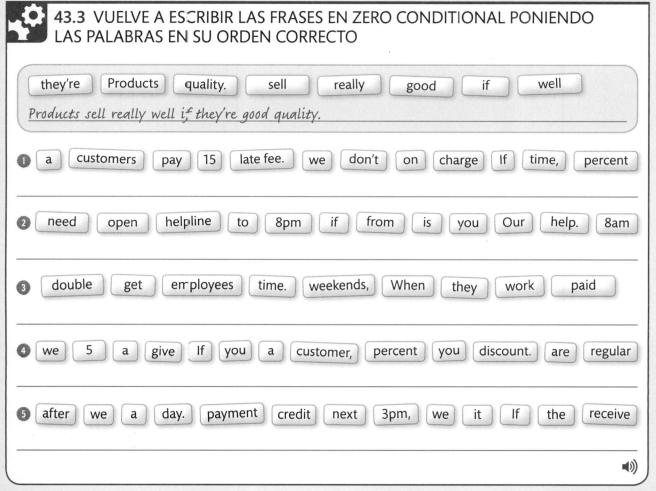

| they're | Products | quality. | sell | really | good | if | well |

Products sell really well if they're good quality.

1 a | customers | pay | 15 | late fee. | we | don't | on | charge | If | time, | percent

_____

2 need | open | helpline | to | 8pm | if | from | is | you | Our | help. | 8am

_____

3 double | get | employees | time. | weekends, | When | they | work | paid

_____

4 we | 5 | a | give | If | you | a | customer, | percent | you | discount. | are | regular

_____

5 after | we | a | day. | payment | credit | next | 3pm, | we | it | If | the | receive

_____

🔊

317

43.4 CONECTA EL INICIO Y EL FINAL DE CADA FRASE

If you book 100 places,

we would give her a verbal warning.

1 If you need help with your computer,

if it was cheaper to do that.

2 We would move production to Europe,

we'll give you a 5 percent discount.

3 We will issue a full refund

we give them a 5 percent discount.

4 If clients are regular customers,

you can call the IT department.

5 If our receptionist was rude to you,

if you return the product to one of our stores.

43.5 VUELVE A ESCRIBIR LAS FRASES EN FIRST CONDITIONAL CORRIGIENDO LOS ERRORES

If you **will order** before 9pm, we'll deliver your goods the following day.
If you order before 9pm, we'll deliver your goods the following day.

1 If you **not** pay on time, we won't send you your order.

_____

2 We'll issue a full refund if **you won't be** happy with our products.

_____

3 If you **will book** two nights in our hotel, we'll give you a third night for free.

_____

4 If Alan's presentation **will go** well, he will get promoted next month.

_____

5 We won't charge you for your stay if you **won't** get a good night's sleep.

_____

6 If you **ordering** over 100 units, we'll give you a discount.

_____

318

43.6 DI LAS FRASES EN VOZ ALTA COMPLETANDO LOS ESPACIOS CON LAS EXPRESIONES DEL RECUADRO

Our standard price for this new model is $200 per unit.

Well, if you lowered the price, _____ *I would buy* _____ 50 units.

1. We'd like the renovations to be finished by the end of next month.

   Well, if you pay for the overtime, _____ the job by then.

2. Is there any possibility you can give us a discount?

   Yes. If _____ 100 units or more, we give them a 5 percent discount.

3. I'm not happy with the quality of your product.

   If you return it to us within 28 days, _____ a full refund.

4. Our new tablet retails for $79 in all major stores. We can do you a price of $69 per unit.

   If _____ a price of $59 per unit, we'd sell it in our stores.

5. Your product is not very good quality.

   We're sorry to hear that. If a customer makes a complaint, _____ it very seriously.

6. We love your product. We'd like to place an order for 100 units a month.

   We can't do that yet. If _____ on extra staff, we'd be able to increase production.

---

we take	we will issue	~~I would buy~~	clients buy
we took	we will finish	you could do	

🔊

319

44 Debatir problemas

Se utiliza el third conditional para hablar de un pasado irreal o de acontecimientos que no pasaron. Es útil para hablar sobre errores en el lugar de trabajo.

⚙ **Lenguaje** Third conditional
Aa Vocabulario Errores en el trabajo
Habilidad Hablar sobre errores anteriores

 44.1 COMPLETA LOS ESPACIOS CON LOS VERBOS EN LAS FORMAS CORRECTAS PARA FORMAR ORACIONES EN THIRD CONDITIONAL

If you __had worked__ (work) late, you __would have finished__ (finish) the presentation.

1. We _____ (sign) the contract if the deadline _____ (not be) so tight.

2. If we _____ (leave) earlier, we _____ (not miss) the train.

3. If the waitress _____ (not be) so rude, we _____ (not complain).

4. If we _____ (order) before 3pm, we _____ (receive) the goods today.

5. We _____ (not lose) the client if we _____ (deliver) the report on time.

6. If you _____ (repair) the printer, we _____ (not cancel) the contract.

7. If I _____ (know) how expensive it was, I _____ (put) it in the safe.

8. The boss _____ (not shout) if you _____ (admit) your mistake.

9. If you _____ (be) more prepared, you _____ (give) a better presentation.

10. We _____ (give) you free delivery if you _____ (pay) on time.

11. If I _____ (know) our competitor's price, I _____ (offer) a bigger discount.

12. We _____ (meet) our deadline if we _____ (employ) more staff.

13. If you _____ (not be) off sick, we _____ (invite) you to the meeting.

14. We _____ (pay) the full amount due if you _____ (not miss) our deadline.

15. If you _____ (sell) more products last time, we _____ (ask) you to lead the pitch.

◀))

44.2 ESCUCHA EL AUDIO Y MARCA LAS COSAS QUE REALMENTE PASARON

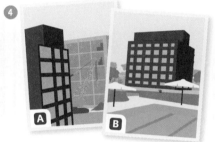

44.3 CONECTA EL INICIO Y EL FINAL DE CADA FRASE

| If you'd left earlier | → | we wouldn't have canceled their order. |

1 If I'd used the spell check,

2 If she'd told the boss about her mistake, → you wouldn't have missed the meeting.

3 If they'd paid on time,

4 If I'd used the latest sales data,

5 If he'd checked the order was right,

6 If you'd ordered more units,

7 If he'd wanted an older model,

he wouldn't have been so angry.

you wouldn't have missed the meeting.

my report would have been up to date.

he would have asked for one.

we would have given you a discount.

my work wouldn't have had so many errors.

his clients wouldn't have complained.

🔊

321

44.4 VUELVE A ESCRIBIR LAS FRASES CON "UNLESS"

If you don't order 500 units, we won't be able to give you a discount.
Unless you order 500 units, we won't be able to give you a discount.

1 Clive will get a verbal warning if his timekeeping doesn't improve.

_____

2 If you don't pay by the end of today, we will cancel the contract.

_____

3 We won't win the contract if we can't offer a better price.

_____

4 I won't get promoted this year if I don't impress the boss.

_____

5 Your warranty will not be valid if you don't register your product.

_____

6 If I don't sell to 100 new customers, I won't meet my sales targets.

_____

7 We won't make many sales if we don't beat our competitors' prices.

_____

8 If I don't work overtime, I'm not going to meet the deadline.

_____

9 His presentation will be boring if he doesn't add special effects.

_____

10 The CEO won't be happy if we don't win the contract.

_____

11 If you don't lower the price, we won't order any more units.

_____

12 We will miss the train if we don't leave now.

_____

44.5 LEE EL INFORME Y RESPONDE A LAS PREGUNTAS

The clients were happy with the product.
True ☐ **False** ☑ **Not given** ☐

1 Customers wanted recipes from around the world.
True ☐ **False** ☐ **Not given** ☐

2 Future Foods didn't offer traditional dishes.
True ☐ **False** ☐ **Not given** ☐

3 Customers wanted evening deliveries.
True ☐ **False** ☐ **Not given** ☐

4 Customers thought that the price was too high.
True ☐ **False** ☐ **Not given** ☐

5 Future Foods will develop more international dishes.
True ☐ **False** ☐ **Not given** ☐

PROGRESS REPORT

Ten months ago we launched our new recipe service, Future Foods, where we send customers the ingredients to cook a new recipe. Sales have been very disappointing, and feedback on the service was not as good as we expected.

WHY? Customers said that they prefer to try a range of dishes from around the world. If we had known that, we would have had less of a focus on traditional meals. They also said that the price could be lower.

WHAT NOW? Unless we reduce the price of our service and listen to customers' feedback, we won't make as many sales as we want. We need to offer a more international, affordable range of foods and recipe packs.

44.6 TACHA LAS PALABRAS INCORRECTAS DE CADA FRASE Y DI TODAS LAS FRASES EN VOZ ALTA

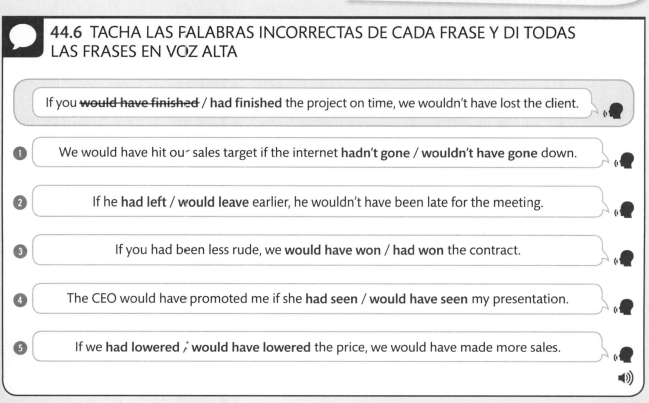

If you ~~would have finished~~ / **had finished** the project on time, we wouldn't have lost the client.

1 We would have hit our sales target if the internet **hadn't gone** / **wouldn't have gone** down.

2 If he **had left** / **would leave** earlier, he wouldn't have been late for the meeting.

3 If you had been less rude, we **would have won** / **had won** the contract.

4 The CEO would have promoted me if she **had seen** / **would have seen** my presentation.

5 If we **had lowered** / **would have lowered** the price, we would have made more sales.

Respuestas

1.1 🔊

1 I'd like to **introduce** you to Marco from IT.
2 You **must** be Paola from Madrid.
3 Gloria, **meet** Julia, our new secretary.
4 Have you two **met** each other before?
5 Great to **see** you again!
6 **Nice** to meet you, Antonio.
7 Sanjay has **told** me all about you.
8 I don't **think** we've met before, have we?
9 It's a **pleasure** to meet you.

1.2 🔊

1 Simone, I'd like to introduce you to **Gerald, our new sales manager.**
2 Hello. I don't think we've **met. My name's Jana.**
3 You must be Selma from the **Chicago branch. Great to meet you.**
4 Hi, Omar. I think we **met at the conference in Dubai last year.**
5 My boss has told me **so much about your work.**
6 This is Colin from IT. **Colin, meet Liam. He's joining our team soon.**

1.3

1 False
2 True
3 Not given
4 True
5 False
6 False

1.4 🔊

1 I **catch** the train to work at 8:15am each morning.
2 We **have** a new printer that is difficult to use.
3 I **am** working at the Guangdong branch all this August.
4 Sanchez **knows** Katie because they worked together.
5 **Are** you enjoying this presentation? I think it's great.
6 Tim **doesn't know** Anna from the Montevideo branch.
7 Marek **likes** the new furniture we bought for the office.
8 How **do you spell** your name?
9 The meeting usually **takes** only half an hour.
10 Doug is really **enjoying** the conference this year.
11 I'd like **to** introduce you to my manager, José Rodriguez.
12 Clara **works** from 8:30 to 4:30 on Thursdays and Fridays.

1.5 🔊

1 Our company **is having** some difficulties at the moment.
2 Pablo, I'd like you to **meet** my wife, Elvira.
3 I usually hate conferences, but I **am enjoying** this one a lot.
4 I **have** two children, a son and a daughter.

5 Michael, **I'd like** to introduce you to Michelle.
6 I **don't think** we've met before, have we?
7 It's so great **to see** you again after such a long time.
8 How **do you pronounce** your last name?
9 You must **be** Harold from Copenhagen. Nice to meet you.
10 Hi, I think we met in Oslo, **didn't we**?

2.1 🔊

1 I was preparing for the presentation.
2 Did Greg work in the New York branch?
3 Akira was living in Kyoto in 1998.
4 I didn't understand the presentation.
5 Pete was reading a book at 9pm yesterday.
6 I was feeling exhausted at work, so I left.
7 Did you enjoy the presentation?
8 Were you working in IT then?
9 Kai wasn't feeling well, so he went home.
10 I found a new job in France.

2.2
(A) 6
(B) 1
(C) 5
(D) 7
(E) 4
(F) 3
(G) 2
(H) 8

2.3 ◄))
❶ Daniel **has worked** for more than five different law firms.
❷ I **have taken** the bus to work all my working life.
❸ The company **has employed** five new people since September.
❹ Peter is a terrible waiter. He **has started** looking for a different job.
❺ Andrea **has worked** here since she graduated in 1999.
❻ The factory **has produced** 15,000 machines this year.
❼ Tim's really happy. He **has finished** his presentation for tomorrow.
❽ We **have sold** our products in more than 25 countries.
❾ I **have walked** to work since my car broke down.
❿ I **have decided** that I'm going to retire next year.
⓫ Dave **has taken** more time than we expected.
⓬ I **have worked** at this office for more than 25 years now.
⓭ Chris **has visited** more than 50 countries so far.

2.4 ◄))
❶ Jim was preparing a presentation **when his boss entered the room**.
❷ I've worked at this company **for more than ten years**.
❸ Chris had to wait for a taxi for **more than an hour**.
❹ Tim moved to New York **when he was transferred to the US office**.
❺ I ran my own software company **before I started working here**.
❻ In 2013, our company **bought a smaller Canadian software firm**.

2.5
❶ True
❷ True
❸ False
❹ True
❺ Not given
❻ True

2.6 ◄))
❶ At 3pm yesterday, I **was discussing** the new software with our IT team.
❷ While Susan **was eating** lunch, her team was working hard.
❸ Karl moved to Berlin when he **lost** his job in Paris.
❹ Alan **was traveling** to work when he received a call from his wife.
❺ In 2007, I **was working** in the company headquarters in Geneva.
❻ I **have lived** in San Francisco since 2003.
❼ Peter **was sleeping** at his desk when his phone rang.
❽ They **have been** based in Frankfurt since 1994.
❾ While I **was living** in France, I worked as a waiter.

❿ Derek **bought** his first house in 2009.
⓫ What **were you doing** at 4pm this afternoon?
⓬ I **was studying** in college when I decided to work as a lawyer.
⓭ Who was in the meeting room when you **entered**?
⓮ We **sold** our first machine in China in 2003.

03

3.1 ◄))
❶ Human Resources (HR)
❷ Information Technology (IT)
❸ Sales
❹ Public Relations (PR)
❺ Legal
❻ Facilities / Office Services
❼ Administration
❽ Research and Development (R&D)
❾ Accounts / Finance
❿ Marketing
⓫ Production

3.2 ◄))
❶ assistant
❷ Chief Executive Officer (CEO)
❸ Chief Financial Officer (CFO)
❹ employee
❺ manager

3.3 🔊
1. to work for
2. to work as
3. to be responsible for
4. to be in charge of
5. to work in

04

4.1 🔊
1. Claude is used to working weekends.
2. Did Paul use to work in San Francisco?
3. I am not used to working in such heat.
4. The team used to go out for lunch.
5. We didn't use to have so many meetings.
6. I used to live in a house near the office.
7. Did you use to work in Paris?
8. I'm used to the new software now.
9. I'll never get used to this operating system.
10. Kerry is used to commuting a long way.

4.2
A. 7
B. 1
C. 5
D. 6
E. 2
F. 4
G. 3

4.3 🔊
1. We didn't use to have so much free time.
2. I'll never get used to driving on the left.
3. Did Anthony use to work in the Frankfurt branch?
4. I am used to having to get up at 6am.
5. Derek isn't used to commuting so far to work.
6. The team hasn't got used to the new operating system.
7. We used to have lunch in the café near the park.
8. Danielle isn't used to giving presentations.
9. Pam used to work in the branch in Cologne.
10. Phil isn't used to wearing a uniform for work.

4.4 🔊
1. She's not used to working long hours.
2. I used to work as a doctor.
3. Dan's used to driving on the left.
4. She's used to getting up early.
5. I'm not used to spicy food.
6. I'll never get used to English weather.
7. I'm not used to working so late.
8. We're getting used to the new boss.

4.5 🔊
1. No, thanks. I'm fine.
2. I'm not used to this hot weather!
3. That would be great!
4. I haven't yet. Is it any good?
5. I'm getting used to the traffic.

4.6 🔊
1. Are you **used to** living in a tropical country yet?
2. I **used to** travel to work on foot before they built the metro.
3. When I lived in Berlin, we **used to** live in an apartment downtown.
4. **Did you use to** work in the Edinburgh branch?
5. I grew up in Japan, so I'm **used to** driving on the left.
6. Arnold's **used to** waking up at 5am every morning.
7. I **am used to** working for a demanding boss.
8. When I was a child, I didn't **use to** like going to school.
9. We **used to** go to Florida each year on vacation.
10. My father **used to** work in a factory until it closed down.

05

5.1 🔊
1. Staff must not smoke in the building.
2. We don't have to go to work tomorrow.
3. I have to go home early on Thursday.
4. You have to do this assignment today.
5. We need to increase sales this year.
6. Jim doesn't have to attend the meeting.
7. The team must not forget their timesheets.
8. Paolo has got to sign up for the course.

9 We will need to hire new staff this fall.
10 We must improve our productivity.

5.2
1 False
2 True
3 False
4 False
5 False
6 Not given
7 True
8 True
9 Not given

5.3 ◄))
1 Would you give Peter a copy of the minutes, please?
2 All visitors must leave their passes at reception.
3 Could you take this letter to the post office, please?
4 Ramon needs to work harder if he wants a promotion.
5 Sharon needs to sign up for the training course.
6 Could you leave a copy of the agenda on my desk, please?
7 You must complete the enrolment form before 5pm on Friday.
8 Staff must not smoke inside the building.
9 Would you send an email to everyone about the meeting?
10 You must finish the project by Wednesday evening.

5.4 ◄))
1 The company must change **if it wants to survive**.
2 I need you to finish **the presentation by Friday**.
3 Could you keep a **record of everything you spend this week**?
4 Would you inform **the team about the recent changes, please**?
5 The company has got to **invest more in training**.
6 You don't have **to finish the assignment today**.
7 We need to think **about closing some of our branches**.

5.5
1 True
2 False
3 Not given
4 False
5 False

5.6 ◄))
1 No, I **don't need** you to finish it today.
2 I'm sorry, Mike. We really **must** have it by Friday.
3 I'm sorry, but members of the public **must not** enter the building.
4 We need them tomorrow. **Could** you call the supplier, please?
5 No, you **don't have** to. The deadline is next week.
6 Well, I **need** it by 1pm today.

06

6.1 ◄))
1 to make a loss
2 to undercut competitors
3 an overdraft
4 overheads
5 sales figures
6 to get into debt
7 to break even
8 an economic downturn
9 income
10 expenditure / outlay
11 an upturn in the market
12 accounts
13 to drop
14 cash flow
15 to peak
16 the exchange rate
17 to go out of business

07

7.1 ◄))
1 Sales **were** good because we **had organized** a good marketing campaign.
2 Sales **had fallen** sharply, so we **decided** to withdraw the product.
3 Aditya **wanted** to try a program that the team **hadn't used / had not used** before.
4 After Peter **had finished** the report, he **wanted** to go on vacation.

7.2 🔊

① Ramon **had written** ten pages of the report when his computer **crashed**.

② Many of our employees **had not** visited the factory before and **were** very impressed.

③ Bob's speech **was** disappointing because he **hadn't prepared** well.

④ Nobody **had told** the conference delegates where their hotel **was**.

⑤ I **hadn't delegated** tasks to Kai before, but I **thought** he did a good job.

7.3 🔊

① The **following** report will explore our new sales strategy.

② As can be **seen** in the table, we have invested $4 million this year.

③ Some of our customers have **stated** that they are not satisfied with the result.

④ Our initial investigation **suggests** that this is not true.

⑤ Our **initial** recommendation is to reduce the budget by 50 percent.

⑥ We **consulted** a number of focus groups for this report.

7.4 🔊

① The purpose of our report **is to review our current sales strategy**.

② The following report presents **a summary of our findings**.

③ Our clients stated that **they were unhappy with the changes**.

④ Based on the initial research, **we should invest more in R&D**.

⑤ Our principal recommendation is to **proceed with the sale of the subsidiary**.

7.5

① 20 miles from downtown

② Rail connections to other cities

③ It is affordable in Alchester

④ Stay in Alchester for over ten years

⑤ A decision has not yet been made

7.6 🔊

① The purpose of this report is to compare the two factories.

② Focus groups had been consulted before we implemented the policy.

③ Sales of our products had fallen in comparison with the previous quarter.

④ Our principal recommendation is to increase investment in R&D.

⑤ Profits had risen by more than 20 percent in the first half of 2015.

7.7 🔊

① In this report we will **present** the findings of our research.

② The **purpose** of this report is to investigate the pros and cons of the new software.

③ This bar chart **compares** the sales figures for the last two years.

④ Our customers **stated** that they had been disappointed with the product.

8.1 🔊

① Of course. Let me see what I can do.

② Certainly. It's ZX42 9JL.

③ We've been having difficulties with our software.

④ We'll offer you a discount on your next order.

8.2 🔊

① Could you **tell me** your reference number?

② **Let's see** what we can do.

③ **We'll offer** you a full refund.

④ Our driver **has been experiencing** problems.

⑤ Could you **hold the line**, please?

⑥ I'm very **sorry to hear** that.

⑦ Can you **look into** to this issue?

⑧ **We'll send you** a replacement.

⑨ Of course I can **help** you.

8.3 🔊

① I'm very **sorry** to hear that, sir.

② Certainly. Let's **see** what I can do.

③ Could you tell me your **reference** number, please?

④ Could you please **hold** the line?

⑤ I'm sorry. Our IT system's been **experiencing** difficulties.

⑥ My order **arrived** dirty and broken.

⑦ Can you **offer** any compensation?

⑧ Of course. We'll give you a **discount** on your next order.

8.4 ◄))
1 Could you look **into** the problem for me?
2 The company **has** been experiencing difficulties recently.
3 Please **hold** the line for a moment.
4 I've been **waiting** all day for my order to arrive.

8.5 ◄))
Nota: Las respuestas a 1, 2 y 4 pueden ir en forma contraída.
1 We **have been preparing** a proposal all evening.
2 Our website **has been experiencing** difficulties this morning.
3 Chris **has been working** on that project for three months now.
4 Our products **have not been selling** well so far this year.

8.6 ◄))
1 Peter has been talking for more than 25 minutes.
2 Have you been getting good feedback from the clients?
3 The company has been losing money for years.
4 Juan hasn't been working at our company for long.

8.7
A 4
B 2
C 6
D 5
E 1
F 3

8.8
4

09

9.1 ◄))
1 social media
2 a website
3 automated
4 to access
5 to work online
6 up to date
7 user-friendly
8 to back up
9 a conference call
10 breaking up
11 to download an app
12 a mobile device
13 to work offline
14 an email has bounced
15 to charge
16 a username and password
17 a network

10

10.1 ◄))
1 I hope all's well **with you and the team in Tokyo**.
2 Would you be free **on Thursday July 7 at 4pm**?
3 Please give me a call if **you can't make it**.
4 Please see the schedule **for next week's conference attached**.
5 If you have any questions, **don't hesitate to get in touch**.

10.2 ◄))
1 I was **wondering** if you could help me prepare my presentation.
2 Would you be free to **meet** on Thursday evening?
3 I'm **copying** Sanjay and Anita in on this email.
4 I **hope** all's well with you and the team in Delhi.
5 Please see the minutes of yesterday's meeting **attached**.
6 If you have any **questions**, please let me know.
7 How **about** joining us at the pizza place later this evening?

10.3 ◄))
1 I just wanted **to** check that you're coming to the presentation.
2 Would you **be** free next Wednesday morning at 11:30?
3 Please find a copy of the report **attached**.
4 If you **have** any questions, please let me know.
5 I'm **copying** Ricardo in on this.

10.4
4

11

11.1 ◄))
1 Mohammed **is meeting** the new supplier to discuss a new deal.
2 Jola **is talking** to Sales this afternoon to agree new discounts.

3 They **are aiming** to have the presentation ready by 5:00pm.
4 I **am writing** to inform you that there is a delay with the part you need.
5 We **are still waiting** to hear from the Chinese partners.

11.2
1 Futuro **2** Futuro
3 Futuro **4** Presente

11.3
1 hesitate
2 obtain
3 confirm
4 inform
5 prefer
6 assure

11.4 ◀))
1 Will you be attending the launch of the new products?
2 I was wondering if we could put our meeting back to tomorrow.
3 We are aiming to send the new designs by Friday.
4 Will you be paying for the order in cash or by card?
5 I was wondering if you would take the clients out for dinner.

11.5 ◀))
1 We are still putting together the final sales report.
2 Will you be giving the presentation at tomorrow's conference?
3 We were wondering if we could postpone our meeting.

11.6
1 Not given **2** True
3 False **4** False

12

12.1 ◀))
1 Can you deal **with** the cleaners, please? The kitchen is a mess.
2 Can we catch **up** later this morning at around 11:00?
3 Is the fridge broken again? I'll **look** into that now.
4 Have we run **out** of paper? There's none in the photocopier.

12.2 ◀))
1 Can we **fix up** a meeting with Marketing and Sales?
2 Have you asked Surina to **fill out** all the paperwork?
3 The printer has **run out** of ink again.
4 I can't **figure out** what Dave wants me to do.
5 I need to **bring up** the topic of punctuality with you.

12.3 ◀))
1 I need to **back** my files **up**.
2 Can you **give** the agenda **out**?
3 Can we **call** tomorrow's meeting **off**?
4 Can you **pass** my message **on** to her?
5 Let me **hand** the minutes **out**.

---

6 I want to **put** my tie **on**.
7 Can you **fix** another meeting **up**?
8 I need to **send** an email **out**.
9 We are **taking** new staff **on**.
10 Can you **set** the projector **up**?
11 I'd like to **talk** the sales plan **over**.

12.4
1 She hasn't backed them up
2 Thursday afternoon
3 Write a report about feedback
4 Deal with some of Amanda's emails
5 A message
6 His best suit and tie

12.5 ◀))
1 Jamil's flight is delayed. I think we'll have to call our meeting with him **off**.
2 All employees have to put an apron **on** before entering the kitchen.
3 We're hoping to give **out** samples of our work at the exhibition.
4 It's really important to back your files **up** every night or you could lose work.

12.6 ◀))
1 Khalil has **filled the form** out.
2 She has just **hung up** on me without saying goodbye!
3 He **put his tie on** because he had an important meeting.
4 He gave **his report out** to everyone at the meeting.
5 They **set a meeting** up for later in the week.

13

13.1 🔊
1 packaging
2 product testing
3 handmade
4 a one-off production
5 labor intensive
6 stock
7 product approval
8 raw materials
9 a prototype
10 a production line
11 a warehouse
12 shipping
13 ethically sourced
14 overproduction
15 a factory
16 mass production
17 a supplier

14

14.1 🔊
1 The media **had been** told about the press launch and were out in force.
2 New models **are being** created to coincide with the premiere of the movie.
3 The design has been **patented** so nobody can copy it.
4 Our coffee is **produced** using the finest coffee beans from Kenya.
5 It is thought that the sandwich **was** invented in 1762.

14.2
A 4
B 1
C 7
D 8
E 2
F 5
G 3
H 6

14.3 🔊
Respuestas modelo
1 Our accounts are audited every May by a separate department.
2 The coffee blends we produce are approved by our professional coffee tasters.
3 All passengers' luggage is scanned by security staff when they go through Departures.
4 All our marketing material for the Asia office is designed by Jane.
5 All the orders are checked by our packing department before delivery.
6 The database is updated with customers' details by Stephen.
7 All our ingredients are bought from Fair Trade suppliers by our cosmetics buyer.
8 New lines are added to our women's fashion range on a regular basis by Nicola.
9 The new product tracking app for customers was invented by Jason.
10 Our new website was launched by our marketing team in January.

14.4
1 False
2 False
3 True
4 Not given
5 True

14.5 🔊
1 These toys can't have been checked.
2 A discount should have been given.
3 The order can't have been taken by her.
4 A free bag can be given to every customer.
5 Faults in the products shouldn't be ignored.
6 Our prices can't be beaten.
7 His order must have been placed late.

14.6 🔊
1 Next, the ingredients **are mixed** together to make a cake mixture.
2 Then the cake mixture **is poured** into cake pans.
3 Next, the cakes **are put** in a hot oven.
4 When the cakes are cooked, they **are taken** out of the oven.
5 The cakes **are left** to cool on a wire cooling rack.
6 Finally, the cakes **are assembled** and decorated with icing.

15.1
OPINIÓN:
fantastic, **amazing**, **excellent**
TAMAÑO:
huge, **tiny**, **large**
EDAD:
ancient, **modern**, **state-of-the-art**
COLOR:
magenta, **crimson**, **black**
NACIONALIDAD:
Indian, **Turkish**, **Chinese**
MATERIAL:
leather, **metal**, **plastic**

15.2 ◄))
❶ It's made by a fabulous, young Indian designer.
❷ I love these fantastic, small, blue china bowls.
❸ We're launching an outstanding new range of clothes.

15.3 ◄))
❶ What a lovely **stylish** desk you have!
❷ Sam asked me to design a **classic** brown chair.
❸ I brought back some delicious **Turkish** candy from my trip.
❹ Do you like this **pretty** crimson watch for ladies?
❺ Do you like our cute **green** teddy bear for our new children's range?
❻ Our competitors are selling **unfashionable** black suits.
❼ Our team is developing an innovative **leather** interior for our executive car.

❽ I love buying large **yellow** flowers for the office.
❾ Jane has bought an **expensive** classic car at an auction.
❿ We have an amazing **Italian** coffee machine in our office.
⓫ I have ordered some of those fabulous **double-sided** business cards.
⓬ We have an amazing **grey** oven in our staff kitchen.
⓭ This is our new **lightweight** digital camera.

15.4
❶ B
❷ A
❸ B
❹ A
❺ B

15.5
❶ False
❷ True
❸ True
❹ False
❺ Not given

15.6 ◄))
❶ Their website is easy to use because it has a **simple**, effective style.
❷ Zander's Pizzeria makes **delicious**, oven-baked pizzas.
❸ I love this **comfortable**, leather armchair.
❹ The new, **full-color** brochure is very bright and attractive.
❺ I like the **clean**, new rooms in that hotel.

❻ Those small, **diamond** earrings are beautiful.
❼ My dad drives a **huge**, black truck.
❽ Ella makes high-quality, **cotton** curtains.
❾ We aim to give **excellent** customer service.
❿ We offer a **unique**, personal experience.
⓫ I don't like those ugly, **wooden** desks. They're hideous!
⓬ This modern, **Japanese** car is much faster than my old one.
⓭ What a **gorgeous**, big photo of all the team!

16.1 ◄))
❶ logo
❷ slogan / tagline
❸ brand
❹ radio advertising
❺ billboard
❻ poster
❼ sponsor
❽ door-to-door sales
❾ copywriter
❿ word of mouth
⓫ coupons
⓬ free sample
⓭ market research
⓮ consumer
⓯ promote
⓰ sales pitch
⓱ merchandise
⓲ social media
⓳ unique selling point / USP
⓴ television advertising
㉑ online survey
㉒ leaflet / flyer
㉓ advertising agency

17

17.1 🔊
EXTREMOS:
enormous, **terrible**, **brilliant**,
furious, **fascinating**, **exhausted**,
awful
ABSOLUTOS:
true, **wrong**, **perfect**, **equal**,
impossible, **unique**, **empty**
CLASIFICADORES:
metal, **electronic**, **scientific**,
woolen, **industrial**, **organic**, **rural**

17.2 🔊
1 The factory was totally destroyed.
2 I was thoroughly exhausted this morning.
3 The warehouse is almost empty.
4 Jon is an extremely good speaker.
5 Peter is fairly good at Spanish.
6 The project is largely complete.
7 Sian is an utterly brilliant swimmer.

17.3 🔊
1 **Fairly** certain. I think I sent it yesterday.
2 Yeah, it's absolutely **fantastic**. I love it.
3 It was very impressive, but **almost** identical to mine!
4 Yes, it's totally **unique**. I have the only one.
5 That's right. **Nearly** everyone likes him.
6 No. It was **absolutely** awful. I almost fell asleep.
7 It was practically **empty**. There were only a few people there.

17.4
1 absolutely fantastic.
2 utterly original.
3 almost impossible.
4 very busy.
5 extremely important.
6 completely new.
7 highly reflective.
8 practically impossible.
9 absolutely amazing.
10 really clever.
11 fairly certain.

18

18.1
1 B
2 A
3 A
4 B
5 A

18.2 🔊
1 There was **such** a large crowd outside.
2 The results were **so** disappointing.
3 We've had **such** a fantastic year.
4 The price for the hotel was **so** high.
5 The week seems to pass **so** slowly.

18.3 🔊
1 This coffee was so expensive.
2 My colleague is so lazy.
3 Clara's presentation was so interesting.
4 That is such a depressing book.
5 The sales were so disappointing.
6 It's such a strange story.
7 It's so important to be on time.

18.4
1 Not given
2 True
3 True
4 False
5 Not given

18.5 🔊
1 Our senior managers think the price of our products is **too** high.
2 This room won't be big **enough** for this afternoon's meeting.
3 The team is **so** excited about tonight's awards ceremony.
4 I thought today's meeting was **such** a waste of time.
5 Jim doesn't speak loudly **enough**. I can barely hear him.
6 Our IT system is **so** old. It's time we invested in a new one.
7 The new intern works **so** slowly. She prefers talking on the phone.
8 Our products were **too** expensive to appeal to middle-market customers.
9 Mary is **such** an ambitious woman. She wants to be a CEO by the age of 30.
10 You shouldn't drive **too** quickly when you're in this part of town.
11 The strikes have caused **such** a problem for our employees who commute.
12 The marketing campaign was **too** boring to appeal to young people.

19.1 🔊
1 You shouldn't work so hard.
2 You could do a training course.
3 You should get some fresh air.
4 You must give him a call.
5 You should order some more.

19.2 🔊
1 You **could** try delegating the task to your team. I'm sure they'd do a great job.
2 Greg **ought to** apologize to his team for his behavior. He was very rude.
3 Antonio really **ought to** employ some new staff, or we'll never meet our deadline.
4 We **should** organize a training course for the interns.
5 The secretary really **should** ask her boss for a raise. She works very hard.

19.3 🔊
1 You **should walk** to work if the train is canceled.
2 You **ought to call** the IT desk about your new password.
3 You **shouldn't eat** your lunch at your desk. Go to a café instead.
4 You **must tell** your manager when you want to book time off.
5 Clare **ought to take** a break if she's tired of her job.
6 You **could do** an English course if you want to learn English.
7 Dave **ought to go** home if he's not feeling well.

8 Pete **shouldn't talk** to the public about company secrets.

19.4
4

19.5 🔊
1 Why don't we **organize** a feedback session?
2 What about **asking** Pedro to do it?
3 Why don't you **hire** some new staff?
4 What about **buying** a new printer?
5 Why doesn't Mabel **go** on vacation?
6 Why **don't** they close the Mumbai branch?
7 What about **inviting** the clients to dinner?

19.6
1 Why don't we file these documents?
2 You should take a vacation for a week.
3 You shouldn't eat your lunch at your desk.
4 What about hiring a new member of staff?
5 Why don't you work from home on Fridays?

19.7 🔊
1. What about asking Pete to do it?
2. What about organizing a workshop?
3. What about selling our products online?

4. Why don't we ask Pete to do it?
5. Why don't we organize a workshop?
6. Why don't we sell our products online?

19.8 🔊
1 What about organizing a workshop?
2 Why don't we arrange a meeting?
3 What about buying a new printer?
4 Why don't we hire a new secretary?
5 What about asking Cyril to help?
6 What about providing free software?
7 Why don't we book a meeting room?

19.9 🔊
1 You ought to ask the clients for more time.
2 How about talking to your co-workers about your problems?
3 We could hire some new interns next year.
4 Why don't you quit your job if you don't like it?
5 You should complete the project before the deadline.

20.1 🔊
1 a bonus
2 an appraisal / a performance review

3 to approve
4 to delegate
5 performance
6 to be promoted

20.2 🔊
1 telephone manner
2 fast learner
3 IT / computing
4 data analysis
5 attention to detail
6 numeracy
7 written communication
8 problem-solving
9 time management
10 work well under pressure
11 able to drive
12 public speaking
13 teamwork
14 research
15 organization
16 leadership
17 decision-making

21

21.1 🔊
1 Tom **can** fix your car this afternoon. It will be ready at 5:00.
2 Karl **can't** drive. He failed his driving test again.
3 Jon used to be really nervous, but now he **can** give presentations.
4 She **can** type really quickly. She types over 60 words per minute.
5 I **can't** work the new photocopier. It's too difficult.
6 Hansa is a really good cook. She **can** cook really nice Indian food.

7 Ali **can't** read my handwriting. He says it's really messy.
8 Ania **can** speak French. She learned it in college.
9 Petra **can't** manage her staff any more. They do what they like.
10 Parvesh **can** write clear reports. They are easy to read.

21.2
1 Pasada
2 Presente
3 Presente
4 Pasada

21.3 🔊
1 Janice **can't** tell me if sales are up until she gets the final reports in.
2 Phil loves meeting new people, so he **can** work in the HR department.
3 Saira **couldn't** type fast, but now she can type 60 words a minute.
4 Ed **can** write reports very well. I'm going to ask him to help me write mine.
5 Keira **couldn't** use the database, but now she trains people in how to use it.
6 For years Alex **couldn't** speak Arabic, but now he has done a beginners' course.

21.4
1 False
2 False
3 Not given
4 False
5 True
6 True

21.5 🔊
1 He would do well in a smaller team.
2 She can manage her new team much better.
3 Before, he wouldn't talk in public.
4 She could train staff to do them.
5 She wouldn't be a good trainer.
6 He could be head of the department.

21.6 🔊
1 David has given his team excellent training. Now they can do anything.
2 Have you seen his brilliant designs? He can create our banners.
3 No one could read the boss's handwriting. It was terrible.
4 Sebastian is a very proactive person and would do well in marketing.

21.7 🔊
1 We think you are very talented and **would** be a great addition to our department.
2 I don't know what is wrong with the coffee machine. I **can't** get it working.
3 My confidence is much better now. Before, I **couldn't** give presentations.
4 Laila couldn't negotiate with her old boss, but she **can** with her new boss.

22.1 ◄))

1 This training is really interesting. It is a lot of fun, **too**.

2 Team-building days are useful. They are **also** fun.

3 Some people always wash their coffee cups, **while** others don't.

4 **Although** Team A did the task quickly, Team B didn't finish it.

5 Team A built the bridge very quickly. Team B was **equally** successful.

6 Team A helped each other, **while** Team B disagreed with each other.

7 Hard work is an excellent trait in a team, **whereas** laziness is terrible.

8 Yesterday's training was useful. **However**, this morning's task was pointless.

9 Some people want to lead a team, **while** others are happy to be team members.

10 It is important to say what we all think. We should listen to each other **as well**.

11 This training is very useful. It is **equally** a good way to get to know people.

22.2 ◄))

1 Although Sam went to the training day, he didn't learn anything new.

2 Team A solved the problem really quickly. Team B was equally successful.

3 This training is useful for managers. It is also useful for team members.

4 Some people want to be managers, while others want to be team members.

5 Laziness is a terrible trait for a team member, whereas honesty is excellent.

6 We'd like all staff to follow our usual dress code for the training. Please be on time, too.

22.3

A 3
B 1
C 6
D 5
E 4
F 2

22.4 ◄))

1 The team-building task was useful and it was also a lot of fun.

2 Team A had to build a bridge, whereas Team B had to make a pizza. / Team B had to build a bridge, whereas Team A had to make a pizza.

3 While Team B completed the task first, they had some problems.

4 Training courses are really useful and they are often fun as well.

5 Team A worked together very well. Team B was equally cooperative. / Team B worked together very well. Team A was equally cooperative.

6 This task will identify your weaknesses, but also your strengths.

7 Our team baked a cake. However, the activity didn't matter.

8 Although the other team came first, we worked well together. / Although we came first, the other team worked well together.

9 Yesterday's task was easy, while today's task was more difficult.

10 Team A finished the task quickly, whereas Team B took its time. / Team B finished the task quickly, whereas Team A took its time.

22.5 ◄))

1 As a consequence, I am now a team leader.

2 Consequently, they all won a medal.

3 For this reason, I was very nervous.

4 As a result, everyone attends them.

5 Consequently, she was promoted last week.

22.6 ◄))

1 Team-building days are great for morale. **Consequently**, the atmosphere in our office is good.

2 We have regular IT training sessions. For this **reason**, everyone has good computer skills.

3 We do team building every year. As a **consequence**, we work really well together.

4 During team building we meet new staff. **For this** reason, we know our co-workers well.

23

23.1 🔊
1 We plan **to launch** our new product range at the conference.
2 Would you consider **organizing** the accommodation for the visitors?
3 I really enjoy **taking** clients out for dinner at famous restaurants.
4 Jenny has offered **to meet** our visitors at the airport.
5 I keep **suggesting** that we should have a staff training session.

23.2 🔊
1 Our clients expect **to** receive good customer service.
2 Would you consider **making** the name badges for the delegates?
3 Colin has offered **to organize** the training program for the new staff.
4 I hope **to impress** our clients when I show them around the new office.

23.3
1 Entertaining clients
2 To receive good customer service
3 They give their honest opinion
4 Their competitors had had one
5 Offer team-building events

23.4 🔊
1 I regret **to tell** you that I can't take the clients out for dinner. I'm very sorry.
2 Do you remember **calling** Dan last month? He has a question about a discount you offered.

3 Sue stopped **to read** the program for the launch event. It looked really interesting!
4 He regrets **telling** her his idea for the event because she copied it.
5 David gave his presentation, and went on **to talk** about new events.
6 I stopped **giving** my presentation because the CEO had a question.

23.5
Ⓐ 4
Ⓑ 1
Ⓒ 6
Ⓓ 8
Ⓔ 2
Ⓕ 7
Ⓖ 5
Ⓗ 3

23.6 🔊
1 I really enjoy entertaining new clients.
2 Sandra invited me to attend the overseas sales conference.
3 My manager asked me to book the accommodation.
4 Tom expects his manager to give him a promotion soon.
5 My boss asked me to give him an update on recent sales.
6 We invited all our customers to come to our party.

23.7 🔊
1. I enjoy entertaining our clients.
2. I remembered entertaining our clients.
3. I remembered to meet our clients.
4. I remembered to book accommodation.

5. She remembered entertaining our clients.
6. She remembered to meet our clients.
7. She remembered to book accommodation.
8. She enjoys entertaining our clients.
9. We enjoy entertaining our clients.
10. We remembered entertaining our clients.
11. We remembered to meet our clients.
12. We remembered to book accommodation.
13. They enjoy entertaining our clients.
14. They remembered entertaining our clients.
15. They remembered to meet our clients.
16. They remembered to book accommodation.

24

24.1 🔊
1 to take minutes
2 to look at
3 to take questions
4 to be absent
5 to reach a consensus
6 to run out of time
7 a strategy
8 main objective
9 action points
10 to give a presentation
11 to send out an agenda
12 to interrupt
13 attendees

⑭ to suggest / propose
⑮ unanimous agreement
⑯ to review the minutes
⑰ a show of hands

25

25.1 ◄))
① She said she could speak Thai and Mandarin.
② She said she needed to talk to Hansa in HR.
③ He said he was working on the sales report.
④ He said he had finished the presentation.
⑤ He said he had been to the Mumbai office.

25.2 ◄))
① She **said (that) the taxi was outside**.
② He **said (that) he needed to call the US office**.
③ He **said (that) she would get the bill**.
④ He **said (that) he couldn't open any emails**.
⑤ She **said (that) she had sent the order to them**.

25.3 ◄))
① She said she was busy that afternoon.
② He said that he didn't like his new boss.
③ They said they hadn't received the delivery.
④ He said he was going to be in Tokyo that week.
⑤ They said they had been to the new product launch.
⑥ She said she would issue an invoice right away.
⑦ He said the company could give a 5 percent discount.
⑧ She said she had gotten along well with the interviewer.
⑨ They said they were designing a new range.

25.4
Ⓐ 5
Ⓑ 1
Ⓒ 4
Ⓓ 6
Ⓔ 3
Ⓕ 7
Ⓖ 2

25.5 ◄))
① He **told** me that he'd been to China twice.
② She **said** that she was going to Montreal.
③ He **promised** that he wouldn't be late for the train.
④ He **explained** that he didn't know how to use the photocopier.
⑤ He **denied** that he had broken the coffee machine.
⑥ She **complained** that the food was cold when the waiter brought it.

⑦ He **confirmed** that the tickets had been booked.

25.6 ◄))
① She **promised** to call me back after 2:30 that afternoon.
② He **added** that he needed a copy of Simon's report about the year-end accounts.
③ She **explained** that the new all-in-one printer wasn't difficult to use.
④ He **confirmed** that he'd like to buy 100 units of the new product.
⑤ He **complained** that he wasn't happy with the customer service he had experienced.
⑥ She **suggested** that we should ask Ameera what she thought.

26

26.1 ◄))
① Selma asked me where you had put the annual report.
② Krishnan wanted to know why I was late for work again.
③ My boss asked me what I thought about the new IT system.
④ Hans asked me where we would have the presentation this afternoon.
⑤ Sophie asked Claude why he wasn't at the meeting.
⑥ Tabitha asked me who had taken her cell phone.
⑦ Fiona wanted to know who had taken the minutes.

26.2
1. False
2. True
3. False
4. Not given
5. True
6. Not given
7. False
8. True
9. True

26.3 🔊
1. make a suggestion
2. get fired
3. make a mistake
4. do your best
5. do someone a favor
6. get a job
7. do research
8. make notes

26.4 🔊
1. She **asked me how many people worked in the company**.
2. He **asked me why I had handed in the report so late**.
3. He **asked me who had gotten / got promoted**.
4. He **asked me who the new senior manager was**.
5. He **asked me which candidate I had chosen**.
6. He **asked me how long I had worked here**.
7. She **asked me why I had been so late this / that morning**.
8. He **asked me what time I got home**.
9. He **asked me where I had had the appointment**.
10. She **asked me which printer I preferred**.

26.5 🔊
1. He **asked me if / whether the package had arrived safely**.
2. She **asked me if / whether I could do her a favor**.
3. He **asked me if / whether he could have a word with me later**.
4. She **asked me if / whether I had finished writing the report yet**.
5. He **asked me if / whether he she could make a suggestion**.
6. She **asked me if / whether I had read last year's report**.
7. He **asked me if / whether I was coming to the awards ceremony on Saturday**.
8. She **asked me if / whether I had enjoyed the presentation**.
9. He **asked me if / whether I had booked a table at the restaurant**.

27

27.1
1. True
2. True
3. False
4. Not given
5. False
6. True
7. Not given
8. True
9. Not given
10. False

27.2 🔊
1. Unfortunately, we have a few problems with our production line.
2. Regrettably, few people have the skills necessary to run a multinational company.
3. So few of our customer reviews are positive that it's becoming a problem.
4. I have little doubt that the conference will be a success.

27.3 🔊
1. **Few** employees have worked for the company for as long as Sofia.
2. We have **a little** bit of time before the meeting ends.
3. So **few** companies offer this service that demand is sure to be high.
4. Very **little** can be done to improve facilities in the short term.
5. We can expect **a little** increase in profits over the summer season.
6. It's great that you have **a few** ideas about how we can improve sales.

27.4 🔊
1 I'm sure all will be well once you've spoken to the customer.
2 All I know is that the order is late.
3 Is that all you need?
4 All we can do is wait for a response from the client.

27.5 🔊
1 There are a few things we can do to improve staff morale.
2 We've had little interest in our new app.
3 Little can be done to improve staff morale.
4 So few people have money to spend on our luxury vacations.
5 Our new app is very popular.

28

28.1 🔊
1 What is our target this year?
2 Who is handling the account?
3 Who is in charge?
4 What is your sales target?
5 Who responds to complaints?
6 Who spoke to Mr. Jones?
7 What is our plan of action?

28.2 🔊
1 Do I need to dress formally?
2 Did you quote this price?
3 What should I tell the client?
4 Who wants to work in New York?

28.3 🔊
1 We should increase our margins, **shouldn't we**?
2 I didn't send you the report, **did I**?
3 She'll be a great manager, **won't she**?
4 I'm not getting a raise, **am I**?
5 We haven't made a loss, **have we**?
6 We're going to win the award, **aren't we**?
7 Louis has worked here since 2012, **hasn't he**?
8 Brett worked late last night, **didn't he**?

28.4 🔊
1 We could launch our product early, **couldn't we**?
2 Jakob ordered the samples, **didn't he**?
3 We can't cut prices any further, **can we**?
4 We haven't achieved our target, **have we**?
5 We need to improve product quality, **don't we**?
6 We're not ready for the meeting, **are we**?
7 They are opening a new store, **are they**?
8 You weren't in London last week, **were you**?
9 You traveled to Paris by train, **didn't you**?
10 I'm writing the proposal, **aren't I**?
11 I emailed the right person, **didn't I**?

28.5
1 Not given
2 True
3 False
4 False
5 False
6 True
7 False

28.6 🔊
1 What was her name? I didn't **hear** it.
2 **Who** is responsible for training?
3 You're not worried about the meeting, **are you**?
4 **What** is our timetable for this project?
5 Sales are better than expected, **aren't they**?
6 Sorry, I **missed** that.

29

29.1 🔊
1 tourism
2 finance
3 energy
4 mining
5 recycling
6 manufacturing
7 agriculture / farming
8 catering / food
9 hospitality
10 fashion
11 electronics
12 real estate (US) / property (UK)
13 chemical
14 entertainment
15 pharmaceutical
16 healthcare

17 fishing
18 transportation
19 education

29.2 🔊
1 organized
2 team player
3 practical
4 responsible
5 motivated
6 calm
7 confident
8 reliable
9 innovative
10 punctual
11 accurate
12 ambitious
13 professional
14 energetic
15 creative

30

30.1 🔊
1 I want to apply for **a** job in **an** office.
2 I've got **an** interview next week for **the** job I told you about.
3 **The** ideal candidate enjoys working in **a** team.
4 **The** deadline for applications for **the** job in IT is next Monday.
5 Please complete **the** form on **the** job page on our website.

30.2
A 8
B 1
C 7
D 5
E 3
F 6
G 2
H 4

30.3 🔊
1 Nurses often have to work very long hours. They are very important people.
2 Working hours are from 8:30 to 5:00. Lunch is from 1:00 to 2:00.
3 Vale loves giving training sessions. The training sessions she gave yesterday were amazing.
4 The job I applied for is based in Madrid. It's in sales and marketing.
5 The people who interviewed me for the job were really nice. They were managers.
6 I have just applied for a job in the finance department at your company.
7 The salary for this job is not very good. I don't think I'll apply for it.
8 The successful candidate will have three years' experience branding new products.
9 Our company is currently recruiting more staff for the Paris office.
10 I have meetings with the CEO and some of our new clients today.
11 Marisha is good at pitching products. It's the thing she enjoys most about her job.
12 This job requires in-depth knowledge of business trends in the wider world.

30.4
1 False
2 True
3 True
4 False
5 True

30.5 🔊
1 We need someone who is willing to travel, and can speak **Spanish**.
2 Tara works in **the finance department** of an advertising agency.
3 Marc and Samantha often travel to China **on business**.
4 The company is based in the UK, but it does business throughout **the EU**.
5 I started looking for a job as **an engineer** after I finished college.

31

31.1 🔊
1 I graduated from college in June 2016 with a degree in chemistry.
2 I am writing to apply for the role of head chef.
3 I heard about the job on your website.
4 I am fully trained in all aspects of health and safety.

31.2 🔊

① Jim graduated **from** college with a degree in physics. Now he is a research scientist.
② He is fully trained **in** all aspects of sales and marketing. I think he'll do a great job.
③ In my role as Senior Program Developer, I reported **to** the Director of IT.
④ Tanya has applied **for** a job in the marketing department of our company.
⑤ I worked **for** the owner of a leading hairdressing salon. I learned a lot from him.

31.3

Respuestas modelo
① Ellie has worked in marketing for more than ten years.
② She developed award-winning campaigns in key markets.
③ She introduced a new customer-focused branding initiative.
④ She is responsible for training junior members of staff.
⑤ She looks after the Europe region.
⑥ She describes herself as energetic, dynamic, and extremely reliable.

31.4 🔊

① skills
② salary
③ a position
④ to apply for a job
⑤ to report to someone
⑥ a team
⑦ a résumé
⑧ an opportunity
⑨ to amount to

31.5

Dear Mr. Chang,

I am writing to **apply for** the position of Senior Sales Consultant, as advertised on your website.

I have **worked in** the sales industry for more than eight years, and am **trained in** selling a range of products to varied markets. In my current position, I am **responsible for** sales to Asian markets, and last year I **looked after** the new market of China, where sales **amounted to** more than $10 million.

I am **passionate about** working in the sales industry and welcome the opportunity to learn new skills. I run the training program for new staff members and ten of the junior sales consultants **report to** me. In their training, I **focus on** developing awareness of the most effective sales strategies.

Please find my résumé and references attached. I look **forward to** hearing from you.

Yours sincerely,
Deepak Singh

32

32.1 🔊

① The person **who** I admire the most in the company is the Sales Manager.
② The office **where** I work is a tall, modern building.
③ The customers **who** gave us feedback were all very positive.
④ The team **that** I lead is fully qualified and highly motivated.

32.2 🔊

① We sell apps **that are designed by IT specialists**.
② We are based in an office **that is in the business park**.
③ I work with clients **who have high standards**.
④ This is the reason **that I applied for this job**.
⑤ Spain and Italy are the countries **where we sell the most**.

32.3 🔊

① Training staff, **which** is my favorite part of the job, is really interesting.
② In my current job, **where** I serve lots of customers, I have learned to deal with complaints.
③ My boss, **who** is very understanding, encourages me to leave the office on time.
④ While I was in college I worked in a café, **which** taught me a lot about customer service.

32.4
- Ⓐ 3
- Ⓑ 5
- Ⓒ 1
- Ⓓ 6
- Ⓔ 2
- Ⓕ 4

32.5 ◀))
1. Last summer, **when** I had just graduated, I worked as an intern in a bank.
2. My teacher, **who** was an amazing person, inspired me to study law.
3. My apprenticeship, **which** I completed in 2016, was in IT.
4. The place **where** I want to work as a tour guide is New York.

32.6 ◀))
1. Tom's team, whose staff are hard-working, hit their sales targets last month.
2. In my previous job, which was in sales, I learned to give presentations.
3. I sometimes work from home as it is the place where I can concentrate best.
4. My clients, who expect good customer service, said my work was excellent.

32.7 ◀))
1. The thing **that gets** me excited is when we hit our sales targets.
2. People **who know** me well say I am customer-focused and give good customer service.
3. I have a can-do attitude, **which means** that I get things done.
4. I would hope to receive more than my current salary, **which is** $45,000 a year.
5. My boss, **who is** quite understanding, would allow me to leave after a month's notice.

33

33.1 ◀))
1. to touch base
2. a change of pace
3. a game plan
4. to be on the same page
5. up in the air
6. up and running
7. in a nutshell
8. to go the extra mile
9. to fill someone's shoes
10. groundbreaking
11. to clinch the deal
12. to call it a day
13. to cut corners
14. to be ahead of the game
15. a ballpark figure
16. to do something by the book
17. to corner the market

34

34.1 ◀))
1. Alex comes up **with** great ideas.
2. Hal looks down **on** his co-workers.
3. I'm **looking** forward to the launch.
4. Fred **puts** up with a lot of noise.
5. She comes **across** as rather superior.
6. The printer has run **out** of paper.
7. Jim's staff get **away** with being late.
8. Shona has to **face** up to poor sales.
9. We need to **keep** up with the schedule.

34.2 ◀))
1. I get along with my team.
2. She comes across as friendly.
3. I can't put up with his music!
4. He comes up with good ideas.
5. Tom gets away with a lot.
6. We have run out of coffee.
7. We must face up to facts.

34.3
Respuestas modelo
1. Some companies think social media is trivial.
2. Social media helps you keep up with trends.
3. ABC Foods uses social media to tell customers news about the company.
4. ABC Foods has previews of its TV ads.
5. The company does this so that subscribers feel they are keeping up with company news.

6 Competitions make ABC Foods stand out from its competitors.
7 Customer loyalty means customers make repeat purchases.

34.4 🔊
1 I'll look **them** up online.
2 Can you fill **it** in?
3 I'd like you to take **it** on.
4 I can't let **them** down.
5 Can we talk **it** over?
6 Could you look **it** over?
7 We are giving **them** away.
8 I need to call **it** off.
9 I can't figure **them** out.
10 The taxi will pick **him** up.
11 I keep putting **it** off.
12 Yola turned **it** down.

34.5
1 Update your website
2 To find new ideas for your product
3 Translating social media use into sales
4 Sharing users' questions and answers

34.6 🔊
1 Cev always comes up with great ideas.
2 Dan and Sam don't get along with each other.
3 The copier has run out of paper.
4 Here's a form. Can you fill it in?
5 Rohit keeps up with the business news.

34.7 🔊
1 I looked **up** the candidates on social media. They all looked very talented.
2 Kennedy's team **gets away with** a lot. It's not fair on the others.
3 You're leading an important pitch today. Please don't **let me down**.
4 Can you take **on** writing the sales report today, or are you too busy?
5 We're giving **away** free books to customers. We hope it will increase sales.

35

35.1 🔊
1 She will get a raise in her new position.
2 You won't get a bonus.
3 We may ask him to become a mentor.
4 We might need to recruit more staff.
5 We may have to fire her.

35.2
1 True
2 True
3 False
4 False
5 True

35.3 🔊
1 Our staff can't use the new database. We might have to provide more training.
2 David has over 15 years' experience and he will lead our marketing department.
3 I need your report by Thursday. You might need to work overtime.
4 Anna's laptop is broken. She will get a new one this week.
5 There is a pay freeze at the moment, so you won't get a raise.
6 If Rita's work doesn't get better, we may have to fire her.
7 We have some meetings in France. You may have to go to Paris.
8 We can't hire any staff at the moment, so you might not get an assistant until March.
9 If your presentation goes well, the CEO might ask you to give it to the board.
10 Tanya has been promoted. She will lead a team next year.
11 Dev has had a bad trading year. He won't meet his sales targets.
12 Paula always goes the extra mile. She will make a great addition to the team.

35.4 🔊
1 He will definitely be promoted.
2 You will probably get a raise.
3 She probably won't need training.
4 They'll definitely get a bonus.
5 I probably won't go on vacation.
6 I definitely won't change jobs.
7 We will probably hire an intern.
8 He probably won't meet clients.
9 It will definitely sell well.

35.5 🔊
1. You will **probably** be promoted.
2. He will **definitely** get the job.
3. She **definitely** won't get a raise.
4. They will **probably** get a bonus.
5. I **probably** won't get a new laptop.
6. You will **definitely** get a company car.
7. I will **probably** move to the head office.
8. You **probably** won't need much training.
9. We will **definitely** hire a new assistant soon.

35.6 🔊
1. Katrina doesn't have much experience. She **will probably** need more training.
2. Meliz has to travel to see clients. She **will probably** get a company car.
3. Mr. Cox has complained about our service. He **probably won't** use us again.
4. The negotiations are going quite well. We **might** clinch the deal tomorrow.
5. You're doing a great job, but our profits are down. You **might not** get a raise.

35.7
Respuestas modelo
1. Isaac met all his sales targets this year.
2. Isaac might be promoted next year.
3. Isaac will mentor two new employees from next month.
4. Isaac will start selling products in Asia.

5. Isaac might need additional training.
6. The company thinks Isaac will perform well.

36

36.1 🔊
1. microphone
2. USB drive / flash drive
3. voice recorder
4. cursor
5. low battery
6. power cable
7. touch screen
8. handout
9. speakers
10. computer
11. laminator
12. video camera
13. lectern
14. keyboard
15. printer
16. cue cards
17. mouse
18. laptop
19. webcam
20. pointer
21. router
22. chairs
23. projector

36.2 🔊
1. report
2. flow chart
3. graph
4. pie chart

37

37.1 🔊
1. Let's now turn to future prospects.
2. My talk today is about building brand loyalty.
3. Do feel free to tweet your questions to me.
4. So, we've looked at our market penetration.
5. To sum up, this year has been difficult.
6. We'll look at case studies, and then I'll take questions.
7. The purpose of this talk is to share sales figures.

37.2 🔊
1. To **sum** up, it's been a very successful year for us.
2. We'll **look** at the competitor's products, then I'll introduce our new product.
3. Do **feel** free to interrupt if you'd like to comment.
4. So, we've **looked** at problems we need to overcome.
5. Now let's **turn** to the solutions to those problems.

37.3 🔊
1. microphone
2. keyboard
3. USB / flash drive
4. cursor
5. handout
6. lectern
7. cord

37.4

1 Not given
2 False
3 Not given
4 Not given
5 True
6 True

37.5

Ⓐ 4
Ⓑ 3
Ⓒ 7
Ⓓ 5
Ⓔ 1
Ⓕ 2
Ⓖ 6

38

38.1 ◀))

1 If we **home** in on our Barcelona store, we can see it is successful.
2 All regions achieved their sales targets, aside from the Southwest.
3 Customer response has been positive, excepting Eastern Europe.
4 Generally speaking, our products are popular in South America.
5 With the exception of February, sales are up.
6 This year the company is focusing on its social media campaign.
7 If we focus on this chart, we can see sales have dropped.

38.2 ◀))

1 Excepting East Asia, our sales **have grown by more than 10 percent**.
2 In actual fact, the consumer group said **they really liked our prototype**.
3 As a matter of fact, I don't think **Alyssa is suitable for the role**.
4 For instance, we've had a lot of positive **feedback about our menswear**.
5 In general, the number of subscribers **to our magazines is falling**.
6 Concentrating on the basics, there are **many areas where we can improve**.
7 Jorge needs to improve key skills such **as dealing with customers**.

38.3 ◀))

1 In **reality**, there is no way of knowing what sales will be like next year.
2 In **fact**, we need to hire about 10 more staff this year.
3 **However**, we can't really afford to hire more staff.
4 **Except** for Janice, all staff in this department deserve a raise.
5 **Actually**, there is little we can do to increase production.
6 **Generally**, staff seem very happy with working conditions.

38.4

1 False
2 Not given
3 True
4 Not given
5 Not given
6 True

38.5 ◀))

1 If we **home** in on profits, we can see growth.
2 If we focus **on** prices, it's clear they're too high.
3 **By** and large, our T-shirts are our bestseller.
4 In **reality**, there's no way we can recover.
5 As a **matter** of fact, I am very disappointed.
6 Except **for** Korea, I've been to most of Asia.
7 **In** general, China is our biggest market.

39

39.1 ◀))

1 This sports car is **the fastest** car on sale today.
2 Our leather jackets are **more fashionable** than our competitors' jackets.
3 This digital camera is **the best** model ever.
4 Our new microwave oven is more efficient **than** any other model.
5 This ice cream maker is **easier** to use than any other on the market.
6 Our customers said our sofa is **more comfortable** than other models.
7 Our organic vegetables are **fresher** than supermarket vegetables.
8 Book a train trip with us in advance to get **the cheapest** fares.

9 Our cake range was voted **the tastiest** on the market in a recent survey.
10 These batteries last **longer** than the leading brand.
11 We think our new winter coat is **the warmest** on the market.

39.2
1 the biggest
2 cheaper
3 more energy-efficient
4 more stylish

39.3 ◄))
1 We will create **the most beautiful** flowers for the tables and the bride's bouquet.
2 Our drink is **healthier** than that brand because it has a natural caffeine substitute.
3 Our fitness tracker is **just as effective as** more expensive models, but is cheaper.
4 We offer **better technical support than** other cell phone companies do.

39.4 ◄))
1 This pizza is as tasty as the leading brand, but much cheaper.
2 Our budget clothing is as stylish as other brands on the market.
3 These store-brand dishwasher tablets are as good as the market leader.
4 Our latest action movie is as exciting as anything you've ever seen.
5 This eco-friendly dishwashing liquid is not as good as the leading brand.

39.5
1 as exciting as
2 more simple / simpler
3 more convenient
4 the healthiest
5 the best
6 just as cheap as / cheaper than

40

40.1
A 3
B 1
C 4
D 2
E 8
F 5
G 6
H 7

40.2 ◄))
1 There has been an increase in complaints.
2 There was a dramatic spike last year.
3 The price is fluctuating wildly.
4 We expect a considerable drop in prices.
5 There was a sharp rise in the share value.
6 The share value has rallied slightly.

40.3 ◄))
1 Staff numbers went **from** 120 to 150.
2 **Between** 15 and 18 percent of stock is unsold.
3 We've experienced a boom **of** 56 percent.
4 Profits have fallen **by** 11 percent.
5 The share price peaked **at** $22.
6 Complaints doubled **in** the last quarter.
7 Our sale was **between** May and June.

40.4
1 Not given
2 True
3 False
4 Not given
5 False
6 True

40.5 ◄))
1 There's been a **dramatic spike** because of a poor harvest.
2 Our sales **peaked at** $200,000 a day in December.
3 Yes, malfunctions have **fallen steadily** since last year.
4 Between **20 and 30** percent of our stock is on sale.
5 Yes, they've **rallied slightly** since last year.
6 There was an **increase of** 10 percent in the cost of electricity.

41.1 🔊
1 Are you able to pay **our fee in installments**?
2 We might move forward with the contract **if you would consider buying in bulk**.
3 I would like to resolve this issue **as soon as possible**.
4 Maybe we could discuss some **alternative options for the design**.
5 We were thinking **that you could design our new logo**.
6 I'm afraid I was hoping for **something more innovative**.

41.2
Ⓐ 3
Ⓑ 4
Ⓒ 1
Ⓓ 6
Ⓔ 2
Ⓕ 5

41.3 🔊
1 I was wondering where I can try these clothes on.
2 Could you tell me when the sample designs will be ready?
3 I was wondering if I could talk to you about Samia's performance.
4 Could you tell me whether I can order this product in store?
5 I was wondering whether you have paid my invoice yet.
6 Could you tell me what the warranty period is?
7 I was wondering how the new product is different from the old one.

8 Could you tell me when the price list will be available?
9 I was wondering if you would be able to offer me a discount.

41.4 🔊
1 I'm afraid **our deadline was missed**.
2 It looks as if **the wrong size was sent**.
3 It seems that **the discount was not applied**.
4 I'm afraid **our order was delivered** to the wrong address.
5 It looks as if **the price was calculated** incorrectly.
6 It seems that **your employees are not very well trained**.
7 I'm afraid **our customers were not satisfied**.
8 It seems that **my order was lost** while it was being delivered.
9 I'm afraid **my steak was not cooked** properly.
10 It looks as if **a mistake has been made**.
11 It seems that **the printer still hasn't been fixed**.
12 I'm afraid **the document was not checked** thoroughly enough.

41.5 🔊
1 I was wondering if **you could** look at my presentation.
2 Could you **tell** me when my order will be dispatched?
3 I was wondering if you **would** be free to meet tomorrow.
4 Could you tell me when **we can** expect our invoice to be paid?
5 I was wondering what time **the store opens**.

6 Could you **tell me** how much the new product should retail for?

41.6
2

42.1 🔊
1 If you ask me, you won't find a better deal.
2 Actually, we are waiting for the factory to send us more of that product.
3 The main thing is that we agree on schedule dates.
4 What I'm saying is that I can offer free delivery on orders over a hundred.

42.2
1 True
2 True
3 False
4 Not given
5 False

42.3 🔊
1. **Actually**, we sent you an email with them this morning.
2. I'm afraid not. If **you ask me**, this is a great deal.
3. What **we need is** an assurance that you can meet our schedule dates.
4. The **main thing is** that we agree on a price that allows enough profit.
5. **I'm afraid** your asking price is too high. Can we say $40 a unit?

43

43.1 🔊 Nota: Siempre se puede usar también la forma contraída de "would".
1. If they **gave** us a discount, we **would place** an order.
2. If the product **was** cheaper, we **would buy** it.
3. If they **moved** the deadline, we **would meet** it.
4. I **would reply** to the email now if I **had** more time.
5. We **would sell** more online if our website **was** faster.
6. We **would send** the package tomorrow if you **ordered** before 9 tonight.
7. If the agency **sent** us better temps, we **would use** them again.
8. If I **worked** late every night, I **would finish** my report for Friday.
9. I **would apply** for the job if the hours **weren't** so long.

43.2
1. True
2. Not given
3. False
4. False
5. True
6. False

43.3 🔊
1. If customers don't pay on time, we charge a 15 percent late fee.
2. Our helpline is open from 8am to 8pm if you need help.
3. When employees work weekends, they get paid double time.
4. If you are a regular customer, we give you a 5 percent discount.
5. If we receive a payment after 3pm, we credit it the next day.

43.4 🔊
1. If you need help with your computer, **you can call the IT department**.
2. We would move production to Europe **if it was cheaper to do that**.
3. We will issue a full refund **if you return the product to one of our stores**.
4. If clients are regular customers, **we give them a 5 percent discount**.
5. If our receptionist was rude to you, **we would give her a verbal warning**.

43.5 🔊
1. If you **don't / do not** pay on time, we won't send you your order.
2. We'll issue a full refund if **you're not / you are not** happy with our products.
3. If you **book** two nights in our hotel, we'll give you a third night for free.
4. If Alan's presentation **goes** well, he will get promoted next month.
5. We won't charge you for your stay if you **don't / do not** get a good night's sleep.
6. If you **order** over 100 units, we'll give you a discount.

43.6 🔊
1. Well, if you pay for the overtime, **we will finish** the job by then.
2. Yes. If **clients buy** 100 units or more, we give them a 5 percent discount.
3. If you return it to us within 28 days, **we will issue** a full refund.
4. If **you could do** a price of $59 per unit, we'd sell it in our stores.
5. We're sorry to hear that. If a customer makes a complaint, **we take** it very seriously.
6. We can't do that yet. If **we took** on more staff, we'd be able to increase production.

44.1 🔊

Nota: Todas las respuestas pueden utilizar también la forma contraída positiva o la forma larga negativa.

❶ We **would have signed** the contract if the deadline **hadn't been** so tight.

❷ If we **had left** earlier, we **wouldn't have missed** the train.

❸ If the waitress **hadn't been** so rude, we **wouldn't have** complained.

❹ If we **had ordered** before 3pm, we **would have received** the goods today.

❺ We **wouldn't have lost** the client if we **had delivered** the report on time.

❻ If you **had repaired** the printer, we **wouldn't have canceled** the contract.

❼ If I **had known** how expensive it was, I **would have put** it in the safe.

❽ The boss **wouldn't have shouted** if you **had admitted** your mistake.

❾ If you **had been** more prepared, you **would have given** a better presentation.

❿ We **would have given** you free delivery if you **had paid** on time.

⓫ If I **had known** our competitor's price, I **would have offered** a bigger discount.

⓬ We **would have met** our deadline if we **had employed** more staff.

⓭ If you **hadn't been** off sick, we **would have invited** you to the meeting.

⓮ We **would have paid** the full amount due if you **hadn't missed** our deadline.

⓯ If you **had sold** more products last time, we **would have asked** you to lead the pitch.

44.2

❶ B
❷ A
❸ B
❹ A
❺ B

44.3 🔊

❶ If I'd used the spell check, **my work wouldn't have had so many errors**.

❷ If she'd told the boss about her mistake, **he wouldn't have been so angry**.

❸ If they'd paid on time, **we wouldn't have canceled their order**.

❹ If I'd used the latest sales data, **my report would have been up to date**.

❺ If he'd checked the order was right, **his clients wouldn't have complained**.

❻ If you'd ordered more units, **we would have given you a discount**.

❼ If he'd wanted an older model, **he would have asked for one**.

44.4 🔊

❶ Clive will get a verbal warning **unless his timekeeping improves**.

❷ **Unless you pay** by the end of today, we will cancel the contract.

❸ We won't win the contract **unless we can** offer a better price.

❹ I won't get promoted this year **unless I impress** the boss.

❺ Your warranty will not be valid **unless you register** your product.

❻ **Unless I sell** to 100 new customers, I won't meet my sales targets.

❼ We won't make many sales **unless we beat** our competitors' prices.

❽ **Unless I work** overtime, I'm not going to meet the deadline.

❾ His presentation will be boring **unless he adds** special effects.

❿ The CEO won't be happy **unless we win** the contract.

⓫ **Unless you lower** the price, we won't order any more units.

⓬ We will miss the train **unless we leave** now.

44.5

❶ True
❷ False
❸ Not given
❹ True
❺ True

44.6 🔊

1 We would have hit our sales target if the internet **hadn't gone** down.

2 If he **had left** earlier, he wouldn't have been late for the meeting.

3 If you had been less rude, we **would have won** the contract.

4 The CEO would have promoted me if she **had seen** my presentation.

5 If we **had lowered** the price, we would have made more sales.

Agradecimientos

Los editores desean agradecer a:
Amy Child, Dominic Clifford, Devika Khosla y Priyansha Tuli por su asistencia de diseño; Dominic Clifford y Hansa Babra por sus ilustraciones adicionales; Sam Atkinson, Vineetha Mokkil, Antara Moitra, Margaret Parrish, Nisha Shaw y Rohan Sinha por su asistencia editorial; Elizabeth Wise por el índice; Jo Kent por sus textos adicionales; Scarlett O'Hara, Georgina Palffy y Helen Ridge por la corrección de pruebas; Christine Stroyan por la gestión del proyecto; ID Audio por la grabación de audio y la producción; David Almond, Gillian Reid y Jacqueline Street-Elkayam por su asistencia de producción.

31901063040283